Advance Praise

Dear readers,

My dear friend, Dame Stan Munro, who I worked with in the early Sixties is the ultimate entertainer with a passion for his act, unbelievable wit, and talent that the audience adores and screams with laughter. A life of wonderful stories and great success. I'm so proud to have worked with and learned from his magic.

Yours sincerely, Carlotta AM.

When drag was dangerous, controversial and out there, Stan Munro was a pioneer bringing it into the mainstream.
Chookas Queen!

Mark Trevorrow
(aka Bob Downe, comedian, singer, actor, broadcaster and journalist)

As someone who produced more than a few drag shows in my time, I insist Stan Munro put the glitter in "The Glittering Mile". Stan knows where the spotlight is the brightest and also where all the bodies are buried!
This is a riveting history and a fascinating record of a lavish, lascivious and lost era.
Highly recommended!

David Mitchell, writer & producer
(Capriccio's, Mike Walsh, Parkinson, Dame Edna, this is Your Life, Dusty, Shout!, etc)

Stan Munro:
Secrets of a Showbiz Dame

With
William Brougham

Copyright © 2026 Stan Munro & William Brougham

Published by Planetary Press and Publishing Pty Ltd

All Rights Reserved. No part of this book may be used or reproduced by any means, graphic, electronic, or mechanical, including photocopying, recording, taping or by any information storage retrieval system without the written permission of the copyright owner except in the case of brief quotations embodied in critical articles and reviews.

Because of the dynamic nature of the Internet, any web addresses or links contained in this book may have changed since publication and may no longer be valid. The views expressed in this work are solely those of the author and do not necessarily reflect the views of the publisher and the publisher hereby disclaims any responsibility for them.

Book design by Planetary Press and Publishing Pty Ltd
Cover design by Planetary Press and Publishing Pty Ltd
Front cover photo supplied by Jodie Harris - 6 Acre Studios
Edited by Keith Howes and Kevin Markwell

ISBN: 978-0-6459044-2-0 (sc)
ISBN: 978-0-6459044-3-7 (e)

Dear Reader,

Darling, let me be clear from the very first line, this book isn't just my story, it's a rallying cry. I wrote it so every young gay person knows that being yourself isn't just okay... it's everything. Anyone who tries to tell you otherwise? Sweetie, they can take a seat.

From a young age, life threw me some fierce challenges, trauma, abuse, and obstacles that could have broken me. But did I let that stop me? Oh, no! I fought, I strutted, I sparkled through it all, staying true to my gay self, just as Nature intended. Every setback, every heartbreak, only fuelled my determination to live boldly, authentically, and unapologetically.

I've spent my life performing, leading, and being a voice for our community. This memoir is my love letter to anyone who's ever felt different, scared, or alone. I want you to see that you can survive, you can shine, and you can embrace your truth with pride.

So, grab your heels, your crown, and your confidence. This is your reminder that your authenticity is your superpower.

Flaunt it, own it, and never let anyone dim your sparkle. Life's too short not to shine, honey!

With love, courage, unshakable honesty and a whole lot of glitter,
Stan Munro

Acknowledgements

Now, let's get one thing straight, this may be my story, but I sure as hell didn't write it alone. It took a village, a few good friends, a lot of coffee, and maybe a glass (or three) of bubbles along the way.

First and foremost, my heartfelt thanks to my brilliant co-author, William Brougham, who spent countless hours/years helping me bring these stories to life. You've been patient, insightful, and just the right amount of bossy when I needed it! I couldn't have asked for a better partner in crime. To Keith Howes and Kevin Markwell, my wonderful editors, thank you for polishing the rough edges, guiding my words, and making sure I didn't go too far off the rails (well, not too far!). Your wisdom and care have been invaluable.

A big thank-you to Lynda Smith, who helped me find the perfect publishing home, and to our fabulous publisher Leanne Murner, who not only believed in this book but made it shine from start to finish. Leanne, you didn't just get it out there you gave it wings, darling.

To the incredibly talented Jodie Harris, the photographer behind the stunning cover image, thank you for capturing not just my face, but my spirit. Your photo holds my quiet strength, my sense of endurance, and a life that's been lived fully. You truly saw me, and for that, I'm deeply grateful.

Of course, my deepest love and gratitude to my best friend and soulmate, Phillip Gadd, who has stood by me through every triumph, tantrum, and tear. You are my rock, my laughter, and my heart.

Finally, to my loyal four-legged companion Bruno, thank you for your unconditional love, your company through the late nights of writing, and for reminding me that a good cuddle (and a treat) can fix just about anything.

To all of you, thank you for believing in me, for helping me tell my story, and for reminding me that even through the darkest times, love, laughter, and a touch of glitter can light the way.

With love, pride, and a wink,
Stan Munro

Foreword - Craig Bennett

If you follow the deliciously outrageous UK born Aussie drag legend Stan Munro on Facebook, you'll know he's always been wildly naughty, even these days, feather boas mostly retired, and living on the edge of a rainforest in the seemingly serene environs of Northern NSW.

But naughty he remains. So much so he'll vanish for months from computer screens and iPhones, as if snatched by aliens, only to reappear claiming he'd been unceremoniously marched off to the horrors of a social media purgatory, where he'd been doing the hard yards in Facebook jail, then requesting his loyal followers 'friend' his new profile.

Yes, it's always a journey when you're naughty. But it's what makes Stan Munro so unfetteredly fabulous.

When Stan's memoir Secrets Of A Showbiz Dame arrived on my desk, I thought: "At last and wow!" Stan's story makes for a ripper read, and is a total page turner - so much so I could not put it down - even cancelling a lunch so as to not interrupt the gossipy tsunami of tales tall or otherwise!

Stan's life, as told in Secrets Of A Showbiz Dame, is screaming to be turned into a glossy TV miniseries or big screen epic, maybe with hunky Welsh actor Luke Evans donning the fetching Dame Munro drag and, hopefully, mastering Stan Speak!

With the assistance of his brilliant co-author William Brougham, Stan has woven stories so compelling and personal, it's like he's in full flight, unstoppably regaling his luscious smorgasbord of shocking, startling, hilarious and eye-popping stories just for you. Strictly entre-nous, of course.

It's a rollercoaster ride - from an ordinary upbringing in Wales, where he describes his hometown Abercarn as bleak, grey, and hideous, to being sexually abused as an 8 year old by someone he knew, singing with the Francis Langford Singing Scholars at 13, to featuring in the provocatively titled Ronnie Corbett movie Fun At St Fanny's.

There's his romance in 1962 with John Inman, who found international TV fame as *Are You Being Served?* legend Mr "I'm free" Humphries. Stan and John remained in touch until John's death in 2007, and he tells me John was as funny off screen as he was on. You get the feeling this was quite the summer fling.

After moving to Australia as a ten pound pom, he shares vivid memories of those gruelling early days in Sydney toiling at the Dairy Farmers shunting yards in Lidcombe. From there it's a quantum leap to the glittering razzle-dazzle of Les Girls and Kings Cross, making such a mark he was cast in the cult movie *Alvin Purple*.

Stan has worked all over the world as a dancer and wonderfully witty drag entertainer, enchanting millions with his talents - and he did it his way, insisting on using his real name, eschewing the trend to concoct some deliciously campy female stage moniker.

I'm thrilled that the secrets of a showbiz dame are secret no more! Bring on the sequel already, I say!

Craig Bennett
Showbiz gossip guru, entertainment bon-vivant seen on TV, heard on radio, and read in the weekly women's glossies.

TABLE OF CONTENTS

Dear Reader I

Acknowledgments III

Foreword - Craig Bennett V

CHAPTER 1
A Queen Is Born 1

CHAPTER 2
The Child Star 10

CHAPTER 3
A Sexual Awakening 21

CHAPTER 4
From Shakespeare to Tap 34

CHAPTER 5
Larry And John 53

CHAPTER 6
The Ten Pound Pom 69

CHAPTER 7
Joining Les Girls 88

CHAPTER 8
Back To Blighty 116

CHAPTER 9
Compering Les Girls 130

CHAPTER 10
See You in Court 145

Secrets of a Showbiz Dame

TABLE OF CONTENTS

Photo Catalogue

CHAPTER 11
The Great Escapes 163

CHAPTER 12
Beirut And Back to Honkers 180

CHAPTER 13
Melbourne Calling 202

CHAPTER 14
The Love of My Life and Alvin Purple 218

CHAPTER 15
Going Solo: TV Beckons 238

CHAPTER 16
The Cheeky Chaps and Carlotta Returns 255

CHAPTER 17
Never Meet Your Heroes: Danny La Rue 269

CHAPTER 18
The Nervous Breakdown: A Career in Tatters? 282

CHAPTER 19
Back On Track 303

CHAPTER 20
To Kyogle with Love 319

Secrets of a Showbiz Dame

CHAPTER 1

A Queen Is Born

I often get asked why I do drag. That's the million-dollar question, isn't it! Drag has been the sparkling, glamorous mainstay of my 65-year career. I enjoyed dressing up and putting on a show from a young age, but I never had any desire to be a woman or live as a woman. Of course, I have been proud to work alongside members of the trans community over the decades and many of those I have worked with are dear friends today. But for me, drag was my craft - the way I made my living.

By throwing on drag, I get to perform and entertain, which is what I love doing more than anything else in the world. Drag is my sparkling, dazzling 'shield of steel' – it allows me to get away with murder on stage (comedically-speaking of course); to push boundaries. I couldn't do any of that out of drag. If I'm ever asked to speak in public as myself without the safety-net of a frock and a wig I simply crumble. The thrill I get from the applause from an audience means more to me than the drag itself. That doesn't mean that I don't love transforming my appearance from that of a man to that of a stunning woman. I do. I love becoming glamorous and fabulous. Drag has treated me very well and enabled me to do the things I love. I love performing. I love entertaining. I always have. This is my story.

'Young Stan, the typical Dame, made a superb job of his part. He had natural stagecraft and held his audience from the very first appearance.' This quote's not from an article about my performance as the female impersonator/compere of the legendary Les Girls show in Sydney or Melbourne but was instead a review of a pantomime I performed in as a 12-year-old boy that appeared in my local paper, the South Wales Argus in 1953.

The pantomime was *Babes in the Woods* performed at the Lyceum Theatre in the Welsh town of Newport. The role of a pantomime dame must have suited me well, even then, and a performer who was appearing in a variety show at the same theatre sought out my Mum and told her how good I was and that he thought that I 'would go far'. At the time I was the only male pupil at the Mitchell & Hammerton School of Tap and Ballet.

The dance school was run by two blonde ladies, Miss Mitchell and Miss Hammerton, who had been dancers in the Second World War; one did tap and the other ballet. I thought they were wonderful, and they put on shows throughout the Welsh valleys where I lived. They even got me my first film role, when I was 13, but more on that later.

The pantomime was my first time dressing in drag and I have had a taste for it ever since. I loved making people happy through my performances.

Soon after I had got a 'taste for the skirt' I dragged up miming to records at a family Christmas dinner. By the time I was 14 my performing for the family had become a regular event. The lounge room was cleared, and everybody would wait for me to make my grand entrance from the upstairs bathroom. I would mime, probably pretty badly, to Rosemary Clooney's fabulous 'Mambo Italiano' or a song of Eartha Kitt's. My family loved it.

Remarkably for the time, my family accepted me dressing up and enjoyed my performances. But there were mixed messages. When I was 9 or 10, I distinctly remember my father remarking on the death of Ivor Novello, who was the composer of 'Keep the Home Fires Burning'. 'He was one of those,' he said to my mother. I wondered what he meant by 'one of those'.

My mother was particularly supportive of my early forays into show business even when I donned the occasional frock, although I didn't fully appreciate it at the time. At the age of 15 I saw an advertisement in a local newspaper for a talent quest at the Lyceum Theatre called *The Carroll Levis Discovery Show*, compered by the talent scout and BBC host, Carroll Levis. I guess you could say it was a very early forerunner to *Britain* or *Australia's Got Talent*, but without the budget.

Rather bravely, given that it was the early 1950s, I decided to perform in drag. I borrowed one of my mum's old dresses and mimed to Teresa Brewer's 'A Sweet Old-Fashioned Girl'. The winner was decided by the strength of the audience applause and although the audience seemed to like me, sadly, I did not win. But what I did have was the support of my Mum, who lent me her dress, encouraged me and came along to support me.

However, although I had parents who allowed me the freedom to dress up in drag and perform both inside and outside our home, I was always on edge, often feeling down and depressed. You see, Mum and Dad were always fighting; there was constant tension in the air which made for an unhappy childhood. It was bloody tough at times and sometimes it felt soul-destroying.

Born on the 21st of January 1941 at the Royal Gwent Hospital in

A Queen Is Born

Newport I was a war baby. Fathers were often away for long periods serving in the armed forces, while mothers were left to bring up children single-handed, surviving on rations and what they could lay their hands on to feed and clothe their children.

I had three brothers, of whom I was the youngest, and a younger sister.

I was brought up in a brick terrace house at 5 Penrhiw Terrace in the small mining village of llanfach perched on the side of a high mountain overlooking the town of Abercarn in South Wales, about 30 kilometers east of Cardiff. The landscape was dominated by coal mines and factories, all of which have now closed.

My mother Emily was born in Bristol to an Irish family who originally came from Cork. Before she married, my mother had worked in Llanfach for a family as their cook, maid and cleaner.

Before the war, my father, Stan Davies, was employed at the Abercarn Tinplate Works. He later found work at an explosives factory further up in the valleys. Mum and Dad met while he was a tinplater in Abercarn and that's where they fell in love. After getting married, they moved into the house in Llanfach where I was brought up. It was a council house, which they initially rented but in the 1950s they bought.

We certainly didn't have much money, but Mum and Dad were houseproud and kept the house very clean. Most of what we had in our home, such as furniture, was not bought outright but was paid off in instalments to the owner of the furniture shop, Mr Brest, who came around once a week to pick up the payments.

I barely saw my father during the war as he was based in Swindon while serving as a military policeman in the Royal Marines until he was demobbed in 1945. My earliest memories of him coming home on leave must be from when I was aged two or three and I recall how important he looked in his uniform.

My very first memory, still so vivid today, though, is hiding under the lounge room table with my siblings as we took shelter from the German Luftwaffe on their way to bomb the coal mines. We were all so scared, but that was just part of my early childhood. I also remember the food rationing. We had such limited choice and there was barely enough to eat. I can still remember seeing and tasting my first banana. It was so sweet and delicious! The first time I ever tasted chocolate was when a woman in the next row of houses was selling it from her back bedroom, on the sly. We don't think twice about buying chocolate and bananas these days, but they were such exotic treats during my childhood.

Following the war, my father was employed at one of the local coal mines where he was in charge of the boiler room. This was where coal was shovelled into the furnaces to power the lift that took the miners down into the underground mines and back up again. He worked three shifts at various times of the day and night. Unfortunately, because of his erratic work pattern we never knew what mood he would be in from one day to the next.

Former neighbours used to comment on my mother's beautiful smile but that smile masked the fact that she was always a bag of nerves and I feel certain that I inherited the propensity for anxiety from her.

A Queen Is Born

My parents would frequently fight, at each other's throats, day in and day out, and the atmosphere was dreadful at times.

Following many heated arguments my mother would frequently go to Bristol with my younger sister to stay with a brother of hers while I would be left at home with my father. Poor mum was even sent to the asylum in Abergavenny on a couple of occasions where she was literally tied down to a bed and received electroconvulsive therapy. I know that she tried to take her own life on at least two occasions. As a young boy, I felt like I was constantly walking on eggshells to avoid triggering any conflict with my dad, in particular. They could be very lonely times.

I am sure my elder brothers were happy to get married and move on and flee the family tensions. I can even remember, as a young boy, crying at the wedding of one of my brothers and wanting to go with him on his honeymoon just to escape. How messed up is that? It may sound dramatic but that is how I felt as a young boy.

Even though I loved to perform, I was a very shy child and because my father was very strict, I had little choice but to be well-behaved. If I put one foot out of line, he would smack my backside; a look from him was usually enough to curl my toes. If Mum was having one of her difficult days and Dad was not at home, she would never stop us misbehaving. She would retreat into her own world. The whole house was a place where moods were made.

Things were so bad so often that when I was young, I wished that I had been born into another family. I think for me, it was so difficult living in a family where my parents fought so hard and so often that I never felt unconditional love. It really seemed to depend on their mood.

I was probably closer emotionally in many ways to my father because he shared my dry sense of humour; and I felt he understood my nature better than my mother. When my younger sister was born, I can remember bursting into tears and exclaiming to my father 'You don't love me anymore'. He replied reassuringly, 'You'll always be my boy.'

However, some years ago my sister showed me notes written by my mother detailing the extent of the abuse against her, which was both physical and verbal. They upset me and I began to see my father in a different light. My mother never touched alcohol and I feel that this was partly because she saw what my father was like when he had had too much to drink, although I would not describe him as an alcoholic. But he liked a drink and when he was tipsy the rows would certainly escalate.

My father could be so brutal when he was angry and was certainly not someone you would want to cross.

I was also abused, sexually, when I was much younger, about eight or nine, by one of my brothers. He robbed me of my innocence. He introduced me to sex long before I was ready and stole my childhood. This went on regularly for a few years, into my early teens. He went on to marry a woman and have a family.

I did not understand fully at the time what was going on or whether it was right or wrong. There was no running to my mother or father to tell them as I thought all hell would have broken loose and that I would have got into trouble. That was the last thing I wanted as our already dysfunctional household did not need any more tension.

At the time I must have thought that was just what guys did with each other. As I got older, I began hearing about cases of child abuse from reading about it in the newspapers or from people I knew. Some of them would tell me that family members had fiddled with them and then I would think or say out loud, 'Well, that happened to me too.' It clicked.

My brother was in his late teens when his abuse started, and I have no idea why he did what he did. Perhaps it was a form of sexual release for him or perhaps he had gay or bisexual inclinations and it was the only way he felt that he could explore his own sexuality. Perhaps it was some warped form of power play where he could pick on someone weaker and more vulnerable than himself. The truth is I will never know his reasons and all the above is pure speculation. It does not in any way excuse his behaviour.

For a long time, I was very angry, but it is now largely water under the bridge. I have no desire to forgive him, but I refuse to let him, and his abuse consume me.

You could be forgiven for thinking that school would provide a welcome escape from the turmoil at home, but it was not to be. Far from it.

CHAPTER 2
The Child Star

The Child Star

I hated my school days in Abercarn. I was unable to concentrate for more than a few minutes and I think I had what would be described today as attention deficit hyperactivity disorder. I was frequently caned and, honestly, there was no pain quite like it. I took woodwork class for three years and while all the other boys were making pieces of furniture, all I ever made was a ten-inch ruler. I found it so hard to focus and got bored very easily. I think it is safe to say that carpentry was not really my thing. Consequently, I was regularly bent over the bench by the teacher who whacked me hard with a wooden T square. Another teacher regularly caned me for my inability to pay attention, slicing the rod across my hand at full force. Oh, the agony! Such brutality and sadism seem so extreme these days but back then it was the norm to use such punishments, even on kids like me whose only 'crime' was to not fit in.

One of my earliest and clearest school memories was of one of the winters we had, when I was about seven years old, which was particularly horrendous. It was made even more so because the village we lived in, Llanfach, was high up on the mountain above Abercarn, which made us even more vulnerable to extreme weather and isolation. We experienced such heavy snowfall that our two-storey house was covered in it. Dad had to dig out the snow from the downstairs of our house. I will never forget those treks, long and treacherous, to and from school in the deep snow. It was one of the worst winters of the last century.

My early school days were uneventful and unremarkable but that was all set to change. At the age of nine I started taking tap dancing and ballet lessons. Yes, I was the Billy Elliot of Abercarn! My sister had begun lessons and because I enjoyed putting on a show at home and miming to records, Mum decided to take me along to my sister's lessons. My sister dropped out, but I kept up the classes, which I loved.

However, all hell broke loose when the other boys found out. They would rip me apart verbally and pummel and kick me daily. I became little more than their punching bag. I was bullied mercilessly by the rest of my class once it became obvious that I was not enough of a 'real boy' for them. Throughout my school years, I don't think I ever had any real friends. Consequently, I detested school with a vengeance, particularly on sports days when we had to play cricket. I always positioned myself near the boys' toilet and if I saw a cricket ball heading my way I would dart into the bog and take cover!

The other boys called me names such as 'pansy' or 'queer' which at the time I did not fully understand. It was horrific but I stuck it out. Some people try to excuse bullying as simply part of growing up, but I disagree. I say that those who bully are cowards and if I met my bullies today, I would not hesitate to tell them what bastards they were for picking on a weaker person. Bullying should never happen. I have never forgotten.

To be honest I think I always knew I was different from the other boys, and I often wondered why I felt that way, but it took me some time before I began to understand who and what I was. As a kid I wanted answers to everything. Then, at about the age of 10 or 11, it clicked, and I had my first inkling that I might have been a homosexual.

The Child Star

Living nearby to us, on a farm, was a boy around my age, called Bobby. He and I kept rabbits as pets, and we used to hang out with each other looking at and talking about our rabbits. I walked round to see Bobby one day to catch up, and lo and behold, he had another guy there to whom he was showing his rabbits. I just turned and walked away and went home. I was really upset and jealous because I had thought Bobby was my special friend. It got me thinking about just why I had been so upset and this is when I think I first started to question myself about my own sexuality. I really didn't understand my feelings towards Bobby, but I knew they were strong, and I liked being with him.

Regardless of how much the other boys bullied me, my dance classes were a way I could escape, at least temporarily, from my regular life in Abercarn. I often felt claustrophobic living up there and I used to imagine those mountains closing in on me and trapping me there forever. I so wanted to escape.

Soon after joining the dance classes, I began performing in concerts with the other pupils around the valleys for charity. The concerts were great fun, I'm a born performer and they provided me with another valuable distraction from the monotony and stress of school. In fact, the classes led to a film role and the chance to work in London.

When I was about 13 my mother received a telegram from my dance teachers. They had seen an advert in *The Stage* newspaper for boys to join a choir which would then appear in a comedy movie called *Fun at St Fanny's*. My teachers had put my name forward and a reply had apparently come back from the producers asking for me to be sent straight away. The film was to be directed by Maurice Elvey. He made over 190 films from 1913 to the mid-1950s and was somewhat esteemed for a few of them, so he was of some stature. This particular movie, an all-boys version of the hugely popular *The Belles of St Trinian's*, was to be shot at Twickenham Studios in South West London and would star Fred Emney, Cardew Robinson, Miriam Karlin, a young Ronnie Corbett, Peter Butterworth and the boxer Freddie Mills.

The choir I was to join was called the Francis Langford Singing Scholars and we were to play the schoolboys in the film. I can remember clearly how I heard that I had got the role which for me came out of the blue. I had gone home for lunch and Mum told me that a telegram had come through from my dance teachers informing Mum I was to be in the movie. She had then walked a mile or so down to the public telephone to ring my headmaster and ask him if I could have time off from school to appear in the movie. Luckily for me, he had agreed.

Her exact words were, 'Stanley, you're going to London this afternoon to be in a film.' My mother had already packed my suitcase. Can you imagine how excited I was? Not only did I get to escape from the daily horrors of school, but I was going to be in a movie! In London!

Mum and I took the steam train from Newport and were met at Paddington Station in London by Monty Sidford, the choir's singing teacher. After a goodbye hug, Mum took the train straight back to

The Child Star

Wales after Monty reassured her that good care would be taken of me. Monty and I then made our way to a boarding house in Clapham, a fairly seedy area in South West London where I met the other members of the Singing Scholars whose ages ranged from about 12 to 16. There were about a dozen of us.

It was about eight in the evening when we finally arrived. I really felt like the Welsh boy from the valleys. Here I was in a room full of strangers in the big city. I did not have a clue and felt so out of my depth.

My general cluelessness was obvious when we sat down at the table for supper. I could not work out whether the person serving us was a man or a woman because he had false eyelashes on, fluffed-up hair and long fingernails. The first thing I noticed were those long, painted fingernails. He was also wearing slacks and a little sweater. I was perplexed and intrigued. I asked, somewhat naively, to one of the other boys, 'Is that a man or a woman?' He replied, 'It's both!' I felt so dumb. I found it so strange as I had never come across someone like that. I was, to put it mildly, gob-smacked, although I was quite happy to throw a frock on and perform in front of an audience. I later found out his name was Jicky, and he had been a female impersonator during the war.

Even though my family did not have much money I was used to living in a clean house and sleeping in a comfortable clean bed. The boarding-house was disgustingly filthy and very run down. There were not enough beds for us boys, so I had to sleep on a smelly old mattress on the floor. Seriously, it was like a scene from *Oliver*!

The next day we took the train to Twickenham Studios where we would shoot scenes for the film for the next few weeks. I found it all so exciting, but I was also terribly apprehensive at first. I had gone from performing in small venues in the Welsh valleys to suddenly working on a film set with famous actors and people I didn't know.

As the days went by one boy told me that he thought I was 'so camp'. I had no idea what he meant and asked him to explain. 'You're one of those, you're so girly,' he told me. It did not take long for it to dawn on me that he meant that I was homosexual. Apparently, he wasn't the only one to think this and it wasn't too long before another boy, Bobby Kent, asked if I wanted to sleep in his bed with him. I was a spoilt Welsh boy who was used to having his own bed so I jumped at the chance as it meant I could sleep in a real bed instead of the stinky mattress on the floor. Well, it didn't take long before he made his true intentions known and he was all over me. It all felt completely natural to me and the greatest thing ever as we explored each other's body. When our lips met in a kiss, I thought I'd died and gone to heaven. This was my first sexual experience that was entirely consensual, and it felt so good.

I fell madly in love with Bobby. I was thirteen and a half and he was a little older, about fifteen or sixteen. His body was more developed than mine, slim, with curly sandy hair. We were pretty inseparable throughout the filming, and I really felt I had found someone who was more than a friend. I even stayed with Bobby and his mother at his home in Wakefield, West Yorkshire after we had both left the choir. We tried unsuccessfully to screw, but he complained that I was so tight that he couldn't penetrate me, and he was worried he would rip his foreskin. Charming! Our sexual relationship might have been short-lived, but it turned into a life-long friendship, and we are still in contact today. Would you believe Bobby became a successful drag queen and worked in clubs in Turkey? Perhaps I should have realised that this could have been a career possibility when he helped Jicky one evening to make up half my face in drag during the movie shoot!

The Singing Scholars was formed by Welshman, Francis Langford. I was only in the choir for about a month but over the years the Scholars performed across the United Kingdom including summer seasons in Blackpool. Francis Langford, who was in his mid-30s, was a tall, ugly, stocky man. One day, during the filming, he called all of us boys into the dressing room and read from a dirty novel. He was quite twisted.

In fact, within a couple of days of my arrival, he invited me into his office, and asked, 'Have you written home to your mother yet?' I replied that I had not. He then asked if I had ever typed to which I responded that I had not. He said, 'Well come and sit on my knee.' You can probably guess the rest. I did not know what to think. He was holding my hand and showing me how to type 'Dear mum'. Then he started to put his hands down my pants and the next thing I knew he had his penis out. The rest is all a bit of a blur but at the time I did not realise that what he was doing was wrong as this had already happened with my older brother. I thought it was natural.

I told Bobby what had happened and he told me that Francis

Langford had done it to the other boys in the choir. He said, 'How do you think we got the job?' Apparently, he had fondled most of the boys. He had boys with him all the time; they were on tap. As far as I know he was never reported to the police. Perhaps he would have been locked up if he had been, but who knows, back in those days, whether anything would have been done.

I feel angry because he took advantage of us boys. He not only abused our trust but that of their parents. I often wonder if Monty Sidford knew what was going on. Several years later I was performing in Finsbury Park in London when I met Monty. We ended up sleeping together and it was the first time that I fucked a man. Thankfully it was a choice I made and there was no pressure.

Fun at St Fanny's was supposed to be the first of a series, but after failing at the box office no other film was made. *The Times* critic described it as a 'farce of the crudest order' while the critic at the *Evening Standard* wrote that it had 'some of the rottenest chestnuts I have had thrown at me in twenty years of film-going'.

Its stars were no kinder. Ronnie Corbett described it as 'One of the most bizarre films ever made'. Years later I bumped into Miriam Karlin in Sydney's Kings Cross while I was working at Les Girls in the late sixties. She was in Australia appearing on the hugely popular *Mavis Brampton Show*. I was in the chemist where all the performers from the show would go to buy their make-up. There was Miriam in the queue; I could not believe it. I approached her and asked if she remembered the film *Fun at St Fanny's*. She flung her hands in the air and shrieked, 'Remember it darling! I've been trying to forget it.' It really was a third-rate British comedy that tried too hard to be an all-male version of *St Trinian's*. For anyone who is a glutton for punishment and can find a copy of the film, I can be seen in the various classroom scenes.

After we finished filming it was time to return to school in Abercarn, but things were never the same. Although I had become homesick, I had had a taste of big city life and I also knew firmly where my affections lay with regards to boys and girls. I found it very difficult to settle down and longed to leave the claustrophobia of the valleys once more.

However, there were some happy surprises from time to time. One day, I would have been 14, I heard from a classmate that some of the other boys would meet by the back of a church in an alcove near the vestry. My ears pricked up and I was very curious. I decided to go along and discovered it was a wanking circle where they would meet and would have a competition to see who could climax first. You can imagine how elated a young teenage boy, discovering his sexuality, felt, with these 'wank-a-thons' taking place, though touching another boy was an unspoken taboo.

We all kept our hands firmly to ourselves. This went on for quite a while until one boy who was a late developer failed to climax and started crying before threatening to go home and tell his Mum that he couldn't cum. We all fled like rats up a drainpipe and were terrified we would be caught. Needless to say, that circle never happened again.

Leaving school could not have come any sooner and at the age of

15 that day arrived, and I was determined to go out with a bang. We were to have a farewell concert, so I decided that it was time to bring out the drag! As I did not have to go back to school the next day, I felt I had nothing to lose. My mother was a whiz on those old pedal Singer sewing machines and she made me a bright red satin frock with ruffles. I wonder how many other mothers back then would have been so supportive, not only letting their son perform as a woman but making their costume. I went on and lip-synched one of my favourite numbers 'Mambo Italiano' by Rosemary Clooney. I was a hit! What a swan song. School was over and I was free.

CHAPTER 3
A Sexual Awakening

My experiences of growing up and schooling in Abercarn had been largely unhappy. I wanted desperately to get out of the place as I had seen a better side of life when I was away filming Fun at St Fanny's. Being a hormonal teenager who had recently started exploring his sexuality in London, I was keen to find others like me. It was not an easy task, although if there's a will, there's a way.

While I was still at school, my Saturday morning dance classes had moved from sleepy Abercarn to Newport, which was the nearest big town, about 12 miles away. These classes also gave me the chance to find other boys and men with similar inclinations. And I'm not talking about dancing! After my classes I would explore the town or go to the Tredegar Hall Picture House to catch the latest film. Musicals were my favourite and I went as often as I could.

It was there at about the age of 14 that I met an older man in his late 30's who was always in the back row every Saturday. We ended up meeting quite often and would fiddle with each other. Although he was much older it was mutually enjoyable and I never felt forced to do anything against my will. I was even rewarded with half a crown, which I used to spend on fish and chips with bread and butter. It was a proper sit-down meal in a restaurant, not just a take-away, which at the time felt very posh because all I had from my parents was my dance class fee and bus fare.

As time went on, I began to meet other young men like me through cottaging and we would hang out together. I would have been about 15 years old. A fellow I had met had told me about cottaging and I loved the excitement and pleasures that I could find easily at some of the public toilets in Newport, even though I was as nervous as hell the first few times I went. My new mates and I would often head to Cardiff, about half an hour away by train and hang out at a couple of bars that were popular with gay and bisexual men. There were no specific 'gay bars' in Cardiff in the 1950s before the passing of the Sexual Offences Act of 1967 which partially decriminalised homosexual acts in private between two males in England and Wales. Being gay could make you vulnerable to assault or blackmail. Consequently, the gay scene was underground.

The covert way we were forced to live our lives brought with it dangers. For example, when I was about 15, I was getting fucked by a fellow who would have been a couple of years older than me at a deserted garage at the back of Newport Station. After he had done his business and I was pulling my jeans back up, out of nowhere I felt the full force of his fist land on my face. And then another. Whack! I was in shock – I couldn't believe what was happening. He began to beat me up; he really ripped into me. As his blows pummelled my head I somehow managed to pull up my jeans as fast as I could and ran for my dear life.

My new pals and I would head into Cardiff on a Saturday evening. Our favourite bar was the Angel Hotel, opposite Cardiff Castle. The front part was frequented by gay men. All I could afford to drink was a Scrumpy cider which was sold at all the bars and hotels around Cardiff and Newport. It went through you like a fast train.

The front area really attracted a broad cross-section of men, boys from the valleys, Cardiff boys and those who were well-to-do. There was one fellow who always sat in the same seat in the corner. He would have been in his early twenties and sat there with one gin and tonic all night. He was very effeminate, but I later found out that he was married and had ten kids. I still find it hard to believe to this day that of all the people in that bar, I would have said he would have been one of the least likely to settle down with a wife and produce so many children.

When I was trolling (that's what we called cruising for men) the Angel Hotel, I wore very tight jeans which left little to the imagination and I was rather flamboyant. Hardly any of the queens spoke to me in the street. When they saw me flouncing up the street they would dart into a doorway or cross the road. I was really what you might call a 'flaming homosexual' and was constantly flapping my wrists. It was all a bit too much and in your face. I was often looking for some action but to be honest I never got much trade out of the Angel. Most of the customers were straight, apart from those at the front and those who were gay or bisexual saw me as little more than jailbait. It would have been one thing to have been caught and outed as a homosexual but quite another to have been considered a pederast too.

However, cottaging was different. The best trade was at a public toilet down a laneway near one of the hangouts, the Ship Inn, in the Cardiff suburb of Tiger Bay where it was every 'gal' for herself. The toilet was very popular with men looking for men for sex; if only those walls could talk. The toilet cubicles had more holes than a block of Swiss cheese. On the inside of one of the doors was drawn the life-size figure of a naked man, which was perfect in every detail. Queens from the Welsh valleys would come down on a Saturday night just to gaze in awe at the glorious image. It became well known among other gay and bisexual men and for a long time no one would dare scribble over it. For us, it became as famous as the Statue of David, until one day it was gone, door and all. The story got around that someone had it removed, and it was hanging in some wealthy queen's apartment as a piece of art. I called it a piece by 'Jackson Bollocks'.

I was falling in love with every bit of trade I met and was always having my heart broken when it only lasted a week or so. The disappointment from these short-lived 'affairs' would get me into a terrible state, to the extent that I worried that there was no future for me. It always felt like the end of my world. To this day I still hate getting hurt. I think I was looking for any sort of affection, something I felt was lacking at home. Unfortunately, the fellows I was meeting really just wanted sex and nothing more. Having said that, however, as a mid-teen my mind was often in my pants, and I thought with my cock.

In Cardiff there was always the possibility of a screw up an alley before rushing to get the last double decker bus home on a Saturday night. I would arrive home after midnight yet, surprisingly enough, Mum and Dad never asked me where I had been or why I was back so late. They never tried to stop me going out either. There must have been times that they smelt alcohol on my breath. If they did, they never said anything. They certainly had no idea I was going to bars popular with men who liked men. Perhaps they thought that as a young man it was only natural that I should go out socialising and sow my wild oats. I was very lucky that no questions were ever asked.

On one occasion I even went to London as part of a two-week holiday to stay with a pen pal who I had met through the kids' pages in a local newspaper. We were both 15 and to be honest I just wanted a male friend. However, as luck would have it, it turned out we both liked each other in more ways than one. And the sex was to die for. We were both young and so keen for it. We had a strong physical connection, and we rarely went out in London as we were having so much fun between the sheets.

He lived with his grandmother who drank a bottle of Guinness every night before going to bed. After a week she asked me if my mother knew where I was. When I said 'no' his grandmother sent me straight back to Abercarn the next day. I arrived home and Mum was in the garden hanging out clothes on the washing line. She looked at me and my little suitcase and said simply, 'Your dinner is in the oven.' I thought she was being smart but there was my dinner waiting for me. She never even asked where I had spent the past week.

Many years later I was in a gay pub in London watching the drag comic Lee Sutton. Sitting near me was a man who came over to me and said, 'It's Stan, isn't it?' It turned out to be my friend with whom I had stayed with all those years ago. We had a good old yak, and it was lovely to catch up after all those years.

A Sexual Awakening

Soon after my experience staying with my 15-year-old friend in London, I started writing to someone else who suggested a cheap guest house where we could spend the night in Cardiff. He was a few years older than me and said that he would drive up in his father's car. I arrived at the guest house on the Saturday evening as arranged. The room had been pre-booked, and I explained to the guesthouse owner that it was for two people. I paid my share of the room and told her that my friend would pay his on arrival.

Not long after I heard a car pull up outside and soon enough my new friend knocked on the door of our room and came in. He was tall and very cute (we hadn't seen photos of each other before we met) and he was eager for fun. There were three beds in the room and for some reason he insisted we have sex in all three of them. After we'd finished the room was in a right old mess - blankets and pillows were all over the place. He then announced out of the blue that he had forgotten something in his car which he needed to get. He also told me he would take the briefcase that he had with him to save him doing that the following morning.

I was so naïve and trusting back then but even I thought this was a bit odd and I had a funny feeling that he was going to do a runner. I watched out of the window as he jumped into his car and sped off. I was flabbergasted. The next thing I knew there was a knock at the door. What's a girl to do?! I was naked as a new-born, so I hid behind the curtain as the landlady entered. 'Oh my God! Look at the mess in here. I know you're in here as I can see your feet.' I coyly stuck my head out and she told me that I would have to leave first thing in the morning without any breakfast. It probably won't come as a surprise that I never heard from my friend again. Or that I never went back to that guest house!

When I grew a few years older I started renting a room on a Saturday night with whoever picked me up. There were plenty of dirt-cheap boarding houses down by the river. I would be broke for the rest of the week after spending my money on accommodation but it was worth it. You might well say that my cock ruled my head, and you would be right. Without doubt! I would have sex whenever and wherever I could get it. I was like a bunny on heat.

My first experience of being fully penetrated was when I was 15, at a cottage in Newport, and it hurt like hell. But practice makes perfect and I soon began enjoying bottoming. Sometime soon after, I was fucked by a man called George in the toilet at the back of the car park of the King's Head Hotel in Newport. This was not just any old fuck. George bred greyhounds but that was not what he was memorable for. He had the biggest penis I have ever seen. It must have been ten inches. He used to scare the queens away with it as it was so huge, but not little ol' Stan. No, I just had to have that monster. It took twenty minutes and half a jar of Vaseline to get it up me. And take it I did.

It was when I was 15 that I also met someone who was to become a life-long friend; someone who became very special to me. Desmond Berry was one of the boys in Newport who I would hang around with. He became my first real friend, my best friend in fact. We met at a busy beat in Carpenters Arms Lane in Newport which was situated between two hotels. Apparently, it had been a popular meeting place for men for at least 100 years. It had eight stalls which were not enclosed by doors where men would go to urinate. Of course, urination was the last thing on many a man's mind.

Some of us would get up to so much mischief there, and not always the sexual kind. For example, one Saturday afternoon before heading to Cardiff I went to Carpenters Arms Lane and I was miffed as no stalls were vacant, it was so packed. It appeared that I was not going to get any action there that night. I left, waited a few minutes, and then went back and yelled out, 'Police'. As you can imagine, havoc ensued, with queens running here, there and everywhere in the confusion. I ran like the clappers only to be caught by a bit of rough trade who I had already had a few weeks before. I was mortified at being found out and he told me off big time

I fell in love with Des pretty quickly. He was the same age as me, about my height, slim, dark hair and dark complexion and such a beautiful boyish smile. He also had a somewhat fragile, elegant, appearance, and I think this combination of vulnerability and cheekiness just completely captured my heart. We slept together for the first time soon after we met while my family were away on holiday in the seaside resort of Barry. I even introduced him to my neighbours and my Aunt Joan! I think I was a bit too erratic for him at first, but we became the best of friends. He became my saviour and guardian angel in so many ways, always there for me and he was my closest confidante for many years. He was also my guide to the gay scene and introduced me to lots of other people. He also loved my dry sense of humour. I loved his, which was wicked.

Once, Des and I were at a party and we went into the bathroom. The host had warned us not to go near the bathtub as he was using it to make elderberry wine. We just found this so funny and could not stop laughing. We could not let this go without causing some sort of mischief, so we both pissed in the bath. Oh, we could be evil!

Des didn't like his straight hair so he would put rollers in it as he wanted to give it some curls. One night he laid down near a three-bar heater, sadly with the rollers in, and promptly fell asleep. He awoke to find that the plastic on them had melted because of the heat. Thankfully, his scalp was not burnt but his hair was badly singed, so we had to cut the rollers out of his hair. He ended up wearing a cap for a few weeks after that. It was the kind of cap that comic strip character Andy Capp wore. The front of the cap was so low down that it would cover Des's eyes. Try as you as you might, you just cannot look swishy wearing one of those.

Des had also been advised by an older queen that he should pinch his cheeks to make them look rosy as he had very pale skin. One evening, he ran out of rouge to put on his cheeks and sat in front of the mirror pinching them for a about an hour. He had never been told exactly how long he should have pinched them for before achieving a healthy glow. The glow never materialised but he did end up with two very bruised cheeks. He ended up staying in that night.

Des could be quite shy and sometimes I liked to tease him about this. By this stage, he had moved from Newport to Bristol, and I was going to go and stay with him for the weekend. We met in Newport and decided to take the train to his new home city. I decided this would be a good opportunity to shock him. I had with me a little bag containing some of my mother's skirts and an old wig that I had bought at C&A. It was really a hat, but it was made of bathmat material and was quite fluffy. Women used to buy it as a wig and comb it into different styles.

Once we were seated on the train, Des asked me what was in the bag, and I told him it was my clothes for the weekend. I then told him that I needed to go to the toilet for a while and asked him to stand guard outside. I locked the door and very hurriedly took off all my boys' clothes before stuffing them in my bag. I put on the skirt and a pair of Mum's stockings. Pantyhose was not around in those days, so I used a bit of elastic to hold them up. I also put on a blouse, a coat, and a pair of high-heeled shoes.

Of course, it was not just about the clothes but the whole look, too. To create the desired effect, I applied some lipstick, eyebrow pencil and some powder, all of which had been 'borrowed' from home. Getting glammed up like this didn't come quickly, and every now and again there'd be a knock at the door followed by Des calling, 'Are you alright Stan?' I would yell back, 'Yes, I'll be out in a minute.' That must have been a very long minute.

Back in the 1950s the carriages in the steam trains had a corridor on one side and seating on the other. I opened the door and came out in drag. Well, Des nearly keeled over and fainted. He was gob-smacked, exclaiming, 'What are you doing? Oh, you can't do that.'

But, after his initial shock had worn off, he laughed. We then stood in the corridor, with me trying to act feminine. The train then pulled into the station before Bristol where it stopped. That had not been the plan as we had intended to take the train directly to Bristol.

A voice came over the tannoy system announcing, 'All change here, the Bristol train is over the footbridge on Platform Two.' We had to get off the train. A man on the platform kindly opened the door for me. I don't think he had a clue that I was a 16-year-old boy in drag! As Des and I began walking along the platform I suddenly felt the elastic that had been holding up my stockings starting to ride down towards my knees. To get to the other platform we had to go over the bridge, no mean feat considering my predicament.

Once we made it to the other side my stockings were down around my ankles. I told Des that I needed to race to the Ladies to quickly adjust them. For a second time that night he nearly passed out. Inside the Ladies there was a girl doing her makeup in the mirror and she did not take any notice. I was very bold about it all and oozed confidence. Little did I realise back then that I would spend the bulk of my career in drag.

Thankfully, we only had to wait about two or three minutes for the next train and when we reached Bristol, we got straight on the bus for the five-minute journey to Des's home. We raced into his flat and closed the door before screaming our tits off. He was immediately on the telephone to our friend Peter saying, 'You'll never guess what Stan's done. He's come all the way from Newport on the train in drag!'

A Sexual Awakening

Des later moved to London where he was in charge of the staff dining room at one of the branches of Marks and Spencer. He had a lovely little flat in Victoria right across the road from the Biograph Cinema, which had become a very popular meeting place for gay men. Some wags nick-named it 'the Biogrope'. So much sex went on in those seats as well as in the toilets. Men would change seats to sit next to someone young and attractive.

The Sunday tabloid newspaper News of the World wrote a scandalous story about it featuring the headline 'Close Down This Cinema of Vice'. The actor Kenneth Williams even mentioned it in his diaries. The Biograph closed in 1983 and was quickly demolished. Another piece of London's gay history gone!

Des eventually left his job at Marks and Spencer and moved to Peacehaven, near Brighton where he ran a successful guest house. Tragically, he died of a brain tumour about 40 years ago. I was lucky to have such a loyal, devoted and loving friend in my life. Nobody has replaced him in my heart. I miss him dearly to this very day.

CHAPTER 4
From Shakespeare to Tap

From Shakespeare to Tap

Towards the end of my time at school my headmaster successfully applied for a grant for me to train at the prestigious Royal Welsh College of Music and Drama for six months. Although I hated school and wasn't a particularly good student, the headmaster had taken an interest in me and knew that I enjoyed performing and I was taking dance and elocution lessons. The grant covered my tuition and then, if I showed any talent or promise, I could continue. The college was at Cardiff Castle, in the middle of town. I was so happy to get the grant as my parents could never have afforded the tuition fees and I felt it was an opportunity to establish a career in performance.

The college's most famous graduate is probably Sir Anthony Hopkins, who of course played Hannibal Lecter in *The Silence of the Lambs* for which he won an Oscar. In fact, Hopkins was probably a student there just after I left, as he graduated from the college in 1957 and I was there in 1955.

I was a born performer, but, alas, Hamlet I was not. I have already mentioned that I had problems with concentration, so I found it challenging trying to put my heart and soul into it. I was so bored doing Shakespeare and having to learn to sword fight using foils or memorising long monologues. I began to realise the college was not for me and I left when the six months was up. I do not think anyone was particularly sad to see me go or surprised as with my lack of enthusiasm, I did not exactly impress the teachers.

However, I was rather more enthusiastic about the extra-curricular activities that became available to me! I spent my lunchtimes trolling nearby Castle Park which was rife with men looking for a bit of action. It had a wonderful public toilet, or cottage as we called it, which was always bursting with life, day and night. Of course, I could not resist having my fair share of fun. It would have been rude not to!!!! Many a time I only made it back to class by the skin of my teeth. On other occasions I missed a class because I was too busy getting down and dirty.

Soon after leaving the college, I saw a job advertised in the *South Wales Argus* that could have given me a chance to mix with not only the British aristocracy but also royalty. The advert stated that Lord Llewellyn was looking for a trainee butler. Mum agreed that it would be ideal for me as I used to do a lot of the cooking at home. Bless her cotton socks but she was not very good in the kitchen so I would often cook. Nothing fancy but things like Welsh rarebit and cakes.

I applied for the job in my best handwriting to work in this Welsh household. About two weeks later I received a reply. The heading on the letter said something like the 'Llewellyn Estate' and referred to me as Master Davies. Sadly, it explained that another candidate had been selected for the job but that they rather liked my handwriting. At least that was something.

I had also applied to become an apprentice pastry chef and was signed up by a large company in Newport called Lovell's Confectionary. About a month later I received a letter from the Llewellyn Estate explaining that the person they had accepted for the role had not worked out. They offered me a full butler traineeship. I could not believe it but unfortunately, it was too late. I had taken on the apprenticeship at the bakery. Later, when details of the relationship between Lord Llewelyn's son Roddy and Princess Margaret were revealed, I wondered if I might have crossed paths with royalty, had I become a butler at the Llewellyn Estate. In the end, though, I worked with more queens than I ever would have done butlering for the Llewellyns!

After a year at Lovell's, I left and began working for Jones Brothers Bakers in the nearby village of Cwmcarn. I would get up at 5am and go into work where I would bake bread the traditional way. We would have to lift all the dough out of a huge round machine and lug it on to a baking table. Then, after cutting and weighing the dough we put it in tins to bake.

However, it did not take long to realise that this was not the career for me, and I felt if I stayed in the job I would be going nowhere fast. That feeling of suffocation once again took hold. I longed to leave my life in Abercarn and the sleepy Welsh valleys behind. By a quirk of fate, my wish was about to come true, and my life was to change course, thanks to a young man who happened to be visiting from a land Down Under.

I was about 17 years-old, when one of the students at the dance school I was still attending told me that an Australian friend of hers, who was driving buses in the town, was keen to speak to me. She also told me that he was a fabulous tap dancer and acrobat. I was sold! I thought this might be a great opportunity to get away from the dreary life I was leading.

Neville, who was from Sydney, was staying with a family in Newport. I was struck by his strange accent which I had never heard before. It turned out that he had seen me perform at a concert with my dance school when he had come to watch his friend. He wanted to know if I would be interested in joining him as the other half of a tap dancing and acrobatics duo for a national music hall tour he was putting together. I was over the moon and, of course, I said yes, without hesitation.

Neville Munro had come over from Australia as part of a dance acrobatics trio with two other Australians. They had performed up and down the country, including London, and had landed in Newport to appear in a pantomime over Christmas. After the season had finished Neville unfortunately broke his foot which meant he could no longer perform as part of the trio. So, he had decided to stay in town to convalesce and earn a living driving local buses. He had also started seeing a female dancer from the panto which no doubt was another incentive to hang around for a while. However, Neville's unfortunate accident was to prove my blessing – and, ultimately, the start of my career.

I was to pretend to be Neville's brother, so from then on Stanley Jeffery Davies became simply, Stan Munro. Neville often reminded me, 'Don't forget you're Stan Munro, my brother. You'll have to try and act a bit Australian.' Not only did I have to pretend to be his sibling, but I also had to pretend to be Australian, accent and all. I had never even met another Australian. I probably attempted to sound like Chips Rafferty but ended up sounding more like Dame Edna. My attempts at an Australian accent were just dreadful.

Once Neville's foot got better, he was keen to perform again. The trio had been acrobatic but, apart from the odd cartwheel, I had no acrobatic experience whatsoever. My expertise was in tap dancing and, to a lesser extent, jazz ballet. That is what Neville had recognised in me when he first saw me perform at the dance school concert. We rehearsed a few times a week for about six months. One of the routines was particularly challenging as it involved dancing on specially constructed suitcases. Neville was a good tap dancer but as I was not a trained acrobat there were limits as to what I could do on that front.

After six months hard work we put a slick double act together. Neville had been an acrobat and dancer from a young age, and he was twelve years older than me. He was like a father figure to me back then. A beautiful man in many ways. I had deep admiration for him professionally, and it probably won't come as a surprise that I also developed strong personal feelings for him. I was a young gay man who wanted to love and be loved. I have never been able to fathom out his feelings for me and he seemed to me that he was a conflicted man. In fact, we remained friends and spoke on the phone quite regularly, until his death at the age of 92 in February 2021. Whenever I spoke of my gay life and issues he would change the subject or end the call.

He was a hard taskmaster, but he needed to be because it was crucial that the act be perfect and that I mastered the discipline of performing shows night after night for many weeks. I will always be grateful for those early opportunities he afforded me as he taught me the importance of aiming for perfection, something which remained with me throughout my career. After we completed the months of arduous training and rehearsals, I bravely gave up my apprenticeship, quit the bakery, left home and, with Neville, headed to London in early 1959.

We called ourselves 'The Two Munros: Tip Top Taps from Down Under'. Once we arrived in London, we had a load of photographs taken and found a lovely agent, a Jewish woman, Beatrice Braham. In London we stayed in digs in Brixton – a real theatrical boarding house filled with showbiz types. It was a little overwhelming at first as I was just a shy Welsh boy from the valleys. I was afraid to open my mouth as my Welsh accent was still so thick (being Neville's 'brother' was just a stage-act, we didn't keep up the charade when we were amongst other performers).

Within a short time, Beatrice got us on the busy Moss Empire Circuit and we performed up and down the United Kingdom and Ireland. Moss Empires was founded as a company in Edinburgh in 1899 and became the largest chain of variety theatres and music halls in the UK. It was a great way to see different cities and work with some of the biggest names in show business. More on those soon.

It was around this time that my friend, Des, and I saw Liberace at the London Palladium. It was during his notorious libel case when he sued *Daily Mirror* columnist William Connor for insinuating that he was a homosexual. Heaven forbid! Liberace came on stage and sat at the piano and said, 'This is the softest bench I've been on all day.' The audience laughed as it clicked that he was referring to his trial at the High Court.

From Shakespeare to Tap

Liberace wore a black dinner jacket rather than the more flamboyant costumes for which he was later known. We loved the show, and he had a wonderful rapport with the audience, which were mostly women of a certain age, who lapped him up. After the show Des and I hurried to the stage door to meet him. He greeted us, thanked us for coming and signed our programs. Our encounter was very brief, and it was the first time that I had seen a felt-tip pen. I remember its fine point very well.

I have fond memories of the places we stayed and the people we met. Recently, thanks to Facebook, I heard from the granddaughter of a couple that Neville and I boarded with when we performed at Butlin's Holiday Camp in Ayrshire, Scotland. Both her grandparents had died, and she came across some letters that mentioned me several times.

It turns out that there were letters that I had written to her grandmother after I had moved to Australia. After moving Down Under in the 1960s I used to correspond with so many people because I wanted to keep them in my life. Clearly, I was not someone who liked to be alone. Some things never change! The granddaughter said that her grandmother used to talk about me all the time and that I had been a big part of her life. The grandmother was the manager of Woolworths in Ayr and her husband was the chauffeur for a very well-known local family. They were a fabulous couple.

While Neville and I were staying up in Ayr they went away for a month, so I invited Des and a friend of his to stay. One night we picked up some local men in Ayrshire and took them back to the house. I ended up dragging up in the grandmother's dresses and then tried on her husband's chauffeur uniform. It was one of the best parties I have ever hosted.

We stayed in Ayr for four months, all through the Scottish summer, performing two shows every night for two weeks as most people came to these camps for a fortnight's holiday. Scotland was never the warmest of places at the best of times and it was not uncommon to have two solid weeks of rain.

In the early days I admit I did wonder about Neville's sexuality. My friend Des certainly had his suspicions about him. Des was unused to the Australian accent and found it rather camp. When we worked in Wales, I introduced Neville to my family and my father gave me a look and asked, 'He's not one of those is he?' When I told him he was not he simply responded, 'Oh! Well, we don't want one of those in the family.' In later years Neville married and brought up a stepson and stepdaughter before he and his wife, Dawn, had a daughter of their own.

Our first job on the Moss Empire circuit was performing at the Liverpool Empire with comedian and actor Max Wall. Also appearing was an Irish vocal quartet called the Four Ramblers, which featured a young Val Doonican, who went on to become almost as famous for his knitted sweaters as his singing.

One of the biggest acts we got to work with early on in our career was the Andrews Sisters from America. We were performing on the same bill as them at the Gaumont Theatre in Southampton. It was an absolute thrill to see them perform and to be working alongside them as I could remember growing up listening to their 78-records on our wind-up gramophone when they had hits such as 'Boogie Woogie Boogle Boy' and 'Rum and Coca Cola.' Maxine, Patty and LaVerne were featured in films starring the likes of Bob Hope and Bing Crosby. I thought I had really hit the big time.

We shared the first half of the show with other acts, there would be an interval and then the Andrews Sisters would occupy the whole second half. They were fabulous and wonderful, and I would watch them perform in awe. I had to pinch myself to believe that these were the very same people I had heard on records and had seen in films.

It was also the first time that I had ever heard a woman swear. Neville and I helped them backstage with their costume changes for each song. On one occasion there was a problem with one of the costumes and I think it was Patty who exclaimed, 'Oh fuck it!' I was taken aback because not only had I never heard a woman say 'fuck' - or any other swear word - but this was one of the Andrews Sisters.

Sometime later, our agent Beatrice got us a gig in Germany touring the US military bases for about three months. I could not believe it as I had never thought I would go overseas. In the late 1950s, it was not very common to do so unless you had a lot of money or were emigrating.

One of my strongest first memories are of the delicatessens and cake shops which I loved. Germans are wonderful at making pastries and cakes. I never saw pastries like that in the UK beyond the odd custard tart. I also loved German pork sausages. You could get a meal at the bar with your beer. Two German sausages on your plate were enormous. They were big and fat and so juicy.

However, sadly I never had the opportunity to experience any German sausage of the human kind or visit any bars popular with gay men. We were on a very tight schedule and spent a lot of time between shows travelling on the tour bus to different military bases. For these reasons we had very little interaction with the military servicemen. We would arrive at each base, do our act (which was well received) and then we were gone.

During those months in Germany, we travelled with a group of variety entertainers. Headlining the bill was Welsh entertainer Tessie O'Shea and English comedian Bobby Dennis, who went on to find success in Australia and who also appeared in the BBC comedy series *It Ain't 'Arf Hot Mum* and *Hi-de-hi*. Tessie used to play the banjo and her nickname was Two-Ton Tessie because she was a rather large woman.

Both Tessie and Bobby were great to work with and very funny. Overall, and even though I didn't get to meet any German men, Germany was a wonderful experience and gave me my first taste of overseas travel.

Back in the UK, Neville and I were given the opportunity to work with some big names including Petula Clark, Helen Shapiro, Anthony Newley, Tommy Cooper and Adam Faith. I loved what I was doing so much, and I thought I had the best job because after many years of being bullied at school I felt I was now truly among friends. We were like a band of gypsies working and touring together. For the most part, nobody judged anyone else. Perhaps for the first time in my life I felt accepted, and my sexuality was not an issue.

My biggest thrill, in 1959, was to perform with English singer, songwriter and actress Petula Clark in the pantomime *Humpty Dumpty* in Southampton. I had followed her career for many years as she had started so young in show business. She was the most beautiful person and so friendly. And she was also tiny: she only came up to my shoulders and I am not tall. She was also half-Welsh which is a plus in my book.

Also appearing in *Humpty Dumpty* was English comedian Tommy Cooper. I knew Tommy off the television, and he was so funny. He was always so friendly and polite to me. I remember him being very tall with huge feet. When he walked it looked as if his feet belonged to a different person, as if they had a mind all of their own. Sadly, in 1984 he was to die, literally on stage, during a live television performance of a heart attack. I had a fling with Tommy's personal assistant during the pantomime's run. I should add he gave me crabs, the personal assistant, not Tommy. I had to shave off all my pubes and the critters were sorted. Happy days!

Neville and I worked with English actor, singer and songwriter Anthony Newley at the Birmingham Hippodrome around 1962. He was a wonderful entertainer. I was a keen photographer at the time, and I used my box camera to record a lot of the other performers. One evening I went into Anthony's dressing room to ask if I could take a photograph of him. He obliged and came out of the room for his close up. Sadly, I have long since lost that picture. When I was in the dressing room, I noticed a striking young woman who I later realised was the actress Joan Collins who he married in 1963. If I had known that at the time, I would have asked to have taken a picture of them both.

Other people we worked with included singer Adam Faith who was the heartthrob of his day. I thought he was adorable. Another performer on the same bill that I got on well with was Des Lane with whom Neville and I were sharing digs. He was often known as the Penny Whistle Man for his ability, funnily enough, to play the penny whistle. We all also worked with the John Barry Seven which was, unsurprisingly, led by John Barry who went on to become best known as the composer for many of the James Bond themes, as well as winning five Oscars for films like *Out of Africa* and *Born Free*.

One of the members of the John Barry Seven who I remember fondly was Les Reed, who would go on to write and co-write songs for the likes of Tom Jones, Engelbert Humperdinck and Herman's Hermits. They were all lovely people. The members of the John Barry Seven were such good friends that working alongside them was such a big hoot. One of the more unusual acts Neville and I were fortunate to work with was a vaudeville act called Wilson, Keppel and Betty, the highlight of which was a sand dance which parodied the postures of people in ancient Egyptian tomb paintings. I was standing in the wings once, talking to one of the male members of the trio. He told me that they could not go out in the sun as they were so pale. He said that if they tanned or burned, they would have to paint themselves white as being pale-skinned was a crucial part of their act.

I also worked with Rex Jameson, better known by his alter ego Mrs Shufflewick, a Cockney charlady very keen on her drink, and, as it turned out, so was Rex. The character would be seen propping up an imaginary bar each night. Rex wrote his own comedy material and was renowned for his perfect timing and delivery. In fact, many of those in the audience were unaware that Mrs Shufflewick was a man in drag as Rex would simply be billed as 'Mrs Shufflewick'. He was very convincing as a woman.

Mrs Shufflewick was a really big name around the variety theatres, music halls and working men's clubs and she became even bigger on radio and eventually television after many of the large theatres closed. I first heard her when I was about 15 on the BBC radio show *Workers' Playtime.*

Some years later she was one of the biggest names performing in gay pubs and I remember my dear friend Des telling me how funny she was when he saw her at the Black Cap in London. He loved the way Mrs Shufflewick dressed like an old barfly and got drunker and drunker. Some years later, in the 1970s, I was fortunate enough to see her perform at the same venue. Her act was a bit cruder than when I had shared the bill with her on the Moss Empire circuit. She would drop the odd 'fuck' here and there to please the queens.

I first worked with Rex Jameson as Mrs Shufflewick at the Newcastle Empire when I was 18. Also appearing on the bill was comedian and actor Max Wall and actor and singer Tommy Fields who was the brother of actress, singer and comedian Gracie Fields. Rex was really great. Then again, each night the material was exactly the same, word for word. On stage Mrs Shufflewick was a real belter and the patter and jokes just kept coming. She was very funny and made the act seem fresh and original to each new audience. Off stage Rex was very shy and retiring. He was a tiny man who reminded me of a pixie.

One of the highlights of my time as part of the Two Munros was touring for six weeks with Ralph Reader's *Gang Show* around 1960. Ralph was an actor, theatre producer and songwriter but from the age of 11 he had dedicated much of his life to the scouting movement. He created the format for the *Gang Show* which featured various sketches and variety acts. One of the songs that Ralph wrote was 'On the Crest of a Wave', which would be performed during the finale of the show.

The idea was very similar to the characters in the BBC television comedy *It Ain't Half Hot Mum* which tells the story of the Royal Artillery Concert Party putting on variety shows for troops in India and Burma. The original Gang Shows were performed by Scouts; today, they are still often performed by Scouts and Guides.

In our show, a professional theatre version, there was a group of singers from Manchester called the Lancashire Lads whose leader was as camp as Christmas. The group featured a young Freddie Starr who became a popular comedian, actor and singer in the UK. In Britain he is still remembered for the 1986 *Sun* newspaper headline 'Freddie Starr Ate My Hamster'. It is a story he always denied and claimed it was cooked up by the late publicist Max Clifford.

Freddie was as mad as an axe, as we say here in Australia, and was regularly having arguments and fights with the rest of the cast. He seemed to be angry and moody all the time. I never knew why. However, a couple of years later Neville and I were the opening act at the Liverpool Empire when Freddie came backstage to say hello after seeing us in the audience. He still talked the talk and walked the walk, but he seemed more mellow and down to earth.

Our Gang Show opened at the Finsbury Park Empire in London and it must have been one of the last productions on at the venue before it closed in 1960. Other towns and cities we travelled to included Brighton and Glasgow before finishing up in Coventry. Neville and I would do our dance and acrobatic act and then would join in with the rest of the chorus when needed.

Ralph Reader was an old queen who would often be seen with a young man who was just a couple of years older than me. None of us was certain whether it was his adopted son or his boyfriend. Let's just say that he and I had a few jumps in the hay and I soon realised it was unlikely he was Ralph's son. He was almost always with Ralph and seemed untouchable but I certainly touched him. He was a beautiful and lovely chap. It was all very hush hush as we didn't want Ralph finding out, and anyway I was also having a relationship with a man called Peter who ran a theatrical costumiers in London's West End and supplied all the costumes for the show.

Peter was in his late thirties and was married but wanted me. During our six-week run we spent as much time together as possible. I even visited his home and met his wife.

When we played in Brighton, I stayed with him at the Grand Hotel on the sea front. One morning the stage manager knocked on the bedroom door and asked if Peter had the 'Welsh Princess' in his bed.

Once the tour was over, we went our separate ways as often happened, given the nomadic world of touring. One of my abiding memories is when he took me to a restaurant in Brighton. It was the first time I had tried scampi. I have loved it ever since.

The leader of the Lancashire Lads troop was a gay man called Alan who made a move on me when we were performing in Brighton at the Hippodrome. I was having none of it as I was still on with Peter. Following our tour, we stayed in touch as I had always found Alan to be very pleasant and we had got on well.

During my time with the *Gang Show* I befriended a man called Eric Mills who was besotted with me, but I was dating Peter. Eric was hanging around with Ralph and was still in the army. About a month or so after I left the *Gang Show*, he left the military and travelled with Neville and me to Scotland where we were performing and got himself a job as a truck driver. He then followed us to Manchester. Eric was still enamoured with me and we enjoyed an on-off affair. My dalliance with Peter had ended when I had left the *Gang Show*.

As I wrote earlier, Neville and I spent a lot of time in Scotland. One year we were performing at the Glasgow Empire in Sauchiehall

Street. There was a man who used to come from Kilmarnock to see all the shows at the theatre. He was known by his camp name Lana Turner. Lana had a deformed foot and wore a built-up boot. Funny the things you remember. One day Lana introduced me to a young man called Johnny Beveridge. Johnny and I fell in love when we first met, and we had a good thing going when I was in Scotland performing at Butlin's Holiday Camp in Ayr for four months.

Johnny was a beautiful person in every sense and the most wonderful lover. He just adored me, and the feeling was mutual. He was very well hung, which I loved. Once again, when our summer season in Ayr was over, we parted ways. He was a busy man with his career and I was travelling with Neville doing our act. Johnny and I lost contact soon after.

However, a year later I was back in Glasgow and bumped into Lana Turner again. I knew that if anyone would know what Johnny was up to Lana would. She told me that Johnny was writing music. I thought that was fabulous and after much searching, I found out that Johnny was working in collaboration with fellow composer Peter Oakman. They wrote 'A Picture of You' which became a Top Five hit for English Cockney singer Joe Brown in 1962.

I have never forgotten Johnny. Several years ago, I tried to find him online but had no luck. So, I contacted his writing partner Peter Oakman to see if he knew what had become of him. Peter told me that Johnny had been living in Los Angeles and used to visit Peter and his wife. He said that the last time he saw Johnny was in 1985 and he was not well but he did not know what was wrong with him.

I later found out that Johnny had moved back to the UK and had tragically died from AIDS not long after. He was a couple of years younger than me; a life taken far too soon.

CHAPTER 5
Larry And John

It probably sounds like I had a long list of flings, admittedly, short-lived, with some of the men I was working with and there is probably some truth to that. I was young, good looking, virile and full of energy. However, they were not all happy liaisons. I was easy pickings for many of the performers who wanted a bit of fun on the side, often away from their wives or girlfriends.

One performer, in particular, manipulated and took advantage of me. I was in my late teens, and he was many years older than me. We performed regularly on the same bill. One evening he called me into his lodgings and the next thing I knew he had dragged me into bed and was having sex with me. This happened many times, but it was always on his terms. Even though he was taking advantage of me, I still fell for him big time.

Sometimes I went to his room begging for sex and he would tell me he was too tired or not in the mood. However, when it suited him, he would take me to bed and pretend as if nothing had happened. He was deeply in the closet and in denial. One time we were sitting on a double decker bus in London, and I tried to talk about my sexuality with him. His response was simply, 'You're sick, son!' As a teenager with raging hormones, I found it all so confusing.

I was so keen to keep in his good books that I would have done anything for him. I even acted as a pimp for him and went to bars and public toilets to find teenagers and young men for him. Once I offered a guy £5 to have sex with him. This performer with whom I was besotted went on to marry and have a family. Looking back, I feel totally used. If there was any silver lining it was that I promised myself that I would never allow myself to be trapped in the closet and would always be proud of who I am. I have stayed true to that to this day.

I do not think I really knew what love was as I did not have much love at home from Mum and Dad. Yes, Mum had encouraged and supported my theatrical side when I was younger, but I never felt much affection or love from her. Perhaps that is just my perception and she did love me in her own way. I thought both my older brother and the owner of the Langford Scholars in London, Francis Langford, loved me when in fact they abused me. I craved affection and would quickly 'fall in love' with whoever I became intimate with. I realise now that I wanted what was lacking at home.

You may well ask where Neville was during all my liaisons and what he thought of them. For much of the time we toured together I insisted on staying in different boarding houses as I did not think Neville would approve of my antics. I really did not need Neville knowing about my various hook ups or who I might be sharing a bed with. His main concern was our double act and that is how I wanted to keep it. It was really a case of out of sight and out of mind…as much on his part as mine I suspect.

He certainly did not get the camp sense of humour that many of those we worked with displayed. Sometimes after a show those of us sharing digs would stay up late and just piss ourselves with laughter into the wee hours. I really do not think dear Neville would have approved. That is not a criticism. Neville was wonderful to me and gave me many opportunities that I may never have experienced otherwise. Above all, he helped me realise my dream of escaping the Welsh valleys. However, we were very different people and I think giving ourselves space between shows was healthy and meant we were not suffocating each other. I never really knew or asked where Neville stayed.

During my time on the Moss Empire circuit, I had two relationships with performers who went on to become stars on British television. Both shared my camp sense of humour and my time with them has formed some of my happiest memories.

I first met Larry Grayson when Neville and I were performing on the same bill as him in 1959 at the Liverpool Empire. Headlining the show was pop heart-throb Adam Faith. In support were Scottish singer Johnny Worth, singing group The Honeys, the John Barry Seven and comedian Don Arrol. Larry wasn't ever well-known in Australia, but he became a huge television personality in Great Britain. His period of greatest fame was in the 1970s and 80s and he hosted an extremely popular BBC game show, *The Generation Game,* which attracted audiences of over 20 million viewers.

The first show of the evening was due to start at about six thirty. Neville and I were getting ready in our dressing room when the door flew open and one of the campest men I had ever seen called out, 'Hello boys!' and as bold as brass waltzed over to the window, which faced a brick wall. He flung open the window and announced, 'Oh, I have always loved this view'. It certainly broke the ice for me, and, in that moment, Larry entered my life like a whirlwind and an instant friendship formed. Larry would have been in his mid-30s, I was 18.

Larry And John

Larry's style of comedy was essentially him having a friendly gossip with the audience. He was amazingly witty but could also bring down a house just with a raised eyebrow or a faux look of shock. He appeared during the first half of the show in a suit, dragging his trademark Bentwood chair across the stage, complaining to the audience about his various ailments and telling them how he had not been well. He then essentially brought the audience into his confidence, gossiping about what his imaginary friends, with names such as Apricot Lil, Slack Alice, Pop-It-In-Pete, Self-Raising Fred and Everard, had been getting up to. His style of comedy was camp but never bitchy but loaded with inuendo.

He often paused during his act and had a sniff or a scratch, exclaiming, 'Just look at the muck in here' or 'It's alive'. His genuine camp nature spilled into his show and he would often look at a young man in the audience, give him a wink and smile before saying 'Seems like a nice boy'. He adopted this as a catchphrase along with 'Limp as a vicar's handshake' and 'What a gay day'. Larry's best-known catchphrase was probably 'Shut that door' which, on the face of it, doesn't sound all that funny, but when delivered by Larry, was enough to get a huge laugh from the audience.

He did not tell jokes like a lot of comedians and instead his act was laden with innuendo and audiences loved it. His timing, mannerisms and intonation were perfect. When he eventually found huge success on TV, the camera 'loved him' because he could create so much humour just with a witty, camp aside, or simply a look to the camera.

During the second half of the show Larry appeared in drag. He wore a blouse and skimpy mini skirt which showed off his skinny legs. He also wore a dreadful wig and beret and wore huge clumpy wedge-heeled shoes.

He immediately created a rapport with the audience, and everyone seemed to relate to him, as if he was gossiping with friends. I thought he was brilliant and hung on to his every word. Everything that came out of his mouth made me collapse into hysterics. I can honestly say he is the only man who has ever made me fall off my chair laughing…on several occasions! And, as I said, his humour was always of an innocent kind, based simply on the observations he made, especially of the imaginary people who populated his imaginary world.

On one occasion Larry and I were staying in a boarding house in Liverpool with the 'Penny Whistle Man' Des Lane, and a blonde music trio, the Honeys, with whom we were performing. Our accommodation faced a church, and from the lounge where we ate lunch, we could see a wedding about to take place with all the guests and, of course, the groom and bride arriving. We watched avidly through the net curtains as Larry gave us a running commentary on each arrival and, in particular, what they were wearing. Comments such as 'Just Look at the hat on her' or 'I would never wear a dress like that to my daughter's wedding' just tripped off his tongue. He just made up the commentary as he went along, and we were rolling on the floor in hysterics. He had us in the palm of his hand.

Larry And John

I remember thinking on several occasions why he was not a star on television. It was not until he was in his early fifties that he found success on television in the early 1970s with *Shut That Door!* Of course, his biggest success came in 1978 with the BBC's *The Generation Game.* By the time he appeared on television he had dropped the drag part of his act, but the rest remained unchanged, including his colourful characters and camp catchphrases. He developed a huge following among viewers who really adored his camp, inuendo laden humour, but it was underpinned with genuine warmth and love. He would invite the audience into this whimsical world that he created on stage or in front of the camera.

Naturally, I was besotted by him. I really was. I stayed with him on quite a few occasions over the years, including on trips back from Australia. For most of the time I knew him closely, he and his adoptive sister, Fan, lived in a tiny one-up and two-down house in Nuneaton in the Midlands. The house had no bathroom but there was a washhouse at the back with neither a shower nor a bath. You would have to run water in the sink and use a flannel to wash yourself.

Larry had been born William White in Oxfordshire to an unmarried couple. At ten days old he was adopted by Alice and Jim Hammond from Nuneaton who had two daughters, Flo, or Fan as Larry called her, and May. Sadly, his adoptive mother Alice died when he was six years old and Fan brought him up. In fact, they spent most of their lives together under the same roof and Fan dedicated her life to Larry. She would do everything for him including cleaning and cooking; nothing was too much trouble. She was lovely, though understandably protective of Larry as she cared deeply for him. Larry would have done anything for her, too.

A regular visitor to his home in Nuneaton was a woman who Larry knew as his Aunty Ethel. I had met her because she used to come round on a Sunday. She was a lovely lady with a warm and beautiful personality. As a boy he had discovered that she was in fact his biological mother. In 1963 when I was on board the P&O ship that took me to Australia Larry sent me a letter as I had told him all the stops on the way so that post would reach me. What a tragic tale that letter contained. Larry explained that Ethel had come to stay. He was thrilled that she was under the same roof as him as it gave them a further chance to bond. However, when he had gone to the upstairs bedroom to check on her, he found to his absolute horror, that she had died.

I held on to that letter since 1963, but I somehow lost it a several years ago on a trip to the UK. I wanted to donate it to the Nuneaton Museum. Larry began the letter, 'I never thought I would be writing this to you' and it was full of emotion as he opened up about his feelings regarding his mum and her death. The letter was typed, and he signed it with a pen, 'Lal'. He wrote and sent me the letter within a couple of weeks of her death. I felt very sad for him, but I was also happy that he was able to confide in me.

He loved company, and his friends in Nuneaton often visited his home where much gossip and laughter would ensue. Larry was a natural entertainer and always so much fun. If ever I was feeling down or had had a difficult gig his companionship was always the perfect antidote. At this stage Larry was known as Larry Grayson in the theatres but in the working men's clubs where he also performed he was known by his other stage name, Billy Breen. His friends would often call him 'Lal' though family members often referred to him as 'our Billy'.

If I was staying at his home, I would accompany him to his gigs at local clubs in Birmingham or Coventry. He was popular and getting regular club work. He would have the club audience in stitches just as he would at the Moss Empire theatres.

Larry introduced me to my favourite type of food shortly after we first met around 1959. We were driving back to his home in Nuneaton after a performance in Birmingham. Inside the car were me, Larry and some of his family. Now, first I must tell you about one of the other performers on the bill that evening, a rather chubby female opera singer. In the first part of her act there were no great surprises. Larry kept telling me to wait and see what would happen later in the evening.

I was intrigued. She came on in the second half, but she had no top on. She had a big ball gown on but was naked from her waist upwards with her great big breasts hanging out. She had a beautiful voice but I was not quite sure of the point, but then Larry and I probably were not her usual audience. It was a bit wasted on us, but we found it hilarious.

Larry liked to eat after the show and if there was a restaurant open late it was often Chinese. However, on our way back to Nuneaton we could not find a Chinese restaurant, but Larry noticed an Indian restaurant that was open. I had never eaten Indian food. So, our group bundled into this Indian restaurant and had this marvellous meal. I have loved Indian food from that moment on. With all the spices and different flavours, I found it such a contrast to the bland plain food to which I was accustomed.

Larry's campness and innuendo-laden humour has led to much conjecture about his sexuality of the 'is he or isn't he' variety. Some people claim that he was closeted about his sexuality while one book I read recently even seemed to suggest he was probably asexual or even sexless. I want to address these claims as I can tell you from first-hand experience that he was none of these things.

Larry was about 18 years older than me, and I simply adored him. It did not take long for a bond to develop between the sheets for us and we slept together many times. I don't think I was very sexually attracted to Larry but he was charismatic and entertaining and that drew me to him. The sexual dimension to our relationship seemed to happen naturally and I would have done anything to please him so happily went with the flow. He was not exactly a Casanova, but I just loved being with him.

Larry later came in for much criticism from some gay liberationists for supposedly being in the closet and not coming out. I find such suggestions really surprising. I do not think that there could have been a closet big enough for Larry because he was so out there. It was never a secret and he never tried to hide it. His friends knew, as did many of his fellow performers. I never saw him attempt to conceal his sexuality and I am not sure he could have even if he had tried, as his act was so camp and full of innuendo. As for complaints about him portraying a 'tired old camp and effeminate stereotype' of a gay man, well that was Larry. Larry was the same off stage as he was on. With Larry you largely saw what you got. On stage he was simply playing himself.

I read a recent biography of Larry which stated that he suffered from depression. I never saw this side of Larry and I find it hard to imagine him being depressed. To me, he had always seemed such a happy person to be around and had this cheerful aura about him. But then again, I was quite a lot younger and probably couldn't recognise depression in older people, anyway. I am sure that trying to keep up a cheerful demeanour all the time could be a bit of a strain. I think he concealed his depression quite well. Throughout much of my life I, too, have suffered from depression and I know that I have successfully hidden it from other people, including friends, by putting on a metaphorical mask of happiness and fun.

Larry became very upset when Judy Garland died in 1969. He adored and idolised Judy. He loved her films and records and had seen her when she had visited London. I was staying with him at the time, and he was beside himself with grief when he heard about her death. I had never seen this sad side of Larry. He had seemed to be on a constant high and it was as if he was on stage all the time.

Back in the 1960s there was no internet of course which made it harder to stay in contact and easier to lose touch and so this wonderful, close friendship with Larry slowly fizzled out although I heard bits and pieces about him from time to time. The last time I saw him was when my partner Phillip and I made a trip to the UK from Australia during Christmas 1974.

By this time Larry had found much success on television as the host of the comedy talk show *Shut That Door*! He had also appeared on other television shows including the first of two cameos on the soap opera *Crossroads*, a soapy he adored.

My mother, who loved him, kept me informed of his growing television success in letters to me in Australia. I had introduced him to my family when we had been working in Bristol and he charmed them as he did so many other people. When he performed at the New Theatre in Cardiff my mother was in the audience. She had sent a message to him to say she was there, and he made a big fuss of her, which she was really chuffed about, and gave her a photograph of himself with a lovely message written on it.

During our 1974 trip back to the UK, Phillip and I decided to see Larry perform the role of Wishee Washee in *Aladdin*, the pantomime, at the Birmingham Hippodrome. I sent a message ahead to let him know we would be in the audience.

As we walked into the foyer of the theatre, I noticed Larry talking to Alfred Marks, who was also appearing in the panto, in the corner. Larry spotted me and after lots of hugging, he insisted we come backstage to see him after the show. Afterwards we went backstage and were offered a drink in his dressing room in which a crowd of people had gathered. Phillip and I were just two among the throng.

Larry seemed somewhat different from the down to earth person I

Larry And John

knew and admired. All Larry did was talk about himself, and none of that impressed Phillip. He seemed to have little interest in anyone else in that room. The spark between Larry and me no longer seemed to be there. He seemed more aloof and distant. I think what changed was that he had become a star. He was certainly the star of *Aladdin* and had top billing. He was making big money and even had his own chauffeur. I think that perhaps fame, money and success had gone to his head. He did not have all of that when I knew him in the late 1950s and 1960s. Perhaps I am being harsh but that was my perception at the time.

As we left the dressing room, he gave me a note and said, 'Ring me, here's my phone number.' I noticed he had left a digit off. I felt at the time that he had done it purposely. Perhaps he felt he had moved on or perhaps without realising I had said or done something to upset him. I never found out but that was the last time I ever saw or had any more contact with him.

I remember watching him on the television when he performed at the Royal Variety Performance in 1994 where he made a surprise appearance on stage in front of the then Prince of Wales. It had been a few years since he had enjoyed any regular television work. His opening words were, 'They thought I was dead' which proved to be quite prophetic. Larry had his familiar chair as his prop, and he uttered his various camp and innuendo-laden catch phrases, and his friend Slack Alice even had a mention. He ended his five-minute stint with his most familiar line, 'Shut that door!' Unfortunately, within six weeks of that performance he was dead after having been rushed to hospital with a perforated appendix.

I treasure the many fond memories I have of Larry and will always be thankful to him as he helped give me the confidence to be myself. He was very much my mentor and teacher and I learned much about timing gags and general stage craft from watching him perform. But above all, for many years he was a dear friend.

John Inman came into my life when we were both performing in Scarborough. John is best known for playing the flamboyant Mr Humphries in the BBC comedy *Are You Being Served*? I never grew as close to John as I did to Larry as I met him less than a year before I moved to Sydney, but he absolutely lit up my life at the time and knocked me out with his dry wit and camp humour.

We met in 1962 when we were both working at neighbouring theatres. He was in his late 20s and I, just 21. I think it was my second or third summer season in the UK. Neville and I were performing at the Futurist Theatre in The *Al Read Show*.

Neville and I did two shows a night and the theatre was packed every evening as Scarborough was the place to go in Yorkshire for a summer holiday, with vibrant entertainment all along the seafront both day and night.

John was appearing in *What a Racket* at the Arcadia Theatre, next door to the Futurist Theatre where Neville and I were performing. It starred the comedian Albert Modley. The play was a comedy about a young lad who was a rock 'n' roll artist and lived with his parents.

John and I met backstage (the two theatres had a shared backstage area) and got to know each other very quickly because we shared the same sense of camp humour. We used to be taken out to lunch on the seafront quite often by a very merry old queen who worked in a holiday camp and who, as it turned out, was quite keen on me. He would pay for everything and sometimes brought along chickens on a rotisserie from the restaurant where he worked. I remember wondering who on earth could afford a whole rotisserie chicken in those days. I had seen them before because when I left school I worked briefly in a restaurant in Newport. I got the sack because the manager caught me and the headwaiter down in the tap room where they changed the barrels. It was the headwaiter who was fiddling with me, but it was me who lost their job.

Anyway, not only did John and I share the same sense of humour, we were both very partial to the liqueur, Tia Maria. How we made it back to some of our shows in time and sober I will never know.

John and I basically had a 'holiday romance' even though we were, of course, both working. I think the holiday atmosphere at Scarborough helped and we had the most brilliant summer together. We had so many fabulous parties which John hosted in his room to which our fellow actors and entertainers would be invited. John was the same in private as he was in public. He could be a bit over the top, as was his later character, Mr Humphries, but I loved all of that. People who were over the top or 'theatrical' were my heroes and I was a bit over the top too. We were simply not afraid to be ourselves.

John and I were inseparable during that summer of 1962. I adored his outrageous sense of humour which I am sure has rubbed off on me. After I moved to Australia, we stayed in touch. When he was filming the disastrous Australian version of *Are You Being Served?* in 1980 at Channel Ten in Melbourne, he came around for dinner with Phillip and me as we lived not far from the studios which were in Nunawading. A few years later I was living back in Sydney when he brought his own stage show out to Australia and I went to see him again. Over the years we stayed in touch with occasional letters and Christmas cards.

In 2003 I received a VHS tape with a label on it written, 'A Christmas present for Stan.' A friend of mine who had put the video together had just returned from visiting England. When I played the tape, I was gobsmacked. On it was John in his dressing room at the New Theatre in Woking near London where he was appearing as Widow Twankey in *Aladdin*.

He wished me a very merry Christmas and recalled our happy time together in Scarborough as well as his visits to Australia where we caught up. At the end of the video John said he would try and find me on his next trip Down Under. Sadly, I never did hear from him again and he died a few years later, in 2007. Recording that video was such a sweet gesture and one I will never forget along with my many other beautiful memories of John.

CHAPTER 6
The Ten Pound Pom

In the summer of '62 while we were working in Scarborough, and while I was happily having my holiday romance with John Inman, Neville dropped a bombshell that was to change the course of my life: 'Son, I think I'll go home to Australia.'

His revelation left me with some serious thinking about my future as Neville had been such a crucial part of my life over the past four years. At 21, I did not yet feel ready to go solo and I knew I didn't want to stay in Wales. Not surprisingly, I never felt accepted there as a homosexual man. To me the valleys were grey, wet and hideous. Through performing with Neville, I had met and worked with people similar to me and I had developed a sense of belonging.

Neville then told me about an initiative called the Assisted Passage Migration Scheme, which had been set up by the Australian government to encourage mainly British citizens to move Down Under. Ten Pound Poms as they were known colloquially would pay just £10 for their fare to Australia and in return, they would agree to stay in Australia for a minimum of two years or they would have to refund the full fare.

There was a more sinister side to the scheme as this was very much part of the country's White Australia Policy though I had not realised it at the time. The Assisted Passage Migration Scheme was a strategy to populate Australia with white migrants. Many non-white and mixed-race British who applied for the scheme were reportedly knocked back.

Famous 'Ten Pound Poms' include the Bee Gees, Jimmy Barnes and John Swan, John Farnham, Olivia Newton-John and members of the Easybeats. Disgraced businessman Alan Bond and former Australian Prime Ministers Julia Gillard and Tony Abbott came to Australia under the scheme with their families.

I decided to explore this scheme as a means of escape to get as far away from the slag heaps of my childhood home as well as to have an adventure. One day I went to a government office in Newport where I filled in lots of forms. Neville's sister in Sydney had kindly agreed to sponsor me and within a couple of weeks I received a letter informing me that I had been approved for the scheme. I was so excited about the adventure that awaited me!

But, to complicate matters, several months before I left for Australia, I met a handsome man called Eddie through Larry Grayson, and we had begun a relationship. Larry had worked with Eddie in the clubs as he was a dancer. Eddie was fully aware that I was committed to go to Sydney and we agreed to make the most of the time that we had left together. Then, the plan was that after I had spent my two years in Australia, I would return to him.

Eddie was very good looking, and we fell in love immediately. We would see each other whenever we could.

Eddie was very supportive of me going to Australia as he wanted me to pursue my dreams. However, he expressed no interest, at that time, in going himself.

Only about a month before we sailed to Australia, I broke the news to my parents that I was leaving. My mum cried but my father was rather stoic about the whole thing. Mum was always rather emotional, like me. I think that is where I get it from. My siblings seemed rather indifferent but then we had never been that close. However, once the initial shock had waned, both my parents were supportive of me going.

A couple of nights before we sailed for Australia, Neville and I had dinner with my parents in a pub in Newbridge. My family liked Neville as they appreciated his Australian openness. They gave us a gift of a pair of Philips electric shavers. I found this a very strange present. I rarely shaved as I had very little facial hair. It was only when I was about 24 or 25 that I began shaving properly and then I would have a wet shave the traditional way. I think I may have used the electric shaver once to remove what few whiskers I may have had. I probably found it more useful for shaving my legs.

Two days later I met up with Neville on a freezing cold February morning at Newport Railway Station and from there we made our way to the Port of Tilbury on the River Thames in Essex. We were to sail on the SS Orion, and it would be our home for the next six weeks or so.

At the time she was built she was the largest Orient Liner, though this was to be her last voyage before she was broken up for scrap metal. She was reportedly the first British liner to be built with air conditioning in all the rooms. The ship carried a maximum of 1,691 passengers.

We boarded her on the 28th of February 1963 to begin our voyage to Australia via the Suez Canal. It was a dull, cold and dreary day and the promise of sunshine and warmth of Australia could not have come soon enough for me. An orchestral version of 'We'll Meet

Again' was playing on the ship's speakers. There were many tears as families and individuals on board waved goodbye to their loved ones left behind on the shore. Brightly coloured streamers connected those on board to those on shore and as the ship pulled away from its mooring the streamers snapped, a sad symbol of the separation that people would feel as their loved ones sailed off on the long voyage to start their new life in Australia. Maybe it was seeing all those streamers stretch and break that set me off, but suddenly I was overwhelmed with this feeling of panic: 'What the fuck am I doing?'

However, it didn't take me long to settle again and any second thoughts were quickly put to the back of my mind as my sense of adventure set in. Neville and I were in separate cabins and I was sharing with four fellow British travellers. I remember little about my fellow travellers in my cabin except that I became rather bored after a short time sharing a cabin and sharing a dining table with the same people for several weeks.

There was very little entertainment beyond bingo in the evenings. I do not even remember seeing a band though I think people may have danced to recorded music. There were some activities such as a swimming pool and table tennis but of course nothing like the stage shows and first-class entertainment you get now on the luxury liners. After all, adults were only paying £10, and kids went free. Thankfully, drinks were cheap, and I would usually have an early dinner before spending the evening at the bar, flirting with bar staff and the occasional passenger.

Things livened up quite a bit when we reached Piraeus, our first port of call. It was here that we picked up many stunning-looking Greek men. I'd never seen so many attractive men, with their dark eyes and hair and olive complexions and beautiful smiles. They were Greek gods! I certainly enjoyed the company of a few during the voyage. In fact, a young Greek took up the spare bed in my cabin and he soon made his intentions known to me. I also enjoyed dalliances with some of the crew. We would suss each other out through eye contact, lingering glances and subtle flirting. I also met up with some of the other Ten Pound Poms as well. On one occasion a man took me to his cabin to have sex. He told me that his wife was in the sick bay with one of his children who was ill.

The ports provided an interruption to my boredom as they usually gave us an opportunity to leave the boat for a few hours. My abiding memory of Piraeus was of prostitutes trying to persuade us to go with them to bars and clubs. I kept having to tell them I was a homosexual. It was pretty full on.

Port Said in Egypt was fabulous. It was my first time outside Europe, and it was so different to what I had known. We were not allowed off the boat, but local traders would pull up their boats next to our ship and show us their wares. They used an ingenious pulley system using a rope. They would put whatever you wanted to buy in the basket and send it up to you. You would then send the basket back down with your money. Typical things they would sell were shirts and sarongs. I found it all fascinating.

One port I will never forget was Bombay. A group of us got dressed up to go ashore that night. It was so hot and humid. I had never seen such poverty or seen so many homeless people sleeping in doorways. Beggars would constantly hassle us by tugging at our clothes and begging for money. It made me feel so sad.

There was cow shit everywhere we went in Bombay, and it stank so much. I was wearing my best white jeans and unceremoniously fell in some of the cow shit. That brought my night in Bombay to an early end and my experience in the city was ruined. It was straight back to the ship after that.

Crossing the equator was a big deal and one of the crew dressed up as King Neptune and demanded to know why we should be given his approval to cross over into the southern hemisphere. He even threw a few passengers and crew into the pool. It was great fun, and the kids received a certificate signed by Neptune himself, authenticating that they had crossed over the equator. It really was a kind of crossing the threshold experience and it made me realise that I was now a long way from home! Seeing Australia for the first time was so exciting as I knew this was the beginning of my new life in the 'Lucky Country'. Our first Australian port of call was Fremantle in Western Australia. By now it was late March, and it was so hot! It must have been about 45 degrees Celsius. I had never experienced heat anything like it. The sky was bright blue and looked so different to that of Wales. It was as if everything was technicolour.

I disembarked the ship with some other passengers and headed straight to the nearest pub. I ordered a beer, but it was so cold it made my teeth chatter as I had never tasted cold beer before.

After just one day in Fremantle, we sailed to Adelaide, where we could again get off the boat and have a look around. I noticed a lot of churches and I started feeling a bit apprehensive. It all seemed a bit too conservative and old fashioned.

We then sailed to Melbourne, which I thought was quite pretty. I loved the old buildings though a lot of them have now sadly gone. We were in Melbourne for the day, and I went to the movies in the afternoon. Although I can't recall the name of the film, I do remember that I had never been to such a large cinema. I had never seen a cinema of that size in the UK even though Neville and I had performed at some huge theatres in the UK and elsewhere, such as the Theatre Royal in Dublin in 1961.

We arrived in Sydney on April 3rd, 1963. It was fabulous sailing through the Heads and seeing the Sydney Harbour Bridge glistening in the sun. I thought it was such a beautiful harbour even though the Opera House had not yet been built. A brass band was playing and once again there were lots of colourful streamers. Lots of families were waiting to meet their relatives on the shore. We disembarked at Circular Quay and our identification documents were checked by Immigration officials. I had not been given a passport (in fact I didn't actually get a passport until a few years later) but a sheet of paper with my photograph and details such as my height and hair colour.

We were met by Neville's sister, Maude, and we went to live with her and her husband in Lidcombe. They had a son and two daughters, but Neville and I were given our own rooms. George worked at a local abattoir, and he would often bring home a sheep and slaughter and butcher it in the garden shed. Fortunately, I never actually saw him kill any sheep, but we did enjoy some tasty home cooked lamb dinners.

My first impressions of Sydney were that it seemed rather old fashioned. Even the clothes seemed behind the times compared to what I had seen in Britain. The men still went to work carrying Gladstone leather bags, for example.

Within a week of arriving in Sydney I found a job at Lidcombe Dairy Farmers where I worked for about a year. It was the nearest factory to where I lived, and it was essentially a bottling plant. I would get up at 6.30am to start work at 7am and finished around 3.30pm. The Dairy Farmers Factory was only a ten-minute walk down the Parramatta Road, so it was quite convenient.

My job was so butch; it could not have been more different from performing in theatres. I worked in the shunting yard where the trains carrying the milk would come in. The milk was transported in long barrel-like tankers. I would undo the bottom part of the tanker and the milk would then be pumped to a central point in the factory. Once it was empty, my job was to climb inside and hose it out with scalding hot and then cold water. I often burnt myself.

It was here that I first experienced 'Pommy bashing' as well as homophobia from my foreman, Dick White. He was a real swine to me and treated me something shocking. He would call me, and a couple of other gay workers, names like 'poofter' and 'shirt lifter'. His favourite was 'pervert'. The few of us who were gay at work did not flaunt our sexuality and simply got on with the job we were paid to do.

He would really let me have it, particularly as I was quite shy and trying to find my way in a new country. I kept a photograph of my Mum and Dad in my wallet and on one occasion, for instance, he saw their pale skin and said, 'Typical looking Pommies!' His barbs were relentless and within a short time I really began to hate him.

Fairly soon after Neville and I had arrived in Sydney, we had established contact with some agents and through them had begun doing our dance show in the Returned Services League (RSL) clubs and other venues in and around the city. The shows went really well, and the audiences responded positively just as they had done in the UK. We were a well-polished act by then.

Working at the Dairy Farmers factory as well as the RSLs kept me rather busy but I was nevertheless very keen to meet other gay men and visit the places where they hung out. Some of the crew I had slept with on the ship over from England had previously visited Sydney and they told me the place to go to meet other gay men was 'the Cross'. Yes, Kings Bloody Cross. It was the 'camp hub' of Sydney well before Oxford Street or parts of Newtown became popular places for men of the homosexual variety.

It did not take me long to head to the Cross and discover the Chevron and the Rex Hotels which were popular with gay men, and they became my favourite venues. The Cross back then was not the seedy, down-at-heel place it became in the 1970s and 80s. It was still bohemian and cosmopolitan, filled with cafes, restaurants, delicatessens, specialised grocery stores, as well as cabarets and hotels such as the newly built Chevron, 'Sydney's Glamour Hotel'. But there was still an edginess to the Cross even then and gangsters and crooked politicians ran all kinds of illicit businesses. I certainly don't want to give the impression that it was 'Pleasantville'.

One of my favourite venues was the Outrigger Bar in the basement of the Chevron in Macleay Street. It was a vast place, but everyone was so friendly and open. It was very easy to tell that you were in a space filled with men who liked men. There was no attitude, and I could pick up easily, standing there sipping innocently from my Bacardi and Coke. The Rex Hotel on the other hand could be a pretty mad place, full of rent boys looking for their next clients. I will never forget that I was in the Rex one night and a fellow walked into the bar with a lobster on a lead. A sailor in the bar yelled out, 'This is an Australian floor show.' I think it was just one of the oddities of the Rex. Anything went.

Pubs closed at 10pm so when the Chevron closed my friends (I had established a small group of friends by now) would leave the bar and stand around the bottle shop to find out if and where we could party on. If there was a party, you would grab yourself a bottle of cheap plonk and head to where it was taking place.

There was one famous party place called the Pet Shop at Petersham. The building had a pet shop at the front and the two boys who ran it lived out the back. They hosted great parties, full of gay men, sometimes up to 20 or so. Everybody just mixed together. Today the different men would probably be classified as twinks, bears and daddies but back then it did not matter. There was none of the labelling of gay men you get now. We were all there for a fun time and that is what we had. It was simply an eclectic group of gay men.

At another party I first laid my eyes on the infamous Rosaleen Norton, the so-called 'Witch of Kings Cross'. I could smell pot before I even entered the party, which was in an apartment at the back of some shops. Rosaleen was sitting in a corner holding court. The air was thick with tobacco smoke and weed. She was giving Tarot card readings to some of the boys. I was introduced to her, and she gave me some vague look of acknowledgement. I found her scary. She looked ugly and she had these funny-looking, protuding teeth. She spooked me a bit with this intimidating look in her eyes. It was all a rather unsettling experience.

However, not every experience that I had of meeting people was as disconcerting. While Neville and I were performing at Redfern RSL club I was lucky to meet a drag performer called Francis Shaw who was our support act. His act, which was 'old school drag' involving beautiful dresses and lots of feathers and sequins, was actually very popular at the various clubs in Sydney.

After our show had finished, we got talking and he invited me to go with him to the Artists Ball at the Trocadero Ballroom, or the 'Troc' as it was affectionately known, in George Street. He also suggested I go in drag, which I happily agreed to. About a week or so later I went to his home in Auburn, which was just up the road from Lidcombe where I was living. I couldn't believe how I looked after he had made my face up – I looked beautiful. It really surprised me how someone with skill and talent could transform my face so much. I also realised that I still had a t shirt on by this stage and so Francis cut it off me with a pair of scissors so that I wouldn't smudge the makeup.

He kindly lent me a pink leotard as well as some white tulle which hung from my backside to the floor. I also wore a pair of beige wedge shoes that I had purchased at Sydney's Paddy's Market.

The Artists Ball, as the name suggests, was full of creative types and their muses and models. It was a hub for many of Sydney's bohemians. These events were inspired by some of the balls that had been held in Europe in places such as the Belle Epoque in the Montmartre in Paris and partygoers would attend in fancy dress.

Many of those attending in Sydney would go in drag and there are stories of drag queens arriving in large removal vans because their costumes and wigs were too large to be transported any other way.

I was so scared and nervous as Francis drove me and another queen called Diamond Lil to the Ball. This was a totally new experience for me as I had never been out in public as an adult in drag and nor had I been to such an event as the one we were heading to. On the way we stopped by a laneway by the Parramatta Road as one queen wanted to take a pee. I found it all so fascinating as she pulled down her corsets and found what she needed to find. It seemed to me that taking a piss in drag was an art form in itself.

Walking into the ballroom was like I was walking into another world. A fabulous, glamorous world. A band played background music as people hugged and kissed each other and, of course, checked out what everyone was wearing. Groups of friends each had their own table which they had decorated in amazing ways as there was a prize for the best dressed table. One of Francis's friends complemented me on how fabulous my legs were. I was ecstatic.

The band started playing dance music and I decided to hit the dance floor and hit it I did. Much to my great embarrassment I slipped over and fell on my back. I really should have spent more time learning to balance on heels. Women have my full admiration. I was mortified but thankfully nobody took any notice though it meant nobody helped me off the ground, which was not easy given the shoes I was wearing. I think the queens were too busy admiring each other's costumes to notice.

To make matters worse I needed to use the toilet, which I found a nightmare. I definitely didn't have the skill I had been admiring earlier in the night when our friend had had to pee on the way to the Ball. I struggled to find a way to pee without wetting myself. In the end I managed to dig deep with one of my hands into the leotard and locate my penis and drag it out. Such a challenge for something that was normally so simple.

There was lots of music, dancing and, of course, queens. Despite my initial setbacks I found the evening was magical! I adored being in drag that night being amongst all the other drag queens.

Francis Shaw was very popular in the RSL clubs and was rarely out of work. He preferred performing to straight crowds as he found the audience less boisterous and more receptive than a gay one plus the money was often better, and he knew he would get paid at the end of the night.

In gay venues you would often be just one of many drag performers and were at the whim of whoever was running the place. They could pretty much pay you whatever they wanted.

I do have an anecdote that Francis shared with me. He used to troll the toilets at Lidcombe train station. On this particular day, Francis was in a cubicle, waiting for some action, peering through one of the peep holes that had been in the partition, hoping he might see an attractive guy on the other side. As he peered through the hole, the fellow in the neighbouring cubicle stuffed some toilet paper into the hole to block his view. This frustrated Francis very much and so he removed the paper. Each time he did so the fellow stuffed it back in.

After a few minutes he heard the guy leave the cubicle and waited, like a hungry trapdoor spider, for the next person to arrive. A few minutes later, he heard the door lock next door, and he hoped his luck might change. The next thing he knew, he was covered in the contents of a bag of flour that had been thrown over the cubicle wall. Fearing that worse was to come, Francis sprung out of the toilets and across the station platform to his car and drove home looking like a white ghost.

He thought it was such a bizarre encounter that he needed to tell his friend Rose about it. Rose had huge breasts because she took hormones, although she was never seen in a frock. She was usually more casually dressed in jeans and a t-shirt. Rose drove a baker's van. So, Francis phoned up Rose and spluttered, 'I've got something unbelievable to tell you…' Rose immediately responded, 'Well let me tell you something unbelievable that happened to me today. At Lidcombe Station there was some queen that kept trying to look at me in the bog, so I went to my van and picked up some flour and threw it over her.' Francis replied in shock, 'You fucking bitch. That was me!'

Attending the Artists Ball had really awakened my interest in drag and soon after I decided to go along to watch my first drag show in Sydney at a recently opened venue called the Jewel Box. It sat above a hamburger joint on Darlinghurst Road in Kings Cross. I was still living in Lidcombe and got there quite early, with a friend of mine, well before any shows were about to start. It was a bit dingy and there was only a small stage with drab curtains. It all looked a bit cheap.

However, things started to change as the glamorous performers began arriving. Electra and Josie Jay were two of the stars that night, who both went on to work at Les Girls. They confidently strode straight across the stage and behind the curtains. I could not believe how beautiful they were or that they had been born male. When they performed, they mimed to some of the top singers of the day. I had never seen anything like it. I was gobsmacked and I loved the whole experience. I found it hard to believe that those performing had been born male yet were able to look so feminine. Their glamorous appearance was vastly different from the drag performers I had seen in Britain such as Mrs Shufflewick or my dear friend Larry Grayson.

One of the performers, Dareille Smith did an excellent Eartha Kitt tribute act. She mimed to Eartha so well you would think she was singing live. She did not do any dancing and stood there miming but to this day I think she was the best lip-syncher in the business.

Grace Kelly, no, not the princess, also performed at the Jewel Box. She was tall and had the best legs in Australia. Just stunning. Seeing these glamourous drag queens began to open up possibilities for me that I had never really considered before. My world was starting to change!

I have never been able to recapture the intense feelings I had of that evening at the Jewel Box. I was now more determined than ever to drag up again and perhaps even make a career out of it. A boy could dream!

And as it turned out, I did not have to wait long before I would have a chance to perform my first drag show in Sydney. As I was leaving a cinema in Pitt Street following the showing of a British comedy a gentleman approached me, telling me that he had noticed that I had laughed at all the English gags. His name was Eddie Tye and we hit it off immediately.

In fact, we enjoyed a bit of a fling though nothing too serious as I was trying to remain as faithful as possible to my other Eddie back in England. I compared every man I met to my Eddie. Anyway, it turned out that Eddie Tye happened to be a drag performer who did shows under the name Tracey Tye. I found it quite funny that he did drag as he was very hairy and had to spend a lot of time shaving before performances or find creative ways to cover up all that fur with his costumes.

When I told him about how amazed I had been at the Jewel Box he suggested I consider doing a guest spot at a recently opened nightclub on Anzac Parade in Kensington called the Purple Onion, often described as Sydney's first gay nightclub. Eddie, who ended up performing quite often at the Onion, had a word with the management and one Sunday night I went along to try out.

The shows and the venue itself seemed to be above the quality of what I had seen at the Jewel Box. In fact, the shows were outrageous though not particularly risqué as the humour was not derived from filth. These shows seemed to attract a largely gay audience who would come in from the surrounding suburbs and so there was lots of camp innuendo and gay in-jokes.

I loved the place and became a regular visitor over the years. The shows featured clever satire and had names such as *The Sound of Mucus* or *A Streetcar Named Beatrice*. They were hysterical. For production numbers they featured songs from the latest Broadway shows before we knew of them in Australia, probably brought over from the States by Qantas flight attendants.

The shows attracted many international names such as Rosemary Clooney and Kaye Stevens. Frances Faye was a particular fan, and I was there the night Dame Margot Fonteyn and Rudolf Nureyev were in the audience. You would go to the Purple Onion, see a show and get pissed. It was a real hoot and it made up for much of the shit you had to put up with as a gay man. Once you were in the Purple Onion you were in just one big gay world.

So later in the night it was my turn to perform. Eddie had done me up and I was confident that at least I looked good. But I was shit scared about performing in front of an audience. This wasn't my family at Christmas time but an audience of ever-critical gay men! I got into my position on the stage to perform a Judy Garland number and I waited for the song to start. And I waited. And I waited but the bloody record would not play. This was my worst nightmare and I stood on stage in the glare of the spotlight, looking like such a bloody fool. I felt absolutely dreadful because, although I had performed overseas for many years, this was my first time performing in drag. I was not doing a tried and tested act as part of a duo, and this was a very different atmosphere.

After what seemed like a million years, the host Karen Chant graciously came to my aid. She came on stage apologising profusely to the audience and me and said there were problems in the sound box, and that the sound guy, Fernando, would have everything fixed as soon as possible.

Eventually, Fernando got the sound working and I performed my song. By this stage I had lost a fair bit of my confidence and I was a bag of nerves. I can safely say that I do not think my performance went down very well with the crowd. You could be forgiven for thinking that my bad experience at the Purple Onion would put me off performing in drag again, but I feel it made me stronger and more determined.

CHAPTER 7
Joining Les Girls

Joining Les Girls

While Neville and I were performing our act at RSL clubs an agent got us two weeks work at the Latin Quarter in Sydney, which was in an arcade off Pitt Street. It was a popular, upmarket cabaret club with a fancy, fine-dining restaurant. However, it was best known for its nightly shows featuring top entertainers and glamorous showgirls. Gangsters and showbiz types would be among the audience.

It was owned by Canadian businessman, Sammy Lee, and his Australian business partner Reg Boom. They also ran the Les Girls Theatre Restaurant in Kings Cross. Sammy had settled in Australia having previously visited the country as a drummer in a band in the late 1930s. He was short and overweight with a bald head and a pencil-thin moustache, and he had a penchant for smoking cigars. I was wary of Sammy at the time because I had heard stories about how he could turn on people at the drop of a hat if they crossed him and had even been known to set his lackeys on to them.

Neville and I were contracted to perform our act with our mix of acrobatics and tap routines, much as we had perfected in the UK. We were part of the late-night cabaret show which also included a singer and other acts such as a juggler or a magician as well as a dazzling group of female dancers. The choreographer was Sheila Cruze who had worked on the Tivoli circuit when she was younger and, as I learned, was also the choreographer at Les Girls. Sheila would have been in her late 40s then, blonde and was regarded as one of the best chorographers working in Sydney at the time.

After our two-week season at the Latin Quarter ended, Neville and I went back to the RSL clubs. It was at one of our afternoon shows at

Randwick RSL that I noticed Sheila was in the audience. She had previously invited me to visit Les Girls but I had not yet had a chance to take her up on her offer. When I saw her in the audience that afternoon it occurred to me that perhaps she might have been looking for more performers and sussing me out. So, I decided to take up her offer and we went along to see what Les Girls was all about.

I was very impressed by what I saw, and it was certainly a step up from the Jewel Box and the Purple Onion. It reminded me of the smart nightclubs I had seen in the West End of London. The venue was essentially a large restaurant. Red was Sammy Lee's favourite colour and it was everywhere. In fact, Sammy's influence and tastes could be seen throughout. Lavish shows were performed on a stage in the restaurant and the colour red featured heavily as there were red tablecloths and red velvet curtains for instance. It was just beautiful and so very glamorous.

The waitresses wore red leotards and a white apron with their breasts pushed up and bow ties around their neck. Diners would have a bottle of wine in an ice bucket on the table and would be served dishes such as sizzling steaks. In later years a bar was opened upstairs where customers could go after the show and sit on lounges, and if they were lucky, hang out with some of the performers. Men would go to Les Girls in dinner suits with bow ties and women would wear frocks and often a corsage of flowers on the top of their dress and around their shoulder. It all seemed so posh back then.

Joining Les Girls

That evening, the shows were compered by Peter Moselle who had come over from England, and featured performers such as Carlotta, Susan Le Gaye and Josie Jay. In those days Les Girls would have fabulous opening music which would often come from Broadway shows. All the girls mimed to the songs and the audience enjoyed a brilliant show. The performances were very much about 'female impersonation': they aimed to create the illusion that these were 'natural born' women on stage even though the audience knew they were men. The 'hook' was the ability to transform a man into a glamorous sexy woman. Gay men well knew that with the right use of makeup, wig and dress, a man could be made to look like a woman, but in those days, straight people were gobsmacked.

The whole experience seemed so professional and glamorous. I loved what I saw, and I think it was the first time that I thought that I could be a part of this. A few weeks later I mentioned to Eddie Tye how much I would love to try my luck at Les Girls despite my disastrous previous performance at the Purple Onion. He wasn't so sure and told me that he thought Les Girls was quite upmarket and a bit above me at that point in my career. Thanks for the vote of confidence, Eddie!

However, I was never one to give up and eventually after much persuasion Eddie suggested that I do a guest spot one night. We turned up late on a Saturday night and had a word with the manager Johnny Mclean.

He agreed to put me on during the guest spot during the third show of the night, which was on at about 1am. Despite my love of performing, I have always been quite shy. On that night I was a bag of nerves as I was so keen to prove myself. I was performing at the top drag venue in Sydney, and I knew I had only one chance to impress.

Eddie did my makeup and provided me with a black leotard from his collection. Then, just after 1am I stepped on to the stage in front of a hundred or so people and began my performance of American singer Eydie Gorme's 'You've Got Hands'. I had always been hopeless at miming but the audience responded well. Then a few minutes later after a costume change, I performed a rather different number. I had devised this comedy skit called the *Tin Can Strip*. It involved me wearing big bloomers and a blouse then me stripping to David Rose and His Orchestra's 'The Stripper'.

Underneath my blouse I had tied two cans to a string which was then tied behind my back. The cans sat on my chest as if they were breasts. By flexing certain muscles, I can make each can move up and down independently or at the same time as the other. I am the only person who has ever performed the sketch or knows the secret of the technique to control the cans. I had perfected the act at parties in the UK. It was definitely an unusual party trick. One time Neville and I hosted a party while we were in Scarborough and John Inman was a guest. He absolutely loved it and thought it was hilarious. However, that night at Les Girls was the first time I ever performed it professionally as part of a show in front of an audience of strangers. Much to my relief, the audience loved it and neither they nor the queens in the show had seen anything quite like it.

Eddie told me I had performed well, and Johnny seemed pleased.

I went home to Lidcombe feeling on top of the world but also wondering if the performance would open doors for me at Les Girls. I need not have worried as a few days later Sheila gave me a call. 'If you ever want a job, I could use you as a male dancer,' she said. Sheila had not been there the night I did my guest spot but Johnny had told her that he had enjoyed my act. As if she even needed to ask!

They may have wanted me as a male dancer rather than as a drag performer, but dancing was what I knew best and this could not have come at a better time as Neville was wanting to get out of the business altogether, as he was wooing a woman and wanted to settle down.

Sheila explained I would have to learn the routines and songs and they would then use me in the show. I had a week of rehearsals which were exhausting. Sheila was very good with me as she knew that I had trained as a dancer for a number of years and worked as a dancer in the UK, Germany, Ireland and, of course, here in Sydney. Following the rehearsal period, it was my time to take to the stage. I did a solo tap dance to 'Me and My Shadow' which was played by an organist at the side of the stage. Even with my years of dance training and experience on the stage I was terrified, but I was boosted on by an adrenaline rush. I also did my *Tin Can Strip* as well as performing as a male dancer as part of the chorus work with the girls. I not only had to dance but I also had to mime the male parts. One of the songs I performed the male voice for was 'Lucky

Pierre' which featured the French-born actor Robert Clary who had starred in the American sitcom *Hogan's Heroes*.

About six months later I progressed to wearing more glamorous costumes and actually became one of the showgirls. I would mime to records that Sammy had brought over from America or that I would find in a record store that I loved on George Street. It really was the life. At that stage I was performing to Sandie Shaw and '(There's) Always Something There to Remind Me', Nancy Sinatra and 'These Boots Are Made for Walkin'', Millie Small and 'My Boy Lollipop', and Rusty Warren and 'Bounce Your Boobies'. Millie Small was actually in the audience one night and although I never got to meet her, I was told by one of the other girls that she loved my tribute to her. I had also decided even at this stage to keep my stage name, 'Stan Munro' even when performing in drag. Danny La Rue was able to achieve great success using a male name, so I decided to keep mine. I was one of the few female impersonators to do this, and it gave me an edge. I never felt pressure from Sammy to work under a drag name, and I've performed as Stan Munro across the length of my six-decade career.

Although I was now doing glamorous spots miming to female singers, I wasn't content with just miming and I was constantly thinking of ways to add a comedy aspect to the songs. I placed small motors in my bra which were attached to colourful plastic propellors which would spin around when I turned a switch and I had another contraption that lit up my crotch. I really wanted to give the audience a laugh and a good time. One sketch in particular that I came up with was copied by other performers at Les Girls over the years though these days it would be considered the height of political incorrectness. It went like this. I would perform Sandie Shaw's '(There's) Always Something There to Remind Me' and it was clear from the bump underneath the dress that I was pregnant.

During the instrumental break in the middle of the song I ran quickly off stage and pulled a baby doll from under my dress. I then came back on stage with the doll wrapped in a blanket though the audience could not see the doll itself, only the blanket. Next, I pulled out an overly long false tit from my dress and started to feed the baby. As I left the stage at the end of the song, I then showed the baby's face for the first time to the audience. The unexpected twist was that it was a black baby and the audiences in those days loved it as did Sammy, himself. In fact, the first time Sammy saw the act he came backstage after the show and told me how much he loved it and said he was giving me the equivalent of a $10 raise. I was overcome with joy and burst into tears.

The cast worked six nights a week with Sunday nights off. Two shows were performed Monday to Thursday with the first beginning around 9.15pm and the second at 10.15. Three shows would be scheduled on Friday and Saturday nights. The shows were changed every six weeks and three weeks after that show started, we began rehearsing for the next one in the days during the week. Sometimes we would not have to rehearse on Fridays as we would have three shows on that night. It was a huge amount of work!

Our choreographer Sheila Cruze always chose the production

numbers where the whole cast performed together but individual performers got to choose their own music for their individual spots. For example, one particular performer only did Shirley Bassey and another only did Lena Horne. Once somebody had their own 'voice', as it was known, nobody else dared do that same voice or there would be one hell of a cat fight.

I believe genuinely that Sammy made drag legit for straight audiences and found a way to make it appeal to everyone from mums and dads to tourists who would all have a fun night out. They could dress up and have an evening of escapism.

About six months after I joined Les Girls, I felt confident enough to leave my job at Lidcombe Dairy Farmers. By this time, I was renting a one-bedroom unit in Granville. Working at both Les Girls and at the factory was exhausting and overwhelming. My days off from Lidcombe Dairy Farmers were during the week so I would work there at weekends and then do three shows on a Saturday night.

Sometimes on weekends I would not get home from Les Girls until 3am and then I would have to be up at 5am for my shift at the dairy. On one occasion I was so tired at the dairy that I fainted. I was leading two very different lives. During the day I was working in the very blokey world of Lidcombe Dairy Farmers and then by night I was in drag. Something had to give. It was not a difficult decision. With drag I had found my true calling.

Sammy was always very hands on and attended the final rehearsals for each new show and he and his lovely wife, Maureen, always attended opening night. He was someone who paid attention to detail, and nothing went ahead without Sammy's seal of approval. He often sat in on rehearsals and if there was something or someone he did not like he would axe it or them. He took no prisoners.

On at least one occasion, for instance, I can remember one of the girls not pulling their weight in rehearsal and Sammy yelling at Sheila Cruze, 'Get that faggot off my stage.' Sammy had a temper but it was because he was passionate about putting on a show that the club's patrons would love. The more that customers loved the show, the more money they would spend and the richer he would become.

He did make us laugh at times because he always struggled to say the word 'sequins' and it would come out as 'sequences' instead.

I adored Maureen from the moment I met her. She had been a Tivoli dancer so understood what it was like to work as a showgirl. I enjoyed her company. She was gorgeous and classy. I cannot say enough beautiful things about her. We are still dear friends today. We spoke on the phone a few years ago and she said, 'Stan Munro – You were Les Girls!' Her kind words brought tears to my eyes.

Although working at Les Girls was anything but ordinary, it was still a job and we had to pay tax, provide doctors' certificates if we were sick and couldn't make a show and we also received holiday pay. Reg Boom's wife Eileen ran the business side of things from behind a desk in the club. If you ever needed cash in a hurry before pay day you could go to her, and she would make you sign a book showing how much you had been given and you would agree that that amount would be docked out of your pay packet the next week.

Reg and Eileen's son Terry was a different story. He was roughly around my age and worked behind the bar but he never seemed to like me. I suspect it was because he knew his father owned half the business and so he felt he had a right to throw his weight around. Frequently after a show he would snarl, 'You're not miming in time with the others. You need to learn the song properly.' I admit I am not the best lip-syncher but I practiced a lot, miming into mirrors or while I did the housework at home, but he seemed to pick on me out of spite. It drove me mad and I found myself not liking him at all. After all he was really only there because of his dad.

However, there was little I disliked about Les Girls apart from the low wages (I would get paid the equivalent of about $25.00 per week when I first started). Sammy paid for the costumes for the production numbers but if you were doing your own spot, you were responsible for buying materials for your outfits. I got my costumes from here, there and everywhere. I have no idea how to sew. I can do buttons and take up jeans but that is about it. Luckily, there were always costumes to be bought off other queens and I took full advantage of the op shops to find anything glittery. I still do. About a year after I joined Les Girls, I began paying Kenny Williams, who was the top dress designer at Les Girls, to put together a chic little something for me.

I met Kenny when I first started at Les Girls and I was completely knocked out by him because he was such a wonderful person. He was a handsome, blond-haired man who lived near the White City

Stadium on Rushcutters Bay Road with his mother who was as camp as a row of tents, and I loved her. She was just so brilliant and accepting of us all. She was great fun and had a wonderful sense of humour. Even though my mum had been supportive and even made drag outfits for me when I was a kid, Kenny's mum was just so accepting and fun to be with that I wished my mum could have been like her. But I also realise that Mum had her own demons she battled with.

Kenny had such flair and creativity. Not only did he make the costumes, but he also designed and operated the lighting. The outfits he created were like something you would see in the Hollywood movies. They were just so glamorous and amazing. They would take your breath away. He was also a brilliant hairdresser and he did my wigs many times. He was always just one of a kind.

Kenny and I hit it off straight away. He had a very sarcastic sense of humour which was similar to mine. His sense of humour was up my street and featured lots of innuendo. If he had gone on stage as a comedian, he would have killed people with laughter. He was hilarious and was as funny as Larry Grayson. We remained good friends until his recent death and I adored him immensely.

When I first joined Les Girls, I was very nervous as professional drag was still pretty new to me. The drag queens could be quite bitchy to me with snide comments or looks. I was not used to it because when I toured on the Moss Empire circuit, I never experienced any bitchiness. People there seemed secure in their roles and jobs, and nobody was seen as a threat. But it was pretty typical drag queen patter which still goes on to this very day and will no doubt continue long after I am gone.

I think I was a bit of an enigma to many of the performers as I was still new in town. The scene was pretty small and many of the queens had known each other or worked together. They must have wondered who this blow-in with a Welsh accent was. However, I did eventually earn their respect and friendship when I proved myself as a performer and we had some great times. Backstage could be loads of fun and sometimes there was just as much partying going on behind the stage as there was out in the audience.

Sheila Cruze and I got on well as she appreciated the fact that I was a trained, professional dancer and I respected her a great deal as a choreographer. All too often she would say to me, 'Oh love, with you I haven't got to teach another drag queen with two left feet.' She not only had to teach them to dance but to also walk and behave like a woman. Teaching men to walk in high heels elegantly is a challenge in itself.

Many years later I was very upset to hear that Sheila had died in Melbourne after being hit by a train. With her was her elderly black poodle, Jackie. Her role in Les Girls should never be underestimated or underplayed as I believe truly that she was responsible for much of the glory and success of Les Girls. It must have been a nightmare for her dealing with new drag queens and their moods, but she had the patience of a saint.

One performer who seemed a natural dancer was Ayesha who joined Les Girls a couple of years after I joined. She mastered the routines very quickly. Ayesha is also the most talented piano player that I have ever heard as she had trained as a pianist. At one time she played piano in a club in Kings Cross. We are still in touch, and we share a wicked sense of humour.

Now, although Les Girls was promoted as an 'All Male Revue' in actual fact most of the performers were living as trans women who were taking hormones to help develop breasts. Some such as Carlotta eventually had gender reassignment surgery. However, about three of us at the time lived as men and simply enjoyed performing in a frock or five.

Peter Moselle, the compere, was one such person who saw himself not as a drag queen but an actor who wore a frock. I recall Danny La Rue writing something similar in his autobiography. Peter's career began in England where he entertained troops during the war. He became particularly popular for his impersonations of Carmen Miranda. After the war he got involved in repertory theatre where he learnt many of his theatrical skills. He toured Europe with Danny La Rue and even played London's West End.

While in London, Peter Small, as he was then known, met an Australian dancer and acrobat called Johnny Stanton and they put together a double act called Stanton and Small. In many ways, Peter and Johnny were like Neville and me: a dancing Brit and an Aussie acrobat who teamed up to put on a double act. They moved to Sydney via New Zealand and became known as the Mad Moiselles which was a play on the word 'mademoiselle'. They soon dropped the 'I' and both took on the surname of Moselle.

Unsurprisingly, many people assumed they were brothers. Eventually, Peter was approached by Sammy Lee to become the compere of Les Girls. I got on well with Peter though I found his comedy rather English and subdued as opposed to my humour which often pushed boundaries. His jokes were very safe and never risqué or offensive.

A typical Les Girls show would start with an overture to signal the show was about to begin and open with a lavish, Las Vegas style production number featuring the girls dancing in beautiful costumes and feathered head dresses. Then the compere Peter Moselle would be introduced. He would step forward into the spotlight in full drag and the magnificent curtains would close behind him. He would essentially do a stand-up comedy routine for about 15 minutes which gave us a chance to change our costumes for the next performance. Then the show would continue with different production numbers from the cast interspersed with individual spots with Peter keeping the flow.

Peter was always pleasant to me, and it was not long before he invited me back to his house in Balmain where he lived with his mother. It will probably be no surprise to you that Peter and I ended up in bed together that night. I was not particularly attracted to him, but I felt that if we slept together, I would be assured of a long run in the show. In those days I slept with anybody if it gave me a leg up (so to speak) or offered job security. It was always good to keep on the right side of people. However, Peter's role was not to hire or fire people. That was left to Sammy Lee or the manager

Johnny McLean with whom I thankfully had a good relationship, and neither of them ever wanted to call in favours of the sexual kind from me.

Peter's signature sign off was that at the end of the show he would take his wig off with a flourish and people would gasp as he was basically bald. He was, however, a trained hairdresser and when not performing he wore a toupee. Before mixing with the audience after the show he would stick this little hairpiece on the front of his head with glue. Apart from the end of his shows where he would reveal his bald head, I never saw him without his toupee which I found odd because we all knew, including the audiences, that he had no hair on the top of his head.

I worked with him in several comedy sketches. Sometimes if I did not hit the right cue for him, he would let me know about it in front of the other girls after the show had finished. One sketch, for instance, involved a brief case as a prop. I can remember that on one occasion I missed my cue. After the sketch was over, I was sitting in the dressing room with the other kids and he threw the brief case into the dressing room and at the top of his voice exclaimed, 'Amateur!'

Peter had much more professional experience, having worked with Danny La Rue and other big stars in the UK and I think he thought we were a bit amateurish at times. If the girls were camping it up too much or being too loud, he would often remark, 'It won't be long now until you're gone.' A favourite phrase of his was, 'You'll be doing the Long Bay follies soon.'

Peter introduced Polari to Les Girls which is a form of slang that was particularly popular among gay men in Britain. He had learned it there and brought it to Australia. Polari can trace its origins back to at least the 19th century and quite possibly further. It borrowed or corrupted words from other languages such as Italian, Romance, Romani and Yiddish. It was also associated with other groups such as travellers, vagrants, sex workers, sailors and actors.

It has often been referred to as a 'secret language' because gay men used it at a time when homosexual activity was illegal to help identify someone as a fellow homosexual and talk openly but also to ensure they were not understood by those in authority such as the police. Polari was popularised by the BBC radio comedy series in the 1960s *Round the Horne* which starred Hugh Paddick and Kenneth Williams. They played a couple of camp unemployed actors and Polari along with rather a lot of innuendo featured heavily. Thus, Polari was introduced to a mass audience.

Polari started to fall out of fashion with the partial decriminalisation of homosexual acts between two adults in England and Wales under the Sexual Offences Act in 1967 and of course the advent of gay liberation when many liberationists frowned upon it as a language borne of oppression.

The first time I heard Polari was as a teenager from my beautiful boyhood friend Des who had been to London and picked up a few words and phrases. I was about 15 and I thought it was fabulous because we could walk around town using Polari and nobody had a clue what we were talking about. We used to chat in Polari and fall about laughing. If a woman went past with dreadful hair we would say 'naff riah' or if we saw a handsome young man we would say 'bona ome, dear'. If we saw another queen mincing down the street we would exclaim 'vada ome palone' which means 'look at that queen'.

My wonderful friend Larry Grayson also used it among his showbiz pals and friends, and I picked up a lot from him.

When Peter joined Les Girls many of the queens picked up the lingo from him. We spoke it all the time and some of the stuff we would come out with was hysterical. It was all just so camp. I do not use it much these days unless I am on the phone to a couple of the people I used to work with at Les Girls.

For a couple of months in those early days, Peter's showbiz partner Johnny Moselle performed in a few sketches with him. He was very funny and did a lot of slap stick comedy. He was also a fabulous tap dancer. One of the sketches they did was very similar to the Old Mother Riley music hall act which had been popular from the 1930s in music halls, in theatres, on radio and then in films and on television in Britain.

In the Les Girls sketch Johnny was the Old Mother Riley-type character and Peter was his daughter.

Johnny was so agile and could tap dance like a maniac. Many years ago, I saw Peter and Johnny perform in Queensland. Both must have been in their late 70s and in the middle of the show Johnny did a back flip. I could not believe it. They were a great double act.

Little did I know that only a few years after joining Les Girls that I would be taking over from Peter Moselle as the compere! He moved to the Gold Coast to put on performances which became known as the *Peter Moselle Show* at the Coolangatta Hotel. Peter died in 2003 but the last time I saw him was in the 1980s when I was on the road with a group of strippers called the Cheeky Chaps, which I'll talk about in a later chapter. I had a couple of days off and visited him in the afternoon and who should be there but another wonderful Les Girls performer called Holly Brown who had also gone to Queensland to work with him when he left Les Girls.

She had just returned from performing in clubs in the United States including a couple of years at the popular La Cage in Milwaukee when I saw her with Peter. I had no idea that she was sick at the time, and she was to sadly die from AIDS soon after we caught up. She was a fabulous performer who sang live. She even made a couple of appearances on *The Michael Parkinson Show* and appeared in a short American film called *Bust Up* which was shown at international film festivals including in Cannes and Montreal.

Holly had a beautiful smile and bright eyes which could light up any room. She was vivacious, friendly and full of life. She partnered me in a few comedy sketches at Les Girls and I loved her as a performer. I feel she has never been recognised in this country for her talent as others with far less seemed to get more recognition. When she died her parents had her buried in a cemetery in Dubbo under her male birth name with no mention of her wonderful talent or her history. She was just short of her 46th birthday when she died.

Joining Les Girls

I really feel fortunate and even blessed, not bad for an atheist, to have worked alongside some wonderful performers in those early years at Les Girls. Of course, many groups often have a figurehead who is the best known and Les Girls was no exception. When people think of Les Girls one name more than any other stands out and that is Carlotta. When I first met her, she was beautiful and slim with thick, dark hair. In fact, I would say she was one of the most stunning performers I have ever worked with. She was elegant and knew how to carry herself on stage.

In her book, *Carlotta, Legend of Les Girls* she described me as a 'fabulous compere', and wrote that I taught her a lot, which was very kind. We learned from each other. We had our egos, of course, but we were also a team, and it was in all of our interests to put on a good show.

In 1964 the ABC broadcast the documentary *The Glittering Mile* which had been filmed just before I joined in late 1963. It helped put Les Girls on the map and brought in a lot more punters. Carlotta was interviewed on the program and it helped make her a star.

Carlotta went on to receive a lot of publicity in 1972 when she had pioneering gender reassignment surgery performed by a visiting English surgeon at Sydney's Prince Henry Hospital. Arguably, Carlotta became Australia's most famous and high-profile transgender woman. Despite all this she was still billed as a 'female impersonator' for many years.

I have always felt that Carlotta deserves to be bigger than she is and perhaps she could have taken more risks with her career. She mimed at Les Girls in those early years but later in her career she sang live as she has a good voice. I think if she had sung live earlier in her career and had spent more time working overseas, she could have been an international star. We may be a large island but Australia is not the centre of the world. Carlotta was incredible. I would say that in those early years of Les Girls that Carlotta was the ultimate in 'female impersonators' and I cannot praise her enough.

We caught up several years ago for the first time in about thirty years when we worked together at a charity event at the golf club in Kyogle, Northern New South Wales, where I now live. I like to say I put the KY in KYogle, but I digress. Carlotta and another performer, a dear friend and former Les Girl, Monique St John stayed at mine for the night. We were awake until the wee hours remembering the old days. It was like we had never been apart. There will never be another Carlotta as she is one of a kind.

Another performer in those early days was Kerry Graham who always looked fabulous. She was slim and petite with beautiful blond hair. Kerry was dating the sound technician at Les Girls who went on to become a very famous prime-time television game show host and radio presenter but who will remain nameless. After all a lady cannot reveal everything…just most things!

One day I said something or other to her to which she took offence, and she went to punch me. Luckily, I ducked and she missed me but hit the wall instead. She broke her fingers and she had to go through the shows all plastered up during the following weeks.

Electra, who I had seen work at the Jewell Box became a stripper at

Les Girls and was in the show for a while before Sammy Lee got rid of her. She could be very volatile and you did not want to get on the wrong side of her. She also had a habit of dating large strong men who would not look out of place cast as a boxer or bouncer in a film or television drama.

Not long after we both joined Les Girls her rough and ready boyfriend at the time grabbed me by the throat and said, 'Don't fucking mess with Electra or you will be for it.' She was clearly marking her turf. One of her favourite sayings was, 'All it takes is one call…' It always put the shivers up me. She ended up having her own shop in Newtown and made drag for all the girls. We stayed in touch right up until her death though I always made sure I never crossed her. Diane Lombard was a dancer and stripper with wonderfully translucent pale skin and an amazing bone structure. You would have had no idea that she had been born into a male body. She was so elegant.

Lilac Haze was a most fantastic performer. She was also a dancer and a stripper, and she had the most beautiful breasts, which she got through hormones, and beautiful legs. She had the most stunning body and was in perfect shape. Unbelievable! We also shared a sick sense of humour so we would bounce off each other with our jokes. It was a pleasure to work with her again a few years later in Hong Kong.

Peter and I were not the only performers who lived as men and frocked up just to perform. When I first started, there was for a short time a showgirl in the chorus called Charlie Porter with the stage name Cherise. He was actually straight and after leaving Les Girls he went on to get married and, by all accounts, he and his wife had several children.

Another performer I worked with in those early days was Susan Le Gaye. She did a lot of Peggy Lee numbers. She was a wonderful dancer and was known as the 'Prop Queen' because of her use of props in her performances.

Her boyfriend was the Les Girls manager Johnny McLean. One day I was mouthing off about Susan to some of the other girls and telling them how she thought she ruled the roost and could get away with anything because she was with Johnny. I got sprung as she overheard everything I said.

She did not say anything as she walked into the room, but I knew she had heard by the look on her face. I simply responded, 'Yes I am talking about you.' She did not say a word. Johnny often gave me a lift home to Lidcombe in his car and one day he hauled me across the coals, scolding me that I should not have said anything about Susan and warned me not to do it again. Susan had told him everything and I have not crossed her since. And yes, we remained friends until her death.

In my early years of Les Girls I moonlighted with Susan, performing shows in Newcastle on Sunday nights. Her sister Elva had been in touch with an agent who found work for us there. We called ourselves the Le Gayes. Sammy didn't seem to care provided we were always available to perform at Les Girls and I think he saw the promotional opportunities that came from us performing up in

Newcastle. When Susan decided to tour Australia with singer Tony Monopoly I did the shows with Les Girls performers Holly Brown and then Simone Troy but my main partner in crime in Newcastle was Monique St John with whom I remained close until her recent death.

She was a wonderful performer and a barrel of fun. Monique and I would pack our gear from the Les Girls show in a couple of suitcases and be driven by a lovely woman friend overnight to Newcastle. It was a very winding road to Newcastle as there was no freeway in those days.

After driving through the night, we would arrive at Monique's mother's house in the early hours of the morning. We'd get a few hours' sleep, have a shower and a bit of brekkie before turning up to the first club at about 8.30am to drag up for a 10am performance. We loved getting to the venue and doing speed or taking a couple of 'Black Bombers' as we called them (slang for a popular weight loss drug that contained amphetamine) to help keep up our energy after being awake all night on the road. It was usually an all-bloke audience on a Sunday morning. They would all be there with their beers but there was thankfully never any drama. You could use any language you liked, and it did not matter. We were there to make them laugh and we did.

Then at about midday we would toddle off to the next club for a 2.30pm performance This one was a more mixed audience. Then after that we would head to our final performance of the day, which usually finished around 11pm. We'd then throw everything in the back of the van and arrive back in Sydney in the early hours of

Monday morning. Then, later that evening we'd take our gear back to Les Girls. We were moonlighting like there was no tomorrow. I could not do it all now but then I could if the money was there. I love knowing I have gelt in the handbag.

I must confess that I did get Monique into serious trouble once a few years later around 1967. I was taking time off from Les Girls to recover from cosmetic surgery to my nose and was offered a gig at a club in Newcastle on a Saturday night and I asked Monique if she would like to appear with me. Monique told me that Sammy Lee would have her shot if she pulled a sickie but somehow, I managed to persuade her to take the night off and perform with me in Newcastle.

Unfortunately, when she went back on Monday night Sammy was waiting for her with a couple of his henchman who began slapping her around in front of the other girls as a warning to them not to cross him. Word had somehow got back to Sammy about her moonlighting, no doubt thanks to some vicious queen who could not keep her trap shut.

Monique kicked one of Sammy's hoons in the balls and took off. She did not return until long after Sammy had died. Sammy's attitude was that Monique, along with others in the show, was simply another showgirl and for every performer that left there was a long queue of hopefuls waiting to join. I have always felt a sense of guilt for my part in Monique getting into trouble and I do hope that over the years she was able to forgive me. We remained great friends so hopefully she did.

Joining Les Girls

When Susan finished touring Australia with Tony Monopoly, she was keen to perform the Newcastle shows with me again. I felt this was unfair as I was working with Monique. Susan argued that we should reunite as the Le Gayes because she was the original person that I had performed the shows with, and I was still using her surname as the act. To make matters more complicated I had her mother Ivy and sister Elva on my back. Elva had been doing a great job of organising our bookings through an agent throughout my time with the Le Gayes, regardless of who I worked with, and I was concerned that I would lose her if I did not take Susan back. In the end we reached a compromise that I would keep doing the Newcastle shows with Monique but I would also do some Sydney shows with Susan.

Conchita was another fabulous performer who I worked with. She was one of the first members of Les Girls to have gender reassignment surgery when she went overseas. A few years later we happened to be both working in Beirut. I visited her at her room at the Crazy Horse Saloon and at some point she asked, 'Darling do you want to see my pussy?' I was astounded as it was the first surgically created one I had seen.

Soon after I joined Les Girls Conchita left for England with Simone Troy in early 1964. I went to see them off on their ship at Circular Quay. I believe that Conchita went on to find success in the UK in the music industry as a manager of pop groups.

Simone, on the other hand, spent a couple of years working in strip clubs in London's Soho before returning to Australia and Les Girls.

She was beautiful and very artistic and creative in terms of the songs she performed and the clothes that she asked Kenny Williams to make. Of course, she later found success with Monique St John in their fabulous Playgirls Revue, but she was also an accomplished compere and performer in her own right. I can remember seeing her at the Newtown Hotel and Imperial Hotel when I was living in Erskinville in the late 1980s.

She was always very direct and if she did not like you, she would tell you. Sadly, she died in 2017 of pancreatic cancer. I read one obituary which said there was a legend that she once drove to a club in Granville because there was a rival act using the Playgirls Revue name. She threatened to return and burn the place down unless they removed the sign and changed the name of the act. I have no idea if the story is true, but it would not surprise me if it were.

I'll never forget attending an awards ceremony in Melbourne in the mid-1990s. Simone had been flown down by the organisers as a guest artist to introduce various segments. One of the segments was a tribute to Les Girls Melbourne where many of the cast from the show got up on stage towards the end of the night to accept an award, which was the reason I had been invited.

One of Simone's riders for taking part was that she had to have a bottle of scotch which she had clearly taken full advantage of before going on stage. During her first segment she was clearly the worse for wear as she started throwing insults at the audience. There are few things worse than a Sydney queen attacking a room full of Melbourne queens in their home city. A drunken rant was certainly not on the agenda of the organisers who had engaged her to simply introduce the various segments.

The second time she went on stage she was met with boos from the audience and she did not go on again. As I was about to go on stage with the other girls to accept the award, I glanced at Simone standing by the side of the stage. She glared at me and said, 'What are you looking at, you cunt???' There was never a dull moment with Simone and she really was a brilliant performer as well as also being a successful businesswoman with a sizeable property portfolio. Another performer gone too soon.

CHAPTER 8
Back To Blighty

Back To Blighty

In those early days at Les Girls, we used to have such fun and would get up to all sorts of mischief. We were earning low wages and I can remember one of the girls asking Sammy if we could have a pay rise. He snapped back, 'You're working. What more do you want?' We especially looked forward to Friday. We would be flat out in rehearsals with Shelia but at about 12.30 in the afternoon, the tradies would come in and put all this food on the large table in the kitchen such as vegetables, huge bags of steak, chicken breasts, eggs and cheese. Everything was put on the table for when the chef arrived at about 4pm to put it all away in the fridges for the weekend.

At the end of our rehearsals, we waited for Sheila to leave before going in the back door of the kitchen to fill our shopping bags with food. On one occasion I put some chicken fillets in my bag, and it was the height of summer. Friday was a three-show night and I did not leave the venue until after 2am. You can imagine that after having been in my bag from around 3 o'clock in the afternoon that those fillets were ready to dance through the Cross.

I got home many times to find that the meat was rotten and it went straight into the bin. The amount of food that the queens used to take on a Friday afternoon was unreal. Huge steaks and chickens all went out the door. There was so much pilfering going on that I have no idea how we got away with it for so long. Nobody ever said anything to us, but after a while the kitchen door would be locked so they must have cottoned on eventually.

I remember Sammy coming to the club one night, demanding a steak immediately. The chef was very busy and was not pleased with Sammy adding to his already stressful workload. The chef wiped his arse with a bit of rump steak, threw it on the grill and served it to Sammy who did not have a clue.

There was a cleaner at Les Girls who was deaf, but the girls used to play a trick on her. She would adjust her hearing aid whenever we would talk with her. We could be very mean and would often go up to her to say a few words, but we would simply mime. She used to get frazzled as she thought her hearing aid was not working. She fell for it every time. We could be wicked but there was no malice intended.

I was also the victim of a prank. On one night a crowd of the girls led by Monique St John grabbed me in the dressing room during the interval and ripped off my underpants for a laugh. I remember Monique saying, 'What a big head you've got!'

Les Girls became more and more popular, and the restaurant was often packed to the rafters. Many well-known people would be in the audience. One regular visitor who came soon after I started at Les Girls in late 1963 was socialite Delly Aldridge who often attended wearing her furs and diamonds. Back then when women went out for an evening, they looked magnificent and dressed to the nines. One night, Delly wore feathers on her shoulder that had come from a bird of paradise from New Guinea.

She gave me two of these colourful feathers which I kept for many years until I gave them to a friend before I moved to Kyogle. Delly loved the queens and was wonderful and outrageous and reminded me of Auntie Mame.

Another regular visitor to Les Girls was the Jewish German-born Australian television and radio personality Dita Cobb who had spent time in Dachau concentration camp. In the 1960s she was an original 'beauty' on Channel 7's *Beauty and the Beast* and she hosted her own show *Dita* with Noel Brophy. Dita also wrote a long running column for the *Australian Woman's Weekly* called 'Ask Dita'.

She was often at Les Girls with a different female companion each time as well as other friends. I found her rather over the top. Everything and everybody was 'dahling' this and 'dahling' that. I can still hear her saying it now.

Some of the biggest fans of the show were the fabulous cast of *The Mavis Bramston Show*, a weekly television comedy sketch revue broadcast between 1964 and 1968. Noeline Brown, Gordon Chater and Barry Creyton were regulars at the club.

Noeline was always very friendly, but I remember Gordon and Barry more vividly. Gordon was fabulous – very jolly, outgoing and a laugh a minute. Gordon Chater and Peter Moselle were very close friends. Gordon and I also became great friends. The three of us used to stand outside the Rex Hotel with a drink before getting ready for the show at Les Girls and Peter would say to me, 'C'mon girl! Quick we've got to get ready as we're on stage soon!'

We would rush around the corner to Les Girls in the Cross and thankfully I only needed to put on some basic foundation and my costume as I was a dancer in the first part of the show, so I was able to leave my fun and frolics at the Rex at the last moment. Then after the opening production number I would put on my comedy makeup, which was easy as it consisted of bright red lipstick, beauty spots and big eye lashes. Peter had his own dressing room but the rest of the cast of Les Girls had to share one and because it was very narrow, we were constantly bumping into each other.

In 1977 I went to see Gordon Chater in a production of the Australian play *The Elocution of Benjamin Franklin* at the Playbox Theatre in Melbourne. I was bowled over by his strong performance. One scene in particular I remember is one where he walked onto the stage stark naked, which was pretty brave for an actor in his fifties. I was so impressed by his whole performance that I wrote to tell him how much I loved it. I was so delighted when he wrote back to say how much he appreciated me coming to see the show that I went back a second time with a friend. Gordon went on to star in the play in an 'Off-Broadway' production in New York as well as in London's West End. It was arguably his most memorable stage role and certainly gave him international recognition. I became quite friendly with Barry Creyton as he used to pop into Les Girls quite often. He was tall and slim and possibly the most handsome man I had ever laid eyes on. With his stunning features he could easily have been mistaken for a Hollywood matinee idol. Today he is as handsome as ever. I found him always down to earth and very easy to get on with.

By late 1965 I had spent more than two and a half years in Sydney. My original plan had been to spend two years in Australia and then return to my boyfriend Eddie who, as you would recall, I had been seeing in England just prior to leaving. I had promised him that I would return, and I missed him dearly. I handed in my notice to Les

Back To Blighty

Girls management, who tried to persuade me to stay, and booked a passage on a P&O ship using money that I had saved up from working hard for the past couple of years.

I was really missing Eddie and hoped that we would click again but as soon as the ship pulled away from Circular Quay I was overwhelmed by these nagging doubts, and I just wanted to get off the boat. I asked myself, 'What have I fucking done?' All I knew was that I was probably doing the wrong thing, but I had little choice than to just make the most of the voyage and hope for the best.

Two things really worried me. The first was going back to someone who I had never lived with, and I had no idea if he still felt the same about me as when I had left England. The second was that I had no idea what kind of work I was going to be able to get because I had been at Les Girls for about two years and did not have an act of my own. It can be tough to go out on your own after working as part of a duo or as part of a team for so long. I was very apprehensive about the future that awaited me back in the UK.

I had fitted in well with Les Girls, but I would once again be starting afresh and did not have the showbiz contacts in the UK that I had had in Sydney. Eddie was doing the clubs with his female partner, tap dancing, and of course I would be able to catch up with my dear friend Larry Grayson, but I was at a loss when it came to trying to come up with my own act. What on earth would I do?

The long voyage was made bearable as I got friendly with a lot of people. One of these was Bert Bates who I was fortunate enough to meet on my second day on the ship. He was travelling with his sister and her husband. They were from Ararat in country Victoria. Bert and I hit it off immediately and we became very good friends. Our friendship was purely platonic but what a friendship it was.

He was so camp that I think he invented the word. We had such a laugh together and he was as funny as a bunch of monkeys. His sister and brother-in-law were also wonderful and seemed to have no issue with Bert's sexuality or either of us camping it up like the queens we were. Our friendship made the voyage so much more enjoyable and helped take my mind off the anxiety I had about returning to Eddie.

On one occasion during the cruise, we entered a fancy-dress competition. I had a few frocks in my luggage so I gave one to Bert and dressed him up like a Charleston dancer. I wore a hula skirt and I had a huge pair of plastic false tits. I won first prize and Bert won second. We were stars on that ship.

Sadly, Bert and his sister and her husband departed the ship in Egypt as they were going overland to Europe. When I was returning to Australia later on, he had written to tell me that he would meet my ship when it stopped in Melbourne on the way to Sydney. He said, 'When I meet the boat, I'll be wearing a sari and if it's a hot day I'll probably be holding a black umbrella.' I really did think he was joking.

When we docked in Melbourne, I looked out for him. I certainly did not think he would be wearing a sari. Then I heard a woman say, 'Look at that funny man down there with the black umbrella.' It was a hot day and there was Bert wearing a green sari and holding a black umbrella. Bert was out of this world, and I loved his dry sense of humour. Thankfully, he had brought a change of clothes in his car which he changed into before kindly showing me around the city.

My father, mother and one of my brothers met me when the ship docked in Southampton and took me to mum and dad's home in Wales. About a week later Eddie came up to meet me. Amazingly, my parents gave up their double bed for me and Eddie, even though I had not officially come out to them as gay. They slept on the single beds in the spare rooms.

I soon moved in with Eddie at his home in Coventry where he lived alone. Before I moved to Australia he had been living with his mother. She never particularly liked me as she suspected something was going on between me and Eddie. One night, she entered the bedroom where we were sleeping and started fumbling around.

Eddie asked her what she was doing, and she said she was looking for matches. He responded, 'I don't have matches. I don't smoke. You know that!' Neither he nor his mother smoked. She staggered out, disappointed in not having caught us at it...so to speak. Thankfully, when I returned to England Eddie had moved out and I never saw his mother again.

At first, everything seemed like the old days between me and Eddie as we reconnected, but it did not take long for me to realise things had changed between us. Looking back, I often wonder why I left Australia at all. I must have been clutching at straws in the wind, thinking everything was going to be lovey-dovey when I got back to Eddie because, to be honest, he had not written to me that much while I was living in Sydney. I was the one making most of the effort to stay in contact; it was me writing most of the letters. I used to write pages and pages of them describing my life in Sydney, but I rarely received any back.

Eddie and I just did not click. In the two and a half years I had been away, we had drifted apart on opposite sides of the world. I think I was naïve, hoping I could just slip back into Eddie's life. He had a huge group of friends and I never felt I was able to fit in with them. I would just sit there when we all got together and say nothing and just sulk.

Tensions between us grew; little things would be magnified resulting in arguments. Many of the arguments were about me not fitting in with his mates. I kept asking myself, 'What am I fucking doing here?' After a few weeks everything just became too much, and Eddie said I would have to leave. It was all a bit tragic, really. I should have followed my gut instincts and stayed in Australia, although this trip did allow me to catch up with Des and Larry as well as my parents.

I contacted my parents when Eddie was at work and my mother, father and a brother turned up at his house in Coventry. I went to greet them, carrying my suitcase. While I was putting it in the boot of the car my father went into the house. I wondered why he went in, but I never asked as I was keen to get away and had a lot on my mind. Mum called out, 'Are we going?' Dad simply came out of Eddie's home and said completely deadpan, 'Yes. I've seen all I need to see!' I have no idea what he saw but I found it very embarrassing. I dared not ask in case his answer embarrassed me further.

I moved back in with my parents in Wales. However, I was so miserable, made worse by the weather which was so dull and dreary compared to Sydney's sunshine and warmth. I found it hard to reconnect with old friends, and compared to my life in Sydney, everyone and everything felt so conservative. I had moved on and they were still stuck in rural Wales. I was so bored. All I wanted to do was get back to the blue skies of Australia and the bright lights of Les Girls as soon as I could. However, the only way to do that was to make some money in order to pay the fare back to Australia.

I found a job at the nearby Hoover factory in Pontllanfraith carrying and packing parts. My sister also found a job there working in another department. She and I often enjoyed a lager and lime after work at a nearby pub. The staff were friendly, and I got on well with everyone but of course I missed performing. Fortunately, a friend of mine who lived on the same street as my parents did the bookings for one of the social clubs in Abercarn, called the Top Club. He told me he would get me some work at his venue and at other clubs in the valleys which he did. He even drove me to the gigs.

I performed in drag miming to songs and did some stand-up comedy like I did at Les Girls, though this was the Welsh valleys and not Kings Cross. I am not sure the valleys were quite ready for a drag queen like me. I was certainly hit and miss with the audiences, though my sister, who often accompanied me, seemed to enjoy my act. One club I was booked at was packed to the rafters. I started my act and gave the audience the full barrel with my saucy humour. I went down like a lead balloon!

One gentleman stood up at the back of the audience and walked down the aisle saying to the audience, 'Are you gonna let this poof talk to us like that?' I finished the first half of my act and came off stage. It was so threatening that my friend who organised the booking advised me not to go back on for the second show. Luckily the manager of the venue agreed that I could leave, and he paid me off. When it came to performing in the Welsh valleys, I think I was just way ahead of my time!

None of this put me off because it was not long before I was to tread the boards at none other than the London Palladium, albeit as part of an audition. I saw an advert in *The Stage* looking for chorus boys for a touring version of Ivor Novello's *The Dancing Years*. I suggested to my friend Des that we should go to London and audition. The only catch was that poor Des had never had a dancing lesson in his life. So, I agreed to teach him a few steps. We started our lessons in his flat near Cardiff in the afternoon and continued throughout the night. We were regularly interrupted by the neighbours below thumping their ceiling with a broom as we were making far too much noise.

Poor Des was a hopeless dancer, but we laughed and shrieked as we were having so much fun. We managed to get an hour's sleep before catching the train to London in the morning. I slept on the couch and when I woke up, I realised that I had lain down on my glasses and cracked one of the lenses. I was not happy but there was not much I could do. We caught the train from Cardiff to Paddington Station where we caught up on some sleep on a couple of benches at the station when we arrived. On waking up I put on my glasses and realised that I had now cracked the other lens when I had been resting on the bench at Paddington Station. Des fell about laughing and so did I as, thankfully, I saw the funny side.

We made our way to the London Palladium in the heart of the West End where we encountered hundreds of other hopefuls also wanting to audition. Eventually, the very camp choreographer who was running the auditions separated us into groups and showed us some steps which we had to copy. I realised that I was so short compared to the other young men auditioning. Des was in another group a few rows back so I could not see him dancing but, in any case, neither of our groups made the cut. At first, I was devastated but when we got outside, Des and I pissed ourselves with laughter thinking about what we had been through.

I had no relationships or flings during my few months back in Wales as my focus was simply to get back to Australia. However, I was still doing the beats and cottages. I used to spend Sunday mornings at the Stowe Hill Baths in Newport. It was very old fashioned with white tiles everywhere. Although the baths were open to all, most of the men there were gay or bisexual and there was plenty of action going on. I went a few times with Des when he had a rare Sunday off from his job as head waiter at the St Mellons Country Club outside Cardiff. At other times I would go with other friends I had known before I went to Australia. Some of the regulars asked me why they had not seen me for so long. I would simply turn my nose up, put on a posh accent and tell them, 'I left the country for a warmer climate.'

It was around this time that I came out to my parents. I say 'came out' but I use the term loosely as I had been performing in drag at home and in my dancing school pantomimes since I was a boy.

I was 24 at this stage and living with my parents was making me stir crazy. I just wanted to get out of the valleys. It all came to a head one day when I had a bit of a meltdown at home during one of Mum and Dad's screaming matches. I started smashing plates, which was usually Mum's party trick when she got uptight. She would go into the pantry and smash them. This was a trait I must have picked up from her and this time it was my turn to do the smashing.

After destroying some of the family's fine china I stormed upstairs in tears with Dad following close behind. I told him, 'Look you have to know I am a homosexual. I like men and I don't like women!' He put his arm around me and gave me a comforting and reassuring hug and calmly said, 'That's ok. Mum and I knew anyway.' It was the only time in our lives that Dad and I shared such an intimate moment and that I felt close to him.

Mum then walked into the room and Dad asked her, 'We knew Stan was different, didn't we?' 'Oh yes,' she responded and waltzed out of the room and got on with her business. I have never been sure what she really thought. Mum never discussed my sexuality with me at any time throughout my life.

I can remember the first time she came to see me in Les Girls in Melbourne, in the mid-1970s. She asked me after the show why she had only seen me at the end when the performers mixed and hung out with the audience. I explained that I had been onstage throughout. It then twigged with her that I had of course not only been in drag but had also been the compere.

After a few months I had saved enough money for a one-way passage back to Sydney and so it was now full steam ahead to return to Australia. Before I left at the beginning of 1967, I did a good deed. The foreman at the Hoover factory announced that the company was going to have to lay off some staff over Christmas. I was well liked at the Hoover factory and worked hard so I was fortunate to have my job saved. However, the foreman said to one colleague that I quite liked that he would not be able to keep him on. I stepped in and asked the foreman not to let him go as he could have my job as I was heading back to Australia. I saved his job.

Before leaving for Southampton to sail to Australia my family had no special dinner or send off for me like before my first trip. It was business as usual. My lasting memory is of Mum and Dad standing on the top of the steps of their home with their next-door neighbour Cora waving me goodbye. It was the last time I would ever see my father.

CHAPTER 9
Compering Les Girls

Compering Les Girls

While working at the Hoover factory in Wales I saved up about £100 for the voyage back to Australia, which took about six weeks. I could not wait to get back to Sydney and I'd lay on my bunk at night thinking, 'For Christ's sake hurry up!' I was so impatient to hit the ground running.

Thankfully, I did have a welcome distraction on the voyage back to Australia to keep me entertained. I enjoyed an amorous fling with an Englishman who had previously toured Australia as Tommy's Steele's drummer. He had loved Australia so much he decided to migrate there. He looked like a skinny version of Leo Sayer, and I found him very attractive.

On arrival in Sydney, we parted ways and lost contact. I guess what happens on ship stays on ship, but our little fling made the voyage more fun and bearable.

I was so glad to be back home, which is how I now regarded Sydney, and soon after arriving I met up with Neville. He was living in a caravan in the backyard of a family in Regents Park. He suggested that I could live with Jim and Alice whose home it was. I already knew them because we had previously stayed with them and their two children in Clacton-on-Sea in Essex when we were doing a two-week gig before I first migrated to Australia. They had since migrated to Sydney too.

I was relieved to find somewhere to live on my return though I cannot say I was too thrilled with having to share a room with their young son. He was spoilt rotten by his parents; whatever he wanted he got. He kept himself to himself and did not seem to want to have much to do with me. Then again, we had nothing in common and I found him rather boring. I found the whole family rather dull and was bored as bat shit living there which probably sounds ungrateful but that is how I felt.

Luckily, I spent as little time under their roof or interacting with them as possible because a few days after arriving in Sydney I made a bee line to see the queens at Les Girls. Thankfully, they welcomed me back with open arms and seemed genuinely delighted to see me. They told me they wanted me back. By this stage Reg Boom had died but his wife Eileen was still helping Sammy run the business side of things. Little else had changed and it was so good to see the girls again. Most of the girls that I had previously worked with were still in the cast with very few changes.

One of the new members of Les Girls who joined around that time was Iris who had previously performed comedy drag at the Purple Onion but had had a falling out with the hostess, Kandy Johnson. At the opening of the show at the Purple Onion there would be a break of a couple of minutes while Iris would go off stage to get changed for her next number which would follow the opening.

Kandy would be on stage telling gags while Iris put on her roller skates, her party trick, to do a comedy number. One night she kept Kandy waiting forever. In the end Iris came on and Kandy said to her, 'You can keep skating. You're fucked!' That is how she left the show and joined Les Girls. She originally settled for pulling the curtains but in time got herself into the show and, surprise surprise, even did a comedy number on roller skates. Iris was certainly a character and had a mouth like a cat's arse.

One of the first things Sammy Lee said to me on my first visit to Les Girls after arriving back in Sydney was, 'When are you coming back, kid?' I was so glad he was happy to see me and wanted me back. This was music to my ears. I told him that I was very happy to start back very soon. He said I should have a word with the choreographer and producer Sheila Cruze who also welcomed me back enthusiastically.

However, before returning to Les Girls, I spent the first month back in Sydney working with my landlord, Jim, on the outskirts of Sydney where he was building a boys' home. My job was to scrub bricks with acid which I hated, and I got badly sunburnt. I could not wait to re-join Les Girls which I did within a few weeks. I got back into the swing of things with my old routine of miming to some of the top hits of the day and doing my tin can strip comedy sketch. Unsurprisingly, I gave up my job on the building site.

When I re-joined Les Girls, Peter Moselle was in the process of leaving, along with Holly Brown, as I explained earlier, to compere a similar type of show on the Gold Coast. His replacement was Tracey Lee who had spent several years performing in some of the top venues in Paris, Amsterdam, Berlin, London and Milan. Many of the queens were in awe of Tracey as she arrived with all these feathers and glamorous costumes from Europe. She got on particularly well with Josie Jay as they shared a dressing room. A few years ago, Josie kindly gave me two feather boas, one yellow and one light lilac, that once belonged to Tracey. Josie, by the way, was a fabulous Streisand impersonator in the show. We stayed in touch until her death from cancer some years ago.

Sadly, the admiration of Tracey by the rest of the cast of Les Girls was not shared by the audience. Simply put, the Les Girls crowd was not her crowd. She was used to performing in swanky cabaret venues in Paris or on the French Riviera. She was a brilliant performer and would sing live or recite monologues, unlike the rest of us queens who would mime. She used to do the likes of Marlene Dietrich and Margaret Rutherford which really went over the heads of the crowd to which we played. Tracey was an absolute professional, but she was just not appreciated by our audience.

I think Tracey's material needed to be more suggestive and out there. It all felt very safe and tame. I was still appearing in production numbers at the time, but I had honed my own stage craft dealing with crowds on the Sunday jaunts to Newcastle. I performed to a working-class audience, and you had to appeal to their sense of humour. A lot of these people would have been going to Les Girls for special occasions. The trick is to know your audience and I certainly knew mine.

Tracey isolated herself from the rest of the cast and rarely mixed with us apart from, perhaps, Josie Jay. You could have a good laugh with Peter Moselle backstage but that was rare with Tracey. Perhaps she felt that performing at Les Girls after working in some of the most glamorous venues in Europe was a bit of a come down.

I think if Tracey could have adapted her act for our audience, she would have lasted a lot longer at Les Girls and could have done more RSLs and clubs around Sydney. She was still doing patter and singing songs from the 1950s. It sometimes felt that she was terribly old fashioned, and she was stuck in another era. She did go on to perform in an old music hall theatre at the bottom of William Street which I think suited her more and the audience responded better.

There were light-hearted moments though during the short time I worked with her. She shared a story with me about her time performing in France, which I still find hilarious and perhaps shows a less serious side to her. She was working at a venue for a couple of days, and she had to stay in a hotel room that had no en suite bathroom. One day she was desperate for the toilet but for some reason she did not want to use the shared bathroom. She held it in for as long as possible. Eventually, she could no longer contain herself and did a massive poo on a piece of paper. She could not believe the size of the damn thing, so she wrapped it in the paper and took it to a local delicatessen and asked the shopkeeper to weigh it. It weighed over two pounds.

Tracey could be very sensitive and was not someone you would cross. I once said to her, 'How are you, you old queen?' I never meant any malice by it and was simply having fun and camping it up. She glared at me and snapped back, 'Never say that again!' I am still unsure if she objected to being called a queen or old or both.

I do not think Sammy liked Tracey Lee very much as he was keen to bring in as many customers as possible. The more customers, the more money. He realised early on that our audience was the wrong one for Tracey. I think Tracey realised it too and left after only a short time in the role. This meant that Sammy needed a new compere. Who could possibly fill such a role?

One day Sammy took me aside and he asked me if I would like to compere the show. I hope that he could see that I had the potential to compere, and he knew that I could hold an audience on my own during my comedy skits. I also had developed an understanding of who the audience was and how I could develop a strong rapport with it. But I also think there wasn't anyone else he could ask! I could not believe my luck and felt on top of the world. When I had first arrived in Sydney a few years before I could not have dreamt that someone like me from the Welsh valleys was going to be the star of Les Girls. I should say here that star billing at Les Girls, both in Sydney, and later, in Melbourne, was given to the show's compere.

However, I was worried about my lack of gags as I did not have much comedy material of my own. I admit that I did 'borrow' a couple from Tracey Lee. I was a pro at performing but compering was a whole new ball game for me. I would go on between the various numbers, tell a few jokes and then introduce the next act. A couple of weeks after I took over as compere Tracey Lee came into the dressing room and asked bitterly, 'Hello dear. Are you still using my material?' It was rather embarrassing, and I was stumped for words. I have a feeling that Josie, with whom she got on well, had dobbed me in.

I cannot blame Tracey. The comedy drag game is a hard one because you find that other comics are always ready to steal your material. It has happened to me so many times during my years performing stand-up comedy. I have even had drag queens sitting in my audience writing down my jokes word for word. However, the vital ingredient to a joke is the timing. If you cannot time a joke, whether it is your original material or not, you might as well give up. My friend, Larry Grayson, showed me the power of timing in the way he delivered his material.

Now that I was compere, I was given my own dressing room, which I shared with Electra, and it felt fabulous. The other queens were my friends, and I was determined not to isolate myself from them as Tracey had so, I would regularly hang out with them in their dressing room. I may have become the compere, but I was still one of the girls. Compering was new to me but over time I fell into the role naturally. My confidence grew, I developed my own comedy material, and I began wearing more and more beautiful gowns designed by Kenny Williams.

Sammy seemed to love me, and I have always been grateful that he had enough faith in me to make me the compere. I have sought validation since a young age, and he certainly gave me that. When I returned to Les Girls after being back in the UK, he explained to anyone who would listen that I had been away several months on a world tour. I am not sure performing at a few bars and clubs in the Welsh valleys quite constituted a world tour but if it was good enough for Sammy it was good enough for me.

Despite being the compere, I also liked being a bit of a clown backstage. One of the things I enjoyed doing was cutting out the heads of people in magazines and sticking them on a totally different body. One evening I cut out a photograph of Sammy Lee's head and stuck it on a photograph of the actress Jayne Mansfield. I put it on the mirror in the girls' dressing room. They found it hysterical. One evening Sammy came into the dressing room and I was terrified that he would see it. He took one look at it and fell about in hysterics.

Alice and Jim, whose house I was staying at, knew I worked at Les Girls, but it was not their thing, and they never came to see me perform. Naturally, I was keen to have my independence and privacy so after a few months I saved enough money to move out, eventually moving to a one-bedroom unit in Lidcombe. I no longer needed to worry about coming in late and waking up the family; but even more importantly it meant that I could bring men back home.

One evening a very attractive man came into Les Girls and we started chatting during the show. He made it clear that he was very interested in me, so I invited him back to my flat. Martin was tall with short dark hair, in his early 20s and was so handsome. The icing on the cake was his sexy Irish accent. He told me that he was a sailor in the Royal Navy and was visiting Sydney. And he happened to be bisexual. Once we got back to my flat it was on for young and old but once we had finished, he told me that he had to leave as his ship was sailing at six in the morning. So, at around 2am he left my place and took a taxi back to his ship.

About an hour later I woke to a tapping on my window. I opened the curtains and there was Martin, smiling up at me in the darkness. His sudden appearance startled me, and I called out, 'Oh my God! Aren't you supposed to be sailing off on your ship!' He responded,

'I've jumped ship! I don't want to go back to sea as I want to stop here with you.' Of course, I felt so ecstatic that this sexy young sailor had jumped ship for me, and he ended up staying with me for about two weeks but my interest in him somewhat waned as I was worried about harbouring someone who had gone AWOL from Her Majesty's Royal Navy. I also didn't want to get too close to him and have my heart broken yet again. Also, by this stage I was thinking of working in Hong Kong having been back in Sydney for around 18 months. I introduced him to Neville, and he ended up staying with him for a while in Chester Hill where he was now living.

Martin spent a couple of years living in Sydney and ended up falling in love with a woman who happened to live opposite Neville. He moved in with her and the last I heard was that he had given himself up to the Royal Navy where he did time in the clink. I would love to know what happened to Martin. He was a beautiful man. It is the only time someone has ever jumped ship for me. How romantic!

During the late 1960s, American servicemen on a 12-month tour of duty in Vietnam were offered seven days 'rest and recreation' leave. Sydney was one of the cities that they were given a chance to visit. Their cash certainly brought in a lot of money to Les Girls, and this made Sammy very happy. In the interval one evening I met an American serviceman. He was about 19 years of age with that cute boy-next-door look, a smile to die for and of course his body was amazing. He invited me back to his room in a high-rise hotel on William Street in Kings Cross. I accepted of course.

I kept my drag on and left my boys' clothes at Les Girls to pick up the next evening as I assumed he wanted me dressed as a woman. But when we got back to his room he said, 'Look I don't want you as a woman. I want you as a man.' This, of course, was easily accomplished. I raced to the bathroom and took off my wig, wiped away my makeup and removed my eyelashes. He seemed to approve of my new, more masculine look and we took to the bed. It was amazing. He really was to die for, and he was a fabulous lover.

A couple of hours later it came time for me to go home. It hit me at that moment that I did not have my boys' clothes with me, or any makeup, and Les Girls was, by this time, closed for the night. Talk about a walk of shame! After saying our goodbyes to each other, I went down in the lift in drag without any makeup or false eye lashes and a wig plonked on my head. I walked across the crowded hotel foyer and headed outside to hire a cab. I was so embarrassed the entire time, but I really hope the young American soldier was not killed in Vietnam and went on to have a happy life.

Image was very important at Les Girls, and we had to look the best we could. I had long felt that I had a slightly large nose of which I was very conscious. It was not huge, but it did not shine a beautiful shadow in the spotlight. Several months after I re-joined Les Girls a German queen called Gigi, who I would later work with in Hong Kong, wandered into my dressing room for a chat. She told us about this wonderful surgeon in Bellevue Hill called Officer Brown who performed nose jobs. I wasted no time in seeing the surgeon who agreed to do mine and make it slightly slimmer. I think the surgery cost me around $300, which would be close to $3000 in today's money.

Compering Les Girls

My surgery was done at a hospital in North Sydney. These days you can be in and out of hospital within a day or two but back then in the late 1960s you could spend up to three weeks recovering in the ward with your nose all bandaged up as I did. Happily, I do not remember being in much pain and I was cared for well in hospital. Sadly, the surgery did not turn out quite how I wanted as my nose seemed slightly off-centre, so I went back about three years later and had it redone by the same surgeon.

During my first stint in hospital Sammy came to see me. After some small talk and asking how I was going, he stood at my bedside and said, 'Listen kid, the rest of the kids in the show think you're getting too fat. You need to lose some weight.' This came as quite a blow because I thought I was pretty slim, and I had never thought about my weight too much previously. Perhaps working at night and having all day to myself helped me gain weight. His comments really played on my mind and planted an obsession that I still have today about my weight.

I saw my doctor and asked him if he could give me something to help me lose weight. He wrote me out a prescription for some pills which essentially contained speed. They took away my appetite and from the moment I first swallowed those pills I began a descent into anorexia. The weight started falling off and I just wanted to keep losing more and more.

To make matters worse I was mixing the pills containing speed with other pills. A waitress at Les Girls suggested that I try some fluid pills called Lasix when I mentioned to her that I was trying to lose weight. These pills are used to treat fluid build-up caused by heart failure and can lower blood pressure. They help you lose fluid around your body and can cause you to lose weight.

Naturally, I went straight back to my doctor. He prescribed the fluid pills but did not warn me of the dangers of mixing them with the other pills that he had previously given me. Consequently, I was high as a kite all day and barely sleeping. I had no appetite and so I was losing weight like there was no tomorrow. The fluid pills were bringing my blood pressure right down, and combined with the lack of food, I was becoming very lightheaded. If I stood up too quickly, I would start to feel faint.

However, I soon realised that I needed at least some food to give me energy but whatever I ate would be minimal. I even bought sugarless ingredients to make jelly. I scrutinised the ingredients of everything I bought.

On one occasion I invited Kenny Williams, his mother and Simone Troy to my home in Lidcombe and cooked them dinner which I really had no appetite for. Sometime during the night, Simone mentioned that when she sailed to England by boat, she ate a whole box of Cadbury's chocolate in her cabin. She said it did not matter as she went straight to the toilet and stuck her finger down her throat before vomiting. I thought that was a wonderful idea as I could enjoy food and chuck it up after. I was now also on my way to becoming bulimic.

I rarely slept as the medication kept me wide-awake. I was up all day and night and would do stupid things like wash the floor to pass the time. Once I even took all the cans out of the cupboard and washed them in order to do something. If I was holding a party where I was serving food, I would make up an excuse to go to the toilet so I could make myself vomit. I dreaded going to restaurants and would do the same thing. There always had to be a bathroom nearby.

I was still able to host the shows at Les Girls and I thought it was wonderful that I could fit into the tight costumes. This only spurred me on to lose even more weight. I loved my new slim and trim figure, and I was wearing heavily sequinned costumes that showed it off. If anyone remarked on my weight loss or how skinny I had become I responded with glee, 'Isn't it Fabulous!' The thinner the better.

One evening I went up to the bar at Les Girls as Sammy was discussing costumes. He said in front of all the girls, 'You're too skinny, kid. What's the story? You're getting so thin.' I snapped back at him immediately, 'One moment you want me to lose weight and then the next you want to put it back on. Do you want me as fat or thin? I wish you would make up your mind.' I stormed off but he never said anything to me as he liked me and probably saw me as a good draw card.

I had no idea what anorexia or bulimia were back then and it never occurred to me that what I was doing was unhealthy or even dangerous. Eating disorders take over your life and so much of what you do revolves around food or rather ways to avoid it.

When I moved to Hong Kong in 1968 there was a public weighing machine in a town square, and I used to weigh myself on it regularly. If I weighed even an ounce more I would panic. At one time in Honkers, I only weighed 8 stone and my partner at the time encouraged me to put on some more weight.

In later years I began taking the diet pills with hash or marijuana as well as grog, which was a recipe for disaster. When I got on to hooch it was terrible because if you had had a few joints, you could eat the leg off a table. I will never forget once going to a party in Melbourne in the 1970s when I was working there. I had a few joints and was so hungry that I ate a jar of pickled onions in the kitchen. I reckon that I ate the lot before going outside into the garden to puke them all back up.

My obsession with food lasted throughout the rest of the 1960s and 1970s and continued into the 1980s. I feel that the combination of anorexia, bulimia, drugs and grog contributed to my nervous breakdown in the 1980s, which you will read about a little later.

Today I still have a fixation on weight because one of the first things I often mention to people when I see them is their weight. It is partly a form of self-loathing on my part. Two of my brothers were large, my father was quite large, and my sister had quite a bit of extra weight.

My eating habits have improved but I am still a fussy eater and I do worry about my weight. We can learn to cope with eating disorders, but I do not think they fully leave you. They remain there in the back of your mind hovering and waiting to resurface.

CHAPTER 10
See You in Court

The 1960s were a dark time for gay men in Sydney. Homosexual acts were still two decades from being decriminalised and the gay rights movement was not yet underway, at least not in Australia. This made us all vulnerable to exploitation, blackmail, bashings and stand-over tactics by thugs, people we fell out with, the police and even our employers. Sammy Lee was generally very good to us, but I have heard of other bar owners using threats and intimidation to keep their performers in line.

There were few places where gay men could meet other gay men for sex. Popular places for meeting were public toilets and parks. I was already familiar with cottaging in the UK, so I was easily able to 'apply my skills' to my Australian environment.

During my first stint living in Sydney in around 1963 I met a man at the toilets at Central Station, which was a very busy beat. It was about 5pm and getting dark and I was on my way to starting work at Les Girls. He was a little older than me, skinny and pretty rough looking, which I loved, and he suggested we go to a lane behind an old brewery nearby. As soon as we had finished our intimate relations, he pulled a knife on me and demanded my money. I was absolutely terrified, and I thought he was going to kill me. I handed him all the money I had on me and he then ran off. Thankfully, I was not physically hurt but I was very shaken. Of course, there was no way I could report it to the police as I would have found myself in lots of trouble, but I did tell some of the other girls I could trust.

A few months went by, and I was walking down an alleyway near Central Station and the same skinny roughian who had mugged me previously, recognised me. He was very apologetic telling me how sorry he had been for mugging me and insisted that he was a reformed man. Naïve me believed him and forgave him – in fact I actually felt sorry for him. I am sure the fact that I was quite horny played a role too. He persuaded me to go back to the same old brewery where once again we got down to business. Lo and behold, he pulled out a knife and demanded my money again. I was just as terrified as before but thankfully the only thing that was wounded was my pride.

Several years passed and in 1970 I was back in Sydney rehearsing for the Les Girls show that was soon to be launched in Melbourne when I saw him again leaning on a window just by Sydney Town Hall in George Street. He looked like shit on a stick and his clothes were torn. I went straight up to him and let out a series of expletives. Once again, he was so apologetic, but the charm and apologies did not work on me this time. I was a bit older and wiser. He told me that he was a changed man and had been recently released from prison. I responded at the top of my voice, 'They should have left you to rot there, you fucking dog!' I said this in front of many people and it felt wonderful and empowering.

People often ask me if I witnessed much police corruption during the 1960s in Sydney. The answer is yes. I was a victim of corruption by the cops as well as entrapment, particularly when they were patrolling beats. Some young fellow (a constable in civvies) would sidle up to you at the urinal and try and pick you up by making eye contact and exposing his penis. The moment you tried to touch him another officer would appear from nowhere to grab you and then arrest you. This happened to me many times. It seemed like I was always in the wrong place at the wrong time. Admittedly, I was often in the wrong place, at the wrong time! I loved the beats.

Usually, the arresting officer would simply ask for a donation to the Police Boys' Club. I would give him whatever I had and of course it would go straight into his pocket. But at least he would let me go. One time I was doing the beat at Central Station toilets and every cubicle door had a little window which would be at about head height if you stood up. Police used to come past and have a good look through the windows, which made it riskier to share your cubicle with anyone.

A police officer must have seen me in a cubicle on my knees having a bit of fun, or at least looking for it, under the partition with the person in the next cubicle. The young constable nabbed me as I left the cubicle and he said that he was taking me to the police station. As we were walking back to the police station he asked if I had any money. I was terrified because this was the one time I had no money on me. Thankfully, he only told me to 'fuck off'. A lucky escape.

However, not all incidents had such endings. During my first stint in Sydney, soon after I had arrived in 1963, I was charged twice with indecent behaviour after being arrested at a beat at Strathfield Station. Both times I was taken to Burwood Police Station and hauled before a magistrate. On the first occasion a very handsome man came in and stood beside me at the urinal flashing his penis.

Naturally, I reached over to stroke it. No sooner had my hand got close to his penis than a police officer came out of one of the cubicles and grabbed me. I ended up charged with indecent behaviour and this was followed by an appearance at the local magistrates' court. I was given a one year's good behaviour bond.

On a side note, I was accompanied to court by my friend Ray Schultz who pulled the curtains at Les Girls and appeared in a couple of sketches out of drag. One evening the English comedy writer and actor Jimmy Edwards was in the audience at Les Girls when he saw Ray in action. He immediately fell for him and asked the manager Johnny McLean to introduce him to Ray. The next thing Ray knew was that he was being swept off to England on the same boat as Conchita and Simone, who were also hoping to make it big overseas.

About six months after the first court case, I was arrested again and ended up once again at the magistrates' court in Burwood, where I was given another good behaviour bond. Fortunately, my first arrest only half a year before was not brought up in court so I had a very lucky escape considering that I was only halfway through my first good behaviour bond.

However, I was not so fortunate a few years later after I returned to Sydney in 1967 and had started back at Les Girls. I had taken a train to Cabramatta one Saturday afternoon and went to a popular beat at a public toilet opposite the train station. When I entered the toilets one of the doors to the cubicles opened. Inside, a young man who was about my height, looked around 18 and was slim with light brown hair, signalled to me to join him.

Naturally, I obliged his wishes and we started fiddling with each other, but something did not seem right. For some reason I had this feeling that it may have been a set up though I don't really know what made me so uneasy. I decided to end our dalliance prematurely and walked back to the train station. As I was waiting on the platform I looked towards my right and I spotted a couple of police officers on the bridge over the railway line looking in my direction.

I thought no more of it but the next time I looked over at the bridge I could see the cops walking towards me. Next thing I knew they grabbed and handcuffed me before walking me out of the train station to their police car. I was mortified. One of the cops got into the back of the car with me; on the other side of me was the young man from the cubicle.

I never found out whether he had been planted to entrap me or not or whether he was just another unfortunate person caught out that afternoon. I had noticed as I walked into and out of the toilets that there was a bicycle just outside and I have often wondered whether he rode to the police officers to inform them as I had seen no sign of police when I was leaving. We were driven to Blacktown Police Station, not too far from Cabramatta. As we pulled up at some traffic lights the officer who was driving turned to the other and said, 'Let's throw the poofta out here and shoot him. We can make out that he was escaping!' It may sound like a cliché but my whole life flashed in front of me. That is the absolute truth. I was terrified and those words still ring in my mind on occasion all these years later.

See You in Court

Soon after arriving at Blacktown Police Station, I was put into an interview room and during the interrogation a police officer slapped me right across my mouth. It was agony but I did not want the cop to see that I was scared, and I was determined not to show any sign of weakness. I was then taken to Blacktown Hospital where my penis was swabbed with a cotton wool bud to see if there was any evidence of ejaculation, which, of course, there was not. Nevertheless, I was charged with buggery and fingerprinted when I was returned to the police station.

The cops allowed me one phone call once I was back at the station, so I phoned Jonny McLean, the manager of Les Girls. to come and bail me out. Johnny was very good to me as he immediately came straight to the police station after I had spoken with him and bailed me out.

I arrived back at Les Girls in time for the shows that evening and I was told to go to the dressing room of Peter Moselle, who was still the compere at the time. Sitting in the room were Sammy Lee, Johnny, Sheila Cruze and Peter. It felt quite intimidating at first and initially I thought they looked like they were sitting there as judge, jury and executioner. Much to my relief, they were very supportive.

I was quite emotional as I told them what had happened and Sammy said, 'Don't worry, kid. I'll look after you.' Sammy liked me very much and wanted me in the show, so he was keen not to lose me to prison. Then I somehow got dressed and did the shows. It certainly felt like a very strange and surreal night. At the end of the night Johnny came up to me and reassured me again, 'Leave it to Sammy. He will fix you up.'

The following week I was asked to go to the Latin Quarter where I sat with Sammy at his table. Sitting with him was a skinny man with auburn hair who turned out to be a corrupt detective that he knew. Sammy introduced us and then left us to it. In a business-like way, the detective proceeded to ask me everything about my arrest and what led to me being charged with buggery.

He told me that he would see what he could do to keep me out of prison but in return I would, of course, have to pay money to him. I was concerned that if I paid him the cash early on that he would simply run off with it so we agreed that I would pay $600 dollars to him before sentencing and $600 after sentencing. The money, he said, would be split between him, a police colleague and the presiding judge.

Converted to present day currency rates, $1,200 was about $12,000 and on top of that I had the legal fees to pay as well. Sammy put me in touch with a solicitor in Macquarie Street who was a tall, elderly man in his 70s. Thankfully, the money I had saved from working at Les Girls and my Sunday stints up to Newcastle was just enough to pay off everyone, but it pretty much cleared out my finances. Everything I was earning was going towards keeping me out of jail! I ended up making three appearances at the Darlinghurst Courthouse. During my first appearance I did not have to say much. My lawyer put in a plea of 'not guilty' on my behalf, which meant I had to come back. I was instructed to return for the hearing a couple of weeks later.

At my next appearance, my solicitor spoke on my behalf. Evidence was also heard from the police and the young man who had been in the cubicle with me. In his statement he claimed that I had put 'white' liquid in him. His claim was, thankfully, dismissed by the presiding judge. No evidence had been found in the hospital that I had ejaculated. The judge then reduced the charge from buggery to indecent assault. My solicitor also told the judge that I was willing to undergo a form of conversion therapy and consent to hormone injections in order to 'straighten' myself out. I was told that I would be required to have weekly injections for the next month. The idea worried me shitless, but I was prepared to do anything to stay out of prison.

Every week I saw the doctor at a clinic in Macquarie Street where I would lay down on my stomach on an examination table. The nurse would bring the doctor a huge needle and syringe containing male hormones, which he injected into the base of my spine. The injections hurt like hell and they certainly did not 'cure' me of anything, though I did grow a bit more hair on my face. To think I was doing all of this to prove to the judge that I was trying to cure myself of my homosexuality.

I was also required to see a panel of three rather stern looking Macquarie Street psychiatrists who never really said much, and I never found out who they were working for. Was it the police or the courts? They gave me what is called a Rorschach ink blot test where I looked at these ink blots and had to say what I thought the images reminded me of. I remember describing one image as a butterfly. I was told that the purpose was to examine my personality and determine what kind of person I was.

About a month after my second court appearance, I returned to Darlinghurst Court for sentencing. My heart was in my mouth, I was so very anxious, I was sick to my stomach. I discretely passed the bribery money to Johnny McLean to pass to the detective and I was then taken to a holding cell below the court which was full of rough looking criminals. As I said, Johnny was very good to me and was there for me at my first and third court appearances. I believe he gave the detective the money quietly behind the courthouse. The detective had previously told me that the judge was retiring after my sentencing so he would have had little to lose by accepting my 'gift' of cash. Still, it would have been quite a risk for the judge because if he had been found out he could have been charged and his reputation would be ruined. But obviously, he was confident he wouldn't get caught.

After a couple of hours of being in the cell with all those hardened criminals eyeing me up, I was brought up to the dock and two stern police officers stood either side of me. I was trembling with nerves and the palms of my hands were clammy with sweat. Remember, I was only 26 at the time and the thought of doing time in gaol was simply unbearable. The judge read out the charges and then my sentence. All I heard were the words 'five years' before the judge paused. My jaw dropped and I was overcome with shock. I felt numb. What must have only been a second's pause seemed to me like an eternity. Then, the judge uttered the word 'Suspended'. A giant wave of relief washed through my body and it felt like an enormous weight had lifted from my shoulders.

The judge had sentenced me to a five-year suspended sentence. Finally, I was able to breathe again but more importantly I was able to get on with my life. I had kept my arrest and court case a secret from Jim and Alice; most of the people working at Les Girls had no idea either. However, the suspended sentence meant that I had to keep my nose clean for that period. Any sign of trouble and I would be locked up. I also had to report to a probation officer for five years. I was of course terrified of doing beats and didn't resume doing them for many years.

My probation officer was affable enough but I'm sure he did not approve of my lifestyle. He certainly looked uncomfortable if anything was brought up about my court case or my career. By this stage I was living on my own in Granville having moved from Jim and Alice's in Regents Park. For some reason my probation officer had my old address and went looking for me there where he told Alice everything. She came to my new home in Granville and was furious. She was absolutely disgusted with me and let me have it with both barrels. I felt betrayed and angry with my probation officer, but I did not want to antagonise him, so I said nothing.

Even when I went to live in Hong Kong, the UK, Beirut and Melbourne I was required to contact him by letter until my five-year sentence was up, giving him an update on what I had been doing. I will never know if the money I paid to the crooked detective ever reached his police colleague or the judge. I never met his colleague, so I have no idea if he even existed. I hope the money I paid to that detective helped me get a lighter sentence, but again, I have no idea if it actually did.

I will also never know if the young man in the cubicle with me was planted by the police to entrap me. I have so many unanswered questions and feel angry and hurt by the way I was treated. All I know for sure is that I narrowly escaped a prison sentence.

I know I was not alone. Many men went through what I did and felt the only way to get a lesser sentence was to give or offer a bribe which many police officers would demand and gladly accept. So many married men had families and risked losing everything. So many lives were destroyed. Perhaps I was one of the lucky ones.

The system, which should have been protecting us, was so corrupt. I have rarely discussed my experiences with the police and have been holding on to this for a long time. It has been more than half a century of torture and is never far from my mind. I think it almost certainly contributed to my nervous breakdown in the 1980s.

I wrote that the male hormone injections did not turn me straight but a few months after the court case something happened to me that may surprise a lot of my friends and people who have known me over the years. I met the only woman I have ever fallen in love with and one of the only women that I have truly loved apart from my mother.

Wendy came into my life around late 1967. She was a nurse at a Sydney hospital and used to come with her nursing friends quite often to see the shows at Les Girls. I thought she was just so friendly, wonderful and accepting. We talked a lot and we got on so well.

I loved her beauty. She had shoulder length jet-black hair and was about the same height as me. Rather surprisingly, I found that I was very attracted to her. Even more surprising, given we met at Les Girls, where I was performing, a romance developed. I do not know how it happened, but it did. Attraction is attraction and love is love regardless of how we may pigeonhole our sexuality or have it labelled for us. I fell for Wendy big time.

I was, of course, still attracted to men and if the two of us were walking down the street I would still take a look on the sly at any attractive men we passed. If Wendy ever noticed she never said anything. However, it was my first proper monogamous relationship, and I was utterly in love with her. At one point, I even considered marrying her and having children with her. She was just so yummy!

I was now living in a two-bedroom unit in Lidcombe and Wendy was living in her nursing quarters at the hospital in the city. I chose the apartment because it was the only one available in the building which was very handy for commuting to work as it was near the train station. I kept all my drag in that flat. There was a small bed in there, too, for the occasional guest. Wendy never moved in with me, but we met up a couple of times a week and she sometimes stayed over. I met her mother at her home on the North Shore and we also got on well. She seemed to accept me as an important part of Wendy's life.

I never told the other queens at Les Girls. It was not that I was in a relationship with a woman, rather, it was because I knew that they would make bitchy and sarcastic remarks. It was also none of their business. I was with Wendy for about four months and I really enjoyed my time with her.

We eventually drifted apart as she was busy training to be a theatre nurse and I was working most evenings at Les Girls as well as Sundays in Newcastle. Thankfully we remained in touch and on good terms. A few months after we split, in 1968, I moved overseas for about 14 months. On my return to Australia, I had hopes of perhaps reconnecting romantically, but it was not to be. We arranged to meet at her mother's place and Wendy announced that she had something to tell me.

It soon became clear that she had moved on quite a lot as she revealed that she now had a girlfriend. Yes, Wendy was a lesbian. When we had been together, I had had no idea that she may have been attracted to other women. Then again, many people would have been shocked that I had found a woman so attractive and had wanted to be romantically linked with one, let alone marry her and have children together.

Wendy and I are still friends today and we talk to each other on the phone regularly. One of the many things I admire about her is that she is the most brilliantly talented wildlife photographer. Her photographs are stunning. She is so talented.

About two months after I spilt up with Wendy, I met a man aged about 20 who I will call Jeffrey. My relationship with him was everything that mine with Wendy was not. Like Wendy, he used to be a regular in the audience of Les Girls. He had naturally blond hair, was very handsome and was a little bit taller than me. We got talking one night and we hit it off. He was living in Guildford with his mother who bred greyhounds. There was a definitely a spark between us, and I fancied him very much. We started seeing each other and after about a month he moved in with me.

At first, things were going well between us but soon after we moved in together things went downhill. Jeffrey always seemed so negative and never got excited about anything. I was working nights at Les Girls for most of the week as well as doing regular shows in Newcastle. In addition, I was also performing drag comedy and compering shows around Sydney on Sundays at RSL Clubs with Neville, Susan Le Gaye and a female dancer who was a friend of Neville's when I was not doing the Newcastle shows. Jeffrey worked at Guildford Train Station as a station master. He often complained to me how lonely he felt without me at home when I left to work at Les Girls.

I thought the solution was to introduce him to some friends of mine to help give him some company. This was a big mistake as one of them did indeed keep him company in a biblical sense, though I did not know it at the time. Jeffrey seemed to be more thrilled spending time with his new friends than me. Back then I could be the jealous type, but I also had pretty good instincts; something did not seem right.

Jeffrey and I became more and more distanced and I did not want to make things worse by having a confrontation with him, particularly when I had no evidence that he had been playing away. However, I decided it was open season or at least used my suspicions as an excuse to have some fun of my own.

My unit was on the ground floor and we had a lockup garage where

Jeffrey kept his car. One night I brought back a young man who had been in the audience of Les Girls to whom I had taken a shine. I knew Jeffrey would be in bed, so we decided to go into the garage. I rarely went into the garage as I had little reason to as I have never learnt to drive. My Lothario for the night and I ended up shagging on the bonnet of Jeffrey's car. We then said our goodbyes and I joined Jeffrey in bed.

The next morning Jeffrey woke up to go to work and I started to panic. I had not had a chance to change out of drag the previous night as the man I went home with had offered me a lift in his car. I would have hated to have missed a free ride...literally. The dress I was wearing had feathers all over its top. The following morning, I became anxious that I might have left a few stray feathers on Jeffrey's car or elsewhere in the garage. While Jeffrey was in the shower, I ran downstairs in my underwear to clear up every feather in sight. Thankfully, Jeffrey did not have a clue.

Things continued to go from bad to worse until one night I returned from Les Girls to find Jeffrey and all his belongings gone. No note had been left and when I tried to call him at work, I kept being told he was not there. I was never given an explanation and believe that he took the coward's way out. We had been together for six months but perhaps we had only been delaying the inevitable and he had in fact done us both a favour. How we even survived that long I will never know.

My instincts about Jeffrey having an affair seemed justified after a friend, the type that loves to gossip, told me a mutual friend of mine and Jeffrey's called Jimmy had been sleeping with him. I was furious and felt betrayed. After performing at Les Girls one night, I decided to confront Jimmy. Two friends of mine drove me straight to his home. The side door was unlocked and so we went in. I told my friends to wake Jimmy up while I waited in the sitting room. Jimmy looked gobsmacked when he saw me; his face said it all. If there were any doubts about his guilt, he was guilty as charged.

I told him that if he wished to continue sleeping with Jeffrey I would go into his bedroom, wake his boyfriend and tell him everything. He immediately confessed that he had slept with Jeffrey but that there was no longer anything going on between them. I left it at that and felt empowered that I was able to have it out with him. Unsurprisingly, any friendship that I had with Jimmy was put on hold for a while though I did see him around the traps after I returned to Australia from living overseas in 1970.

I was still not fully over Jeffrey and was keen to try and win him back one last time. It was September 1968 and Jeffrey was about to celebrate his 21st birthday. In all my wisdom I thought that it might be an idea to organise a surprise party. I spoke with my friend Elva who was Susan Le Gaye's sister, and we hatched a plan. Elva would take Jeffrey out for a drive and would suggest that they drop in on me on the way to their destination.

I organised a cake and invited 20 of our mutual friends around. When Jeffrey arrived, he did not seem particularly surprised or excited; but then again, he never got excited about anything. He barely spoke to anyone, looked moody and only stayed for a short time. I think we both had a lucky escape. We were just too different and not compatible. Jeffrey went on to pull the curtains and perform in drag at Les Girls in Melbourne in the 1970s before going on to work in Europe for a while. We are in touch today and get on a lot better as friends than lovers.

Soon after Jeffrey, I found myself young, free and single. I was ready for my next challenge which came in the form of two words – Hong Kong!

Photos

Stan the Man

Les Girls Sydney
with Cilla Black

Melbourne Cup - 1974

Les Girls - Sydney 1963 - 1970

Photos

Les Girls Melbourne
1970 to 1978

Photos

Publicity shot for my Show 1978

On tour with my one man Show

The Two Munro's with the Famous Andrew Sisters - 1960

Hong Kong

Photos

Phillip and Me - 1972

Les Girls - Sydney 1963 - 1970

Stan Munro & Roman Tam

Stan Munro with Neville Munro

Photos

While filming Back roads, ABC - 2020

The Castlemaine RSL Victoria - 2010

Stan - 1980

2018

Stan Munro Show at Kyogle Memorial Institute 2022

William and Stan in Katherine, Northern Territory 2024

Stan, Phillip & Danny La Rue

Photos

Stan in Wales with statue of Tommy Cooper

Stan in Wales
Photos taken by Jane Beechey
2023

Photo taken by Jodie Harris who is a photographer of Yamatji descent living and working in the Northern Rivers NSW on Bundjalung Country. This image was entered into the National Photographic Portrait Prize where Jodie was selected as a finalist - 2025.

Photos

Stan was a joint winner of the Arts and entertainment award at the ACON Hero awards 2024

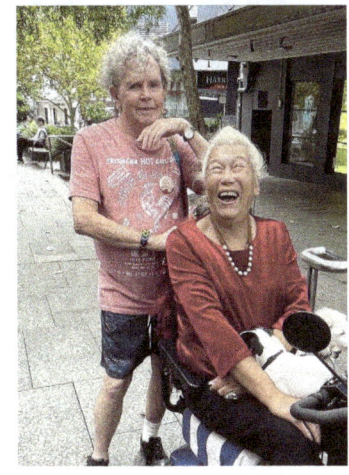

Me age 84 - February 2025
These photo's taken by
William Brougham between 2022 - 2025.

Stan Munro with former Les Girl Ayesha Kazan

CHAPTER 11
The Great Escapes

While at Les Girls I heard from some of the other girls about a similar show to ours in Hong Kong called Playgirls. It all sounded wonderfully exotic, performing in the Far East.

I was enjoying working at Les Girls, but the thought of Playgirls and Hong Kong was never far from my mind, particularly as some of the cast of Les Girls had gone over there to work and were enjoying themselves. Towards the end of 1968 I heard on the grapevine that Carlotta, who had been compering Playgirls for a few months, was planning to return to Australia. I thought that this was my golden opportunity to try my luck and get in on the action.

However, there was one major obstacle – Sammy Lee! He had always been good to me and had given me the opportunity to be the star of Les Girls. In fact, I had recently signed a new contract with him at his home in Elizabeth Bay. Naturally, it felt wonderful that he was on my side and wanted me to continue but signing that contract only made it more complicated if I wanted to go to Hong Kong. I really did not want to let him down but the chance to work in Hong Kong was too good to miss.

I knew that I had to get in fast before someone else was found to replace Carlotta. I nervously approached Sammy about being released from my contract early. You can probably imagine his answer. I knew that Sammy was not someone you crossed and that he would not make things easy for me. However, I was not going to take no as an answer.

I saw Col Joye, who was actually the agent handling bookings for Playgirls, at his booking agency in North Sydney, and he confirmed to me that Carlotta was leaving the show. He also added that he would love to have me in Playgirls. Col was sometimes in the audience at Les Girls and knew my work and what I was capable of. The following week I returned and signed a contract for six months with a six-month extension if both management and I agreed.

Col organised my flight tickets and told me that Mike, the Playgirls Manager, was handling the Hong Kong side of things and that it would be a good idea to speak with him. How brazen was I? I used the phone backstage at Les Girls to call him overseas! The phone was usually used to speak to staff at the front-desk, so I was hoping that nobody was listening in. It was quite a risk.

I contacted the people from whom I was renting my Lidcombe apartment to let them know that I was leaving. I packed up everything I had and threw some of it in the tip and gave some bits and pieces to Neville. The only people at Les Girls who knew that I was fleeing to Hong Kong were Simone Troy and Kenny Williams. The fewer people who knew the better as I could not afford to let Sammy find out - and queens do love to gossip.

I performed what was to be my last Saturday night at Les Girls and then packed up all my costumes into a taxi. This didn't arouse suspicion as everyone assumed I was taking them to wear for my regular Sunday jaunts to Newcastle. My friend Robert spent the night at my place before driving me to the airport. For some reason I didn't have an alarm clock so the plan was that he would have a few hours' sleep and then I would have a few hours' sleep before he would wake me up in time for him to drive me to the airport so I could catch my flight. As it turned out an alarm clock certainly would have been more reliable than Robert, who promptly fell back to sleep when it had been his turn to stay awake.

When I woke up panic immediately set in when I saw him sleeping like a baby. 'Fuck! We are running late for the airport,' I yelled. We threw my luggage into his car and set off down Parramatta Road to the airport, with me screaming at Robert while he was bawling his eyes out. I will never forget it because tradies in their trucks were staring at us. We put on quite a show.

I was terrified of missing my flight and having Sammy catch me at the airport. I had arranged with Simone to contact Kandy Johnson on the Monday morning to let him know that there would be an opening in the show at Les Girls. I am not sure that Kandy ever took up the offer as it was Karen Chant's face that replaced mine on the menus.

Simone loved to put the willies up me and had told me that Sammy would be waiting for me at the airport. She later told me he had been at the airport with a gun and that I should never return to Australia if I thought my life was worth living which was, of course, utter nonsense.

Panic set in when we got to the baggage counter and were informed that my plane had left half an hour before. I started panicking again and began shouting at Robert that it was all his fault. Thankfully, I was told that there was an Air New Zealand plane leaving in half an hour that I could board. I was so relieved. This was when I first gained the nickname 'Stella Escapee' as it was the first of a few narrow escapes I would make.

After several hours of travel, I arrived in Hong Kong where I was met by the charming and friendly, Mike Friedman. He drove me to my apartment in Kowloon which was on the third floor of a large block of flats perched on a hill. On the bottom floor was a furrier's shop. Some of the girls in the show would go there to get their fur coats made. Apart from that short excursion to Bombay during the first voyage to Australia, this was my first time in Asia. Everything was just so different – the sights - the smells - the sounds - from what I was used to. Outside the building there were lots of chickens running freely about. It struck me as quite a poor area. I thought it resembled a slum district. It was definitely not the glamorous place I imagined it to be, and I began to wonder what I was letting myself in for.

The third-floor apartment contained many rooms in which the girls would sleep, and I was very relieved to see that I had my own room. The other girls had named the building 'Cockroach Castle' and not without good reason. As soon as I put my suitcases down in my room a huge cockroach flew in through the window. I burst into tears and thought, 'What have I done???' The acrid smell of wax was a constant in the place because the queens, all of whom were Australian, used it to remove the hair on their face.

Our apartment came with two maids and a head maid who looked after us. Some of the kids in the show treated them as little more than slaves and talked down to them. The worst culprit was someone with whom I had worked at Les Girls. She would ask for breakfast in bed and if she was in a terrible mood, she would throw things at them. I felt dreadful for those maids.

The venue hosting Playgirls, which was down an arcade in the grand Miramar Hotel, was quite spacious. We performed on a stage which was shaped like a curve which extended into the audience. There were two shows on each night at 8.30 and 10.30. The show was similar to Les Girls and included chorus numbers and solos but unlike Les Girls, there were no comedy skits so I did not do my tin can strip. My role was the compere and, fortunately, I was able to perform spoken comedy gags in between introducing the various acts. I lip synched a popular song of the day at the beginning of the shows, which were lavish and very well costumed by a dressmaker from Sydney. By this stage, our songs would be recorded on to reel to reel tapes and Sandy, who was the sound technician, was developing skills in splicing different songs together. It was certainly a step up from performing to records at the start of my career. We were getting US$150 per week which was also another big step up from what I was getting paid at Les Girls.

We certainly had our fair share of stars in the audience. The actress Honor Blackman, *Goldfinger's* Pussy Galore, invited me to join her table one evening. Honor looked so beautiful and delicate, like a porcelain doll. Sitting with her was the ruggedly virile actor Stanley Baker, star of *Zulu, The Guns of Navarone* and other action films. They were in Hong Kong filming *The Last Grenade* which also starred Richard Attenborough and John Thaw. It was such a pleasure to meet Honor and Stanley, particularly as he was a fellow Welshman.

After some banter with them both Stanley and I talked about where we were born in Wales. At the next table sat a group of Pommy sailors who were eyeballing Stanley's hairpiece. In their drunken state they yelled, 'Show us your wig, Stanley!' I was mortified. I stood up and told them to quieten down which thankfully they did. Phew! I imagine that it was not a common occurrence for Stanley, known for his many macho roles, to have his reputation defended by a cock in a frock.

Our audiences were mainly American and British soldiers and Hong Kong residents who were mostly expats from the United Kingdom. I felt particularly sorry for the American soldiers who were in Hong Kong for a week's rest and relaxation from fighting in Vietnam. It was awful seeing their smiling faces and knowing that they would soon be back fighting such a wasteful war and putting their lives at risk.

Many of the soldiers enjoyed the company of Chinese bargirls who were employed by the club to help the lads empty their wallets. The bargirls sat on stools at the bar waiting for their next prey to come along and buy them drinks while helping to increase the profits of the club's owners. While the soldiers seemed to love our show, the bargirls weren't as interested and would turn away. They just wanted their latest victim to keep buying drinks. The more drinks they bought, the more money the girls would see.

I was the only member of the show living as a man as the others were living as trans women and were usually on hormones. Most had had breast surgery. I always strategically carried a photograph showing me out of drag to share with anyone who I fancied or who showed an interest in me. That way they would know what they would be getting if they wanted to meet me after the show. I didn't want any misunderstandings, and besides, this was my point of difference to the other girls. I had a few one-night dalliances with American and British soldiers. They were fun but I didn't lose my heart to any of them. I must have been developing a tougher skin.

There was quite the drag pipeline between Sydney and Hong Kong, and I was fortunate to work with three girls who I had worked with at Les Girls – Monique St John, Lilac Haze and Ayesha. There was another queen from Newcastle called Honey West, who went on to appear in Les Girls in Melbourne, as well as Gigi who had recommended the surgeon who gave me the nose job back in the early 60s.

Gigi was one interesting character! She had very thin calves which she desperately wanted to look round and voluptuous. She eventually found a doctor in Hong Kong who pumped her calves full of some oil-like substance, possibly silicone. Following the procedure, Gigi went straight back to work that night but halfway through the show the goo was leaking out of her legs. I kid you not. It was like superglue, and it was sticking to her pantyhose. I do hope she got her money back.

Gigi was always the first act on and whenever I was preparing to introduce her, she would scream from backstage in her strong German accent, 'Not ready, darling!' Her delay in getting ready became longer and longer each night and I would be left on stage having to tell more and more jokes.

Rather bizarrely, she kept a long length of wood under her dressing table and from time to time would threaten us with it, often without any provocation, in order to exert control over us. She would often say, 'You queens, I'll fucking kill you.' I think the fact she kept me waiting on stage was her way of letting me know that she was the boss.

One particular night she kept me waiting and waiting. I was trying to come up with more and more comedy patter and she kept saying that she was still not ready. Finally, I saw red and said to the audience, 'Oh she's not ready, ladies and gentlemen. That's because she's got a 10-inch cock and she takes so long to tuck it away.' The audience loved the line, but it was the worst thing that I could have said as I could hear her screaming from backstage. When I got back to the dressing room it was an absolute mess as she had pulled all my costumes off the rack and thrown my makeup on the floor in a fit of rage. However, I decided not to say anything but get revenge instead.

I always arrived at work first in order to open up the dressing room and get ready. The kids would drift in soon after having done their makeup at home. One night I got in quite early, and Gigi was the only other person there. She was down at the other end of the dressing room, and I thought that this was my time to give her some of her own medicine. I walked over to her and picked up her piece of four-by-two at her feet and I said to her, 'You gonna hit me with this?' She responded casually, 'No dear.' This wound me up even more. 'Right, we're going to have it out, you fucking bitch,' I shouted in her face.

I dropped the piece of wood and grabbed her around the head. I was gobsmacked as what I thought was her hair came off in my hands. I thought that I had pulled her hair out, but it was in fact a wig. I had no idea that Gigi was completely bald underneath. She was screaming for help and some waiters ran in. As soon as she saw them, she screamed again even louder for them to get out as she did not want them seeing her bald scalp. It did the trick. She never threatened me again with her four-by-two and she was always ready to come on stage when I announced her.

Hong Kong was such a lively place; non-stop seven days a week. I was working every night. Sometimes I didn't even know what day it was. As I performed every night it meant that I did not have much spare time, but I would often go to a bar in a hotel where a lot of gay men, including soldiers, would be looking for action. I was always out of drag, of course, but I still picked up plenty of hot young studs. The one-night stands with the soldiers were of course lovely but I need not have worried long about looking for anyone special because not long after arriving in Hong Kong I met a lovely man at that bar who would later go on to become an iconic pop star in Hong Kong and other parts of Asia and has even been dubbed as the 'Grand Godfather of Cantopop'. His name was Roman Tam, and he was very cute and wonderfully charming. He also had the most beautiful white teeth I have ever seen, and I absolutely adored him. Roman was such a sweet and lovely person with a good nature.

We spent about five months together and we were so very much in love. We spent every spare moment with each other. I even bought us matching sweaters and we'd wear them proudly when we were out and about. He was performing in a band called Roman and the Four Steps when we met. The group was known for covering a lot of popular British and American songs of the day rather than performing in Cantonese. Roman was a huge fan of the Beatles so the band would cover a lot of their songs. I used to help them with their English pronunciations, and I sometimes accompanied them to the TV studios on a Saturday afternoon where they had a regular gig.

As with most of my previous relationships it petered out after a few months, largely because of our busy work schedules. I was working seven nights a week and his career with the band was taking off as they were getting more and more gigs. We lost touch but Roman went on to have a very successful solo career in Hong Kong and elsewhere in Asia. He produced around 56 albums and recorded the theme songs to several popular television series. He even sparked controversy by performing on stage in drag and posing naked for a magazine. That's my boy!

In the 1980s I found out that he was in Australia performing some shows for the Chinese community. I was tempted to get in touch, but I felt that a lot of time had passed. After all, you cannot warm up yesterday's mashed potatoes and expect them to taste as good. Sadly, he died in 2002 of liver cancer. I knew Roman only for a short while, but I loved the time that we spent together. I will never forget him.

The Great Escapes

One night in April 1969, I was literally about to go on stage at Playgirls when I was handed a telegram sent by one of my brothers telling me that my father had died. I was devastated, particularly because on my previous trip back to Wales we had bonded for the first time when he hugged me after I came out to him. I had felt a connection. However, the show had to go on and I went on stage like a trooper and gave it my all. I have always believed that when you are on stage you leave your personal problems off stage, and you should give the audience your best performance.

I felt that I needed to be there for Mum and that I had a duty to go back to Wales. I waited a couple of days before telling Mike. He was not particularly sympathetic and promptly reminded me that I was under contract. However, I was not going to let Mike deter me and decided it was time to bring back Stella Escapee and hatch a plan.

I phoned my friend Robert in Sydney as I knew he was hoping to visit the UK soon. I asked him about his plans, and he told me that he had not yet set a departure date. I suggested to him that he should come to Hong Kong in about a week and see the show and then we could slip away together the next day. Having him with me would give me a bit more courage to make the move.

I contacted Col Joye, out of courtesy, to let him know that I was planning to leave Hong Kong. I explained the delicate situation that I was in to him and he was concerned understandably about me leaving Mike and the girls in the lurch. I told him about my friend Eddie Tye in Sydney and suggested that he would make a good replacement. I knew I was taking a risk telling Col before I left Hong

Kong in case it got back to Mike but I was certain that I could trust him.

I phoned a mutual friend in Sydney and asked him to tell Eddie the situation and for him to get in contact with Col. I knew that recommending and approaching Eddie was taking a bit of a gamble as he had only previously performed to a gay crowd but thankfully, he was up for a new challenge.

All in all, it had taken me about three weeks to plan my departure following my father's death. Robert came to see the show as planned, before going to stay the night in a hotel, and the next morning I met him at the airport for our flight to London Heathrow. I managed to slip out without the other girls noticing as they had all been fast asleep. They would often go partying until three in the morning and not rise until well into the day. This time there was to be no running late for the airport or missing our flight like my previous escape from Sydney.

Once we got to Heathrow, Robert and I were met by one of my brothers who drove us to my mother's home in South Wales. Mum was glad to see me but was, of course, distraught following the death of my father. Although I had missed his funeral, I wanted to try my best to comfort my mother, so I spent most of my three months back in Britain living with her. Robert also stayed at her house. However, I realised early on that I needed to financially support myself and get some work if I was to spend time back with Mum. Money does not grow on trees!

While I had been working in Hong Kong, I contacted a booking agent at the Embassy Club in London's Mayfair to ask if they ever put on female impersonators. I was asked to send some photographs. Thankfully in Hong Kong I had looked my best and was at my slimmest and had had some glamorous publicity shots taken by an excellent photographer. My look was very much that of a glamorous young woman in her late twenties. There was no exaggeration of features using makeup – I simply looked like a beautiful young woman. I sent these to the agent, and he must have been impressed because he agreed to let me perform for a couple of nights when I was back in the UK.

About a week after returning, Robert and I travelled to London, and I performed at the venue for two nights. It was a very upmarket venue, and the male clientele all wore suits. Many of the women were hostesses employed by the club to persuade the men to buy them drinks. It was similar in that sense to Playgirls in Hong Kong. Unfortunately, my act did not go down all that well at all as the audience members seemed to be rather more captivated by the young women on their arms. Needless to say, I never performed there again.

But sometimes work just falls into your lap in the most unexpected ways. My brother Les had recently divorced his wife and had a fiancée who he was soon to marry. They invited me along to a club called the Pantside Social Club in Abercarn. I suggested going in drag and neither my brother nor his bride-to-be seemed to mind. While we were having drinks, a chap in his fifties approached our table and asked me to dance. I was flabbergasted but went along with it. He seemed to have no idea that I was a man in drag.

Later in the evening I asked to see the club's manager about possibly getting some work there. I was more than a little surprised when it turned out that my dancing partner was, in fact, the manager. He asked me what kind of act I did, and I told him that I was a female impersonator. 'If you can fool me, you can easily fool this mob,' he said. We agreed on a price, and he booked me for the following Saturday. But he warned me that there would be another female impersonator performing that night who was not as glamorous as me.

I turned up the following week and walked into the dressing room. Who should be sat there downing a pint of Guinness but none other than Rex Jameson in drag as Mrs Shufflewick. I introduced myself to him, but he was quite stand-offish. I was busting to tell him that we had shared the bill many years before at the Newcastle Empire when I was still part of the Two Munros. However, I said nothing as Rex seemed to be in no mood to chat. Perhaps he felt a tad peeved at having to share the stage that night with a younger, prettier and more glamorous performer – one who is modest too! I had to follow Mrs Shufflewick that night. Thankfully, the audience seemed to like me.

I went on to find similar work to what I had done at the Pantside Social Club in other venues around the Welsh valleys so that I could support myself financially. I was lucky enough to have the same friend drive me to my shows in the valleys as on my previous trips to Wales, which made things a lot easier as I've never driven a car.

Robert and I also spent about a month, on and off, staying with my friend Larry Grayson in Nuneaton. This enabled me to also perform a few shows in the Midlands within easy reach of Larry.

One of the highlights of being back in Britain was seeing American drag star Ricky Rennée. She was appearing at a club in the Midlands on the same bill as Larry. I thought Ricky was a brilliant performer and really set the benchmark for other female impersonators. Stunning to look at and every move and expression perfectly choreographed and timed. After the show Larry introduced me to Ricky who was very friendly and reminded me of a slimmer version of Cliff Richard.

At one time she had even fronted a club in London's Covent Garden modestly called Ricky Renée's, which sadly closed after only a few months. Apparently, there were just not enough customers, and the club did not make enough money, though the shows were loved by those who attended, many of whom would return repeatedly. Thankfully, this did not hamper Ricky's career and she went on to appear in films such as *Cabaret* and *Goodbye Gemini*. It really was an honour to see Ricky on stage and to meet her, however briefly.

After about three months back in Britain I began to grow restless. My visit was never supposed to be long term, anyway. I was glad to be spending time with Mum, but I felt it was time to move on to pastures new as I could feel those Welsh valleys once again closing in on me. I think that was largely part of the wandering gypsy in me. Thankfully, in July 1969 I bought myself a copy of *The Stage* newspaper which covered the entertainment industry and still exists today. An advert looking for a female impersonator to work at the Kit Kat Club in Beirut immediately caught my eye. This simple advert proved to be my ticket out of the valleys. My salvation had arrived!

CHAPTER 12
Beirut And Back to Honkers

I phoned the promoter and explained my history as a performer to him. He must have been impressed because he invited me to meet him in London. The next day Robert and I drove up in his old car to a rehearsal hall in Soho where we met the promoter. I showed him my photographs from Hong Kong and asked if he would like me to audition. He said there was no need and offered me the job there and then.

I decided to try my luck and asked if Robert could accompany me as my sound engineer. I must have been quite convincing as a few days later tickets arrived for us both to fly to Beirut. I had enjoyed spending time with my mother and catching up with friends such as Larry and Des, but I was ready to move on for more adventures and they accepted that. Robert and I set off from Heathrow Airport to begin our new adventure, in a place I knew virtually nothing about.

One of the first things that hit me on arriving in Beirut was the unbearable heat. It was so very hot and dry. At the airport we hopped in a taxi to take us to the hotel, which also happened to be owned by the owner, a very wealthy Lebanese businessman, of the Kit Kat Club. A couple of minutes after we set off from the airport the driver who looked to be in about his mid-thirties beckoned me to sit next to him in the front. Ever-so-obliging, I climbed over from the back seat to the passenger seat as he was driving. He started playing with my legs and I returned the favour. He stopped the taxi at a stall where a man was selling garlands of flowers. He bought one and said, 'These are for you,' before putting it around my neck. That is as far as it went, and it was very sweet. I was to find out I would have no problems getting sex in Beirut.

Beirut was beautiful and I loved the old buildings. It was unlike anything I had ever experienced before. The colours, the smells and the scenery were all so different. Yes, Hong Kong had been a new experience, but this took things to a whole new level. Beirut was then known as the Paris of the Middle East and palm tree fringed boulevards took you down to the sparkling Mediterranean and its golden beaches. Five-star hotels accommodated the rich and famous including Brigitte Bardot and Peter O'Toole. However, unlike Hong Kong, there were no British or American expats or soldiers to chat to and people spoke either French or Arabic, neither of which I understood. I was like a fish out of water, but I found it all so exciting.

Sadly, I did not get to enjoy the sights and delights of Beirut as much as I would have liked to as I was working seven evenings a week and it was far too hot to go out for long during the day. The heat was so intense that many local people retreated to the cooler mountains in the summer months. So many of those in the city were tourists from countries such as France as well as other parts of the Middle East. I spent much of my time in my room where the best air conditioning was. When I did venture out it would be to do little more than visit a local market and buy some fruit. Robert was a tall, slim fellow and so he stood out like a sore thumb in his tight pink mini-shorts and shaved legs. Yes, he did like attention! Many of the Lebanese would do a double take and Robert loved their reactions.

Our hotel was about half a kilometre from the Kit Kat Club, which was on the waterfront next to the St Georges Hotel which had been built in the late 1920s. Apparently, it had been the place to go in the 1930s and 1940s. The Kit Kat Club was, at the time I was working there, a male-only venue as I do not recall any female patrons when I worked there. When I first arrived at the club one of my glamorous pictures from Hong Kong was hanging on the wall with the word 'Travesti' underneath. I was quite confused and told the owner that my name was Stan Munro and not Travesti. He explained to me that the word travesti was the French word for a transvestite or female impersonator. Yes, I was still that boy from the Welsh valleys. Clueless! It was all such a learning experience. But it was also clear that I was going to be a very exotic asset to the Club as I was the only female impersonator working there at the time.

The Kit Kat Club was in its own building and located downstairs. The stage was a semi-circle that reached out into the middle of the auditorium surrounded by chairs and tables. The band was positioned behind the stage. A number of side rooms with booths ran off the auditorium where the patrons could enjoy rather more privacy. The Kit Kat Club was very upmarket, and the clientele tended to be wealthy businessmen and Arab sheikhs. You were unlikely to find your average local Lebanese worker there.

Alcoholic drinks and a very thick, dark, strong and bitter tasting Lebanese coffee, often referred to elsewhere as Turkish coffee, were served.

My working night began at 9pm every evening when I arrived at the club and signed in to start my shift. At midnight I performed my solo show which went for about 40 minutes as part of the program which also included dance acts with real women. On my first evening I arrived in a rather glamorous gown with lots of beads. One of the English dancers took me aside and quietly advised me I should dress down when beginning my shift and save my best showgirl costumes for the show in order to wow and dazzle the audience. She kindly lent me a more modest frock to wear.

I was the only female impersonator and solo artist at the Kit Kat Club, and I had two roles: as a performer on the stage and also as a hostess, working the audience in the hours before my midnight show. I would either go to the tables of our opulent customers or sit by the bar and work my magic in the hope that they would part with their money and buy expensive bottles of champagne. The French word for it was 'consummation'. They all knew I was a 'travesti'.

If I was offered a drink, I always accepted but I'd discreetly pour it on the carpeted floor or in a flowerpot when nobody was looking. The more champagne that customers thought was being consumed the more likely they were to buy another bottle. For each bottle sold I made a small commission. I never felt comfortable trying to wrangle money out of customers this way. I was a stage performer but felt like a high-class hooker. And indeed, it was not unusual for me to pay a visit to one of the booths in a side room where I would get on my knees under the table and perform fellatio on a wealthy Arab. This happened every few nights. I hated it as it really messed up my wig! I would crawl under the table looking beautiful and emerge resembling Lenny the Lion.

The audiences were a mix of Christian and Muslim customers. The fact I was a cock in a frock and that they were buying copious amounts of alcohol did not seem to be an issue for any of them. If anything, it seemed to be an incentive judging by the amount of champagne bought and the number of wealthy businessmen and sheikhs who I was obliged to service. Service with a smile, of course!

But naturally what I enjoyed most was actually performing on stage and entertaining the audience at the Kit Kat Club. My midnight spot lasted around 40 minutes. I told some jokes, mimed to a few songs and did a 'glamorous strip' to my panties and bra. Telling jokes was especially tough at the Kit Kat Club where much of the audience had only a limited grasp of English and did not get many of the jokes. Thankfully the customers enjoyed my mime spots. One of my favourite numbers and theirs was Marilyn Monroe's 'Diamonds Are a Girl's Best Friend'. After the show had ended for the night, I would change out of drag and head out for a drink at a small bar called the Rendez-Vous, run by a German woman and popular with gay tourists. I would usually be in bed by 3am before rising at 10 or 11am.

Robert and I had spent the past few months together since leaving Hong Kong and barely a day went by when we had not seen each other. We were very much in each other's faces though, thankfully, we had our own rooms. Robert just did not appear to be enjoying himself in Beirut and seemed bored. We started to argue increasingly over petty things, not helped by the extreme heat.

One evening he suggested I go on ahead to the Club and that he would join me later. Shortly before the show there was still no sign of Robert and so I phoned our hotel. The man on the front desk told me in broken English that Robert had packed his cases and had left for the airport. He had done a moonlight flit on me. Perhaps it was karma for my own escapes from Sydney and Hong Kong!

I was not at all happy about this as I had vouched for Robert and persuaded the management to employ him and fly him to Beirut to work as my soundman. To top it all I would have to explain his disappearance to the boss. He was not happy but agreed to keep me on but told me that I would have to repay Robert's airfare. Thankfully it was not too expensive as they had flown us out on a bloody cargo plane.

The sex really was rampant in Beirut. In the kitchen at the back of the club a very good-looking young man of about 19 years-old made Lebanese coffee. He was lean, had an olive complexion and dark hair and eyes to match. When I arrived at the club, he often followed me up to my dressing room where we would enjoy intimate relations. He was very passionate, or as passionate as he could be without smudging my make-up and he would usually fuck me. On one particular evening I arrived at work and passed the kitchen as I always would and noticed my young friend was not there. Instead, another man of a similar age was making the coffees. I thought little of it and made my way to the dressing room. However, not long after closing the door I heard a knock. I opened it and there was the young man I had seen a few moments earlier. He explained that he was the cousin of the man who usually worked in the kitchen, who, he said was having a night off. Surprise surprise, in no time the same thing happened, and we had it off with each other.

Many of the Arab men could not get enough of me, including those in uniform. Sometimes I wouldn't be let out of a cab until I'd gone down on the driver. It was quite hectic! One day while I was in my hotel room, I received a phone call from the boss. He told me he had a very important friend coming over whom I had to service. Service being the operative word. I felt I was in no position to argue, I was basically obliged to service the men in the Club as well as any others my boss instructed me to. I never spoke to any of the other girls about it, but I'm pretty sure they were in the same situation. My boss told me that I had to make myself look presentable. I took this to mean that I should wear makeup and dress in drag. Perhaps that was because of how I appeared at work.

Later that evening, he arrived at my apartment. He was an older man, in his late 40s or early 50s, wearing an army uniform and he was clearly a bigshot in the military. He was a big bloke and when he took off his coat, I gasped a little gasp when I saw that he was carrying a gun on his hip which he proceeded to lay on the table in full view for me. There was I in full drag and there was he in his military uniform. Goodness knows what anyone walking in on us would have thought. I was not attracted to him. It was a frightening experience, and I got no enjoyment from it.

On another occasion I had forgotten about the 2am curfew that had been imposed. I had been at the Rendez-Vous but when I realised I would be violating the curfew I rushed back to my hotel by the back streets. As I walked past the Swiss embassy a Lebanese soldier came out of the front gate and demanded to know what I was doing out after the curfew. I explained to him that I had honestly forgotten that it was on. He then asked for my passport and the details of where I was staying and where I worked. At the mention of the Kit Kat Club his eyes lit up and he directed me to follow him into his office. I was terrified but he had his wicked way with me and then sent me away. He must have enjoyed the experience a lot more than I did because he kept calling me at my hotel to meet again. I did not return the calls.

After about three months in Beirut the novelty of men in uniform and night curfews had worn off. I also no longer felt safe. It was still a few years before the civil war began in 1975 but I could certainly feel the tension in the air. I was fed up looking over my shoulder, let alone performing sexual acts on wealthy customers or friends of the owner or indeed amorous soldiers in order to stay out of trouble. I wanted out!

I told the owner of the Club that I wanted to leave but he told me that if I left there and then that I would have to pay back my airfare. I had already re-paid Robert's airfare, so I was not going down that road again. We agreed that I would work a few more weeks and he could take any money that he thought I owed out of my pay. The wage situation was very strange. At Les Girls and elsewhere I had worked I had been used to receiving my wages on a certain day. At the Kit Kat Club I would have to ask for my pay and then they'd ask how much you needed. I found it all very odd.

I needed to obtain a tax clearance before leaving the country by a particular date. Drama must follow me around as I could not get a flight out of Beirut on that date so I went to the airport at around midnight and slept overnight on a bench so that I could catch a flight at 7am the next day. I woke up early and watched as an ancient-looking four propeller Russian aircraft landed. We were informed that we had half an hour to board.

As I was about to board the plane an immigration officer stopped me in my tracks. He had noticed that I had overstayed my visa by a few hours. He told me that I needed to report to his colleagues in an office in a nearby building. I was frantic with worry as I had seen my luggage being loaded onto the aircraft and I was concerned that the plane would take off with all my possessions, but without me. I rushed to the office where, thankfully, I was only asked a couple of questions about why I had overstayed and then they checked my identity documents. For once there was no demand for sex. I was just so over it. I was not detained for long and I ran like lightning back to the departure gate and just made the flight by the skin of my teeth. I was just so stressed that for the first time in my life I felt a sudden need to vomit and promptly did so in a sick bag on board.

The flight took me to Frankfurt where I was to catch a connecting flight to London Heathrow. It really is a small world because on arrival in Germany I heard a voice call out, 'Stan Munro, what are you doing here?' It turned out to be a gentleman who recognised me from Australia. He used to perform at the Lido in Melbourne and had seen me perform at Les Girls in Sydney. He was on his way back to Australia after spending time in Europe.

After all my recent anxiety and uneasiness about life in Beirut it felt such a relief to be met by my mother and one of my brothers at London Heathrow. Not a soldier in sight! I hugged my mother and my brother when I saw them. When I hugged my brother, he immediately recoiled and pushed me away. He had been the brother who had abused me when I was a young boy. Perhaps I read too much into it, but his instinctive reaction struck me as peculiar and extreme.

I spent the next few weeks living with my mother in South Wales and did a few shows around the valleys. A friend told me about a club in Cardiff which was popular with the gay crowd and suggested that I contact the owner. I arranged to meet up with its owner, Lenny, and take a look at the club. He seemed to know the ins and outs of the entertainment business and said I was welcome to perform on Saturday nights. The fee was not great but at least it was a foot in the door.

On Saturday night I tarted myself up and left Mum's home in full drag as the dressing room at the club was very small. I caught the bus from Abercarn to Cardiff Central bus station where I walked to the club. Nobody had taken a blind bit of notice of me. Before going on stage Lenny suggested that if I wanted a huge laugh I should send up a man called Barry who came from a Welsh Jewish family of boxing promoters. Barry's name came out of the blue and was a bit of surprise to me because I had actually had a bit of a fling with him before I had moved to Australia. Stupidly, I took Lenny's advice and made a gag that involved Barry. The audience loved it, but it was bad move!

It turned out that Lenny and Barry were arch enemies as I found out the next week when a very handsome young man asked to speak to me after the show. He told me that word had got back to Barry that I had made a fool out of him the previous week and that I must never do it again or I would be in serious trouble. He gave me Barry's phone number and told me to ring him at the earliest opportunity.

The young man then asked me how I was getting home and I told him that I was going to catch the bus. He insisted on driving me and I accepted. I found him so good looking that I tempted fate and asked him if he would like to stay over. It turned out that, he like Barry, was a boxer. And, more pleasingly, he, like Barry, was up for some fun. We had the most fabulous sex – there wasn't a gun in sight - and in the morning I made him some tea before seeing him on his way. Before leaving he kindly reminded me that I had to call Barry.

Later that day I stopped off at a telephone box and rang Barry. He went off like there was no tomorrow, making lots of threats. He was furious and was so different to the Barry that I remembered.

I tried to remind him that I had known him several years before and he responded, 'I know who you fucking are and I know where you and your fucking mother live.' He said that if I dared mention his name again on stage, he would slice me up like pork. This particularly terrified me and sounded even more sinister as he came from a Jewish family. At that moment, I decided that maybe it was time to leave Wales again and go crawling back to Hong Kong with my tail between my legs, while I still could. I didn't want Barry the Boxer converting me to luncheon meat.

I decided to bite the bullet and ring Mike Friedman in Hong Kong and ask him if I could get back in the show. Understandably he was furious with me for walking out on Playgirls but as luck would have it, I phoned at the right time because they were looking for a new compere. The kids in the show later told me that things had not worked out with Eddie and that Josie Jay was filling in until they found a permanent replacement.

He offered me my old job back but told me that I would have to surrender my passport to him to prevent a repeat of my previous escape. I thought that was a fair enough compromise and was just happy to be returning to Hong Kong and getting out of Wales. I had only been back in the valleys for about six weeks but was relieved to be leaving.

I flew out of Gatwick Airport on a really cheap flight and as I boarded the plane, I could see that the only passenger seats were in the centre of the plane in four rows: the rest of the plane was carrying cargo. It was the most cramped and uncomfortable flight on which I have ever travelled. It was frightful and I wondered if Mike had booked me on that flight as a form of revenge.

When I got to the club that night, I was delighted to find out that Josie Jay, Debra Le Gae and Julie London had joined the cast. Monique St John and my old foe, Gigi, had left to go on a tour of the

Far East together. Lilac Haze had also left. This time I had to share a bedroom with Josie. We manoeuvred a wardrobe down the middle of the room so we could each have a little privacy.

Within a week of returning to Hong Kong, Mike Friedman came backstage to tell me that the American actor and director Burgess Meredith (remember he played The Penguin in the ridiculously camp *Batman* series in the 1970s) and his wife (the fourth, Kaja Sundsten) were in the audience and they wanted to meet me. Apparently, Burgess was directing a movie in Hong Kong and he had a role that he thought would be perfect for me. I was beside myself with excitement, as you could imagine, and so it was with a mixture of anticipation and mild terror that I somewhat anxiously joined Burgess and his wife at their table after the show to find out what he was planning for me.

Burgess told me how much he enjoyed my performance and asked me if I would be interested in playing the role of a madam in a seedy nightclub. He explained that the character had originally been written as a lesbian but having seen me that night he thought that I would be ideal. He told me it was only a small part, but it did involve some dialogue. Called *The Yin and the Yang of Mr Go* the film starred James Mason, a young Jeff Bridges, Jack MacGowran and Peter Lind Hayes. Burgess Meredith himself played a Chinese acupuncturist – hardly politically correct by today's standards.

In a nutshell, the movie's plot involves Jeff Bridges's character, a draft dodger and aspiring writer, who becomes entangled with a notorious criminal mastermind portrayed by James Mason. They then conspire to blackmail a closeted gay American weapons scientist (Peter Lind Hayes) into providing secrets for sale to the highest bidder.

Burgess explained to me that they would be shooting my scene the very next day, so presumably the actor playing my role must have suddenly become unavailable, and that the whole movie was being made on a tight budget. He told me that I would be paid US$150. It was not a lot of money, but it sounded like an exciting opportunity and a chance to work on a film with some big names. So of course, I said yes. We sat for a little while longer talking about the film. I was beside myself with joy!

I woke up at 5.30am the next morning to catch an early ferry from Kowloon to Hong Kong Island. The location for the filming was a Chinese nightclub which was given the name the Neptune Bar in the film. I was handed the script and I could see that my character only had a couple of lines and a few stage directions. I rehearsed these in the dressing room. I had borrowed a rather stunning purple see-through dress off Ayesha and tied a pair of plastic tits around my chest, using a length of string. The makeup artist on the set offered to do mine but I insisted on doing my own. After all I had been wearing it for years! He was happy with the end result and didn't need to touch it up.

My character ran the nightclub and she also played the piano, which I had to fake as I cannot play a note. I had two scenes. The first was me putting on my blonde wig and making my way downstairs to the club. This was to leave viewers in no doubt that my character was a man in a frock, albeit a rather glamorous one. It also set the scene for Peter Lind Hayes's character taking that of Jess Bridges to a rather quieter nightspot, suggesting that it may be a bar popular with gay men.

In my second scene I walk over to Jeff and Peter's characters who are sitting at their table and tell them, 'Upstairs is vacant when you're bored, sweetie.' My 'breasts' are very visible through my purple dress. Jeff's character asks if I use any special kind of glue to keep my boobs on. 'No! Just some special kind of will power,' I reply, cheekily. I then ask Jeff's character if he has a special song he would like to request and he asks me to play 'I Like What You Like' which I then start playing.

It was a very simple role, and it was fun to film. I was basically playing myself with a piano and I got to chat up the very sexy 21-year-old Jeff Bridges in his debut role in a feature film. I think you'd agree it wasn't a bad gig. And I got paid for it! I did not have a lot to do with Peter and Jeff apart from filming my scenes, but they were friendly towards me in between takes. Peter actually asked me for reassurance that the way he was playing his character's sexuality – a gay scientist who has his eyes on Jeff's character – came off as authentic. I reassured him that his portrayal came across as convincing as it was subtle without camping it up.

After filming my scenes, I hung around the set waiting to be paid. I then spent the $150 on a pair of long pants and a beaded coat that I had seen in a shop window in Kowloon before boarding the ferry earlier that morning. The money did not last long but as far as I am concerned it was money well spent.

Unfortunately, the film was later panned by the critics. I watched it for the first time several years ago and it was every bit as bad as the critics described. I actually saw it for sale at my local two-dollar shop here in Kyogle, northern NSW where it was sitting on a 'sales table' on the footpath. I took it home and watched it. It was truly dreadful. The script was all over the place and the acting terrible despite the fact it had a cast of well-known actors. I thought I did OK, though.

During this second stint in Hong Kong, I went out much more as the bars were really jumping with good looking young American soldiers enjoying some R&R during the Vietnam War. I had been back in Hong Kong several weeks and was loving it, but I was also really keen to get back to Sydney eventually. Sydney had been where I had been happiest, and I had now been away for more than a year. One day I was in a shopping arcade in Kowloon and who should I see walking towards me but Sammy Lee. I came out in a cold sweat and made a quick exit so that he would not see me as I was unsure how he would react. Apparently, he was in the audience at Playgirls that very night, but I had no idea. At least he did not set his henchmen on to me. However, I was even more nostalgic to return Down Under.

One night after the show I was in our shared apartment and down the long corridor I heard Josie Jay on the phone saying, 'Hi Johnny McLean, how are you?' My ears pricked up immediately and I went up to Josie and whispered that I wanted to talk with Johnny. I spoke with him, and he told me that Sammy was putting a show together to take to Melbourne and that rehearsals would soon be starting in Sydney. I decided to once again take the plunge and suggested that I could be the new compere. Luckily, he thought that this might be a good idea and would be an opportunity to bury the hatchet with Sammy.

I asked him what Sammy would be like if I rang him but he said I would have to find out for myself. With some trepidation I went to an international phone booth at the Kowloon ferry terminal and rang Sammy at his home in Elizabeth Bay. I expected him to be angry, but he was not. I tried my best to impress him with my recent role in the film directed by Burgess Meredith, but he was utterly unimpressed and abruptly told me that it had no relevance to Les Girls or Sydney.

With a deep breath I plucked up the courage to ask if he would take me back at Les Girls and whether he would consider me as the compere for the Melbourne cast. To my utter surprise and relief, he said he would but that I would have to apologise to the choreographer Sheila Cruze for leaving her in the lurch – she was fine with me when I got back. He made it clear that I would have to pay my own fare back to Sydney, which I thought was fair enough.

I was relieved that Sammy had guaranteed me the role of compere, but I was now faced with the dilemma of how I would plan my escape from Hong Kong. I was up front with Mike and told him that I wanted to return to Sydney but of course he was having none of it. He angrily reminded me that he had my passport, which he would give back to me in another year once my contract was up. 'You're not doing any tricks like that ever again. We've got you now. We've got you,' he scolded me.

I tried to argue with him and explained that I felt exhausted and needed a break. All he said was that he would allow me a bit of time off to go to hospital for a few days to rest. None of this was going to help me get back to Australia so I needed to hatch one of my now notorious escape plans. A couple of nights later I got chatting to this friendly tall, blond, Australian chap in his mid-thirties who was sitting with a woman in the audience at Playgirls and who was working for the American government in Hong Kong. I sensed an opportunity and explained my sorry situation to him: 'No worries. I will get you out!'

I rang him the next morning as he instructed me to do. I was curious as to what his intentions were and if his remarks about helping me escape were simply the words of someone who was a bit tipsy after a few late-night drinks. Thankfully, he was true to his word and had not forgotten our conversation. He invited me to meet him in his hotel foyer about an hour later after breakfast.

He took me to a passport office in Hong Kong run by the British and explained that I was his younger brother and that I had lost my passport and I was desperate to return to Australia because of family problems. He laid it on really thick, but it did the trick as I was issued with a travel document which was simply a sheet of paper with my photograph attached that was stamped. I could not believe that I now had my 'passport' out of there. It's incredible what we could get away with in those days.

I wasted no time in booking a one-way flight to Sydney with Qantas that same afternoon. I also phoned my friend Bobbie Kent in the UK, who I had become friends with during my time with the Francis Langford Singing Scholars, asking if he would like a job in Hong Kong. After I had convinced him that I was not kidding, he jumped at the chance. I suggested he phone Mike Friedman the next day, once I was safely on the plane to Australia, to ask about a job. He actually got the job and a couple of days later he was living and working in Honkers.

I told my Australian saviour that I still needed a bit more help from him. I needed to get all my stuff from my room as well as from the club without anyone noticing. We agreed that he would get a taxi to my place the next morning and I would race down with my luggage before heading to the club and then to the airport.

Thankfully, the next morning he was waiting outside my apartment building in a taxi, and I came down as fast as I could from my third floor flat with my heavy case. I was terrified that one of the queens would notice and would be on the phone straight away to Mike Friedman. As I was leaving the head maid saw me and I panicked. In a split-second I decided to pull the loose-fitting cord of our telephone out of the socket. It was all very theatrical! Luckily, she hardly reacted and simply walked away before I rushed out as fast as my legs could carry me. The metal trunk carrying all my belongings must have made such a noise as I dragged it behind me down the stairs but none of the queens stirred. They rarely did before midday anyway!

We drove the short distance to Playgirls to pick up some of my dresses, which had I taken the previous evening would have aroused suspicion. I was pretty confident that Mike Friedman would not be there as it was still mid-morning, and he only ever came in during the evening. When I arrived, it was dimly lit inside and some of the staff were cleaning up from the night before. They all recognised me and called out, 'Hi Mr Stan.' I have no idea if they found it odd to see me there at that time of day or suspected that I was up to something. They did not let on if they did.

I then went backstage to the dressing room. Unfortunately, I had forgotten something rather important. Each night after the show a huge steel gate was pulled across at the side of the entrance to the dressing room so that nobody could get in and pilfer anything when the shows were not on. It must have been around nine feet high and had bars with a gap at the top. Thankfully, I was very nimble and agile in those days, so I climbed up the bars and scrambled over the gap. I then had to throw all my costumes over the steel gate before walking casually, so as not to arouse too much suspicion, through the club and to our waiting taxi.

After we had driven a couple of blocks my Australian friend asked the driver to stop. He said to me, 'Stan, I'm going to leave you now. I've helped you as much as I can. You're on your own now.' I thanked him profusely before I was driven the rest of the way by the taxi driver to the airport to catch my flight.

My Australian friend really had been my saviour in my time of need. A couple of years later in 1972 I was compering at Les Girls in

Melbourne when someone brought me a note that said, 'You probably won't remember me, but I helped you escape from Hong Kong.' I could not believe it. As I went on stage to perform, I looked into the audience and there he was. I couldn't believe it. I told the crowd that there was someone in the audience who had once helped me out of a very difficult situation. He stood up and everyone gave him a round of applause.

CHAPTER 13
Melbourne Calling

It was early 1970. Once back in Sydney I moved in with my long-standing friend and former dance partner Neville who was now living in a large, converted garage near where Susan Le Gaye and her family were living.

I started rehearsals for the Melbourne show about a week later at Sammy Lee's Latin Quarter. There were about eight of us in the cast and we rehearsed hard five days a week for six weeks. I had never worked with any of the other girls except Josie Jay, who I had worked with in Hong Kong. Other members of the cast included Angelique, Debra Le Gae and Ruby.

At one stage during rehearsals, Sheila Cruze and some of the girls and I went out for a break to get some coffee. As we were sitting in the coffee shop who should walk in but Eddie, you know, Eddie, who I had returned to the UK for. He was one of the last people I expected to see, and I could not believe it. 'What on Earth are you doing here?' He told me he had come over while working on a ship as an entertainer and had applied to stay. He still lives in Australia, and we remain in touch. It was such a surreal moment.

The show's format was very similar to that of Sydney Les Girls. I would continue to do my comedy patter, solo and chorus numbers and of course my tin can strip sketch. During the time I was rehearsing for the Melbourne show I had a brief affair with a wonderful dancer called Vivian Walker who was appearing in the Sydney cast of Les Girls. His mother was the celebrated indigenous poet and activist Kath Walker/Oodgeroo Noonuccal. I fell in love with Vivian immediately. He had beautiful smooth skin and a smile to die for. He must have been about 17 or 18 and I was in my late 20s.

I have very fond memories of our time together but we had to end things when it was time for me to move with the other girls to Melbourne. I was so sad to leave him as I really loved him. Years later I was touring Queensland in 1982 with the male stripper group, the Cheeky Chaps, when we were unexpectedly reunited. While in Brisbane I saw in the local newspaper that the film *A Star Is Born* starring Judy Garland was being shown. Thankfully, I had the Sunday afternoon off as it seemed did every other queen in Brisbane who flocked to the matinee.

As I entered the cinema a man walked towards me and exclaimed, 'Stan Munro!' It was awkward as I did not recognise him. He then introduced himself as Vivian. I could not believe it as he had changed beyond recognition. We hugged and then talked for a while, and he told me that he had had a difficult life in the intervening years. It showed. He had gone from this beautiful fresh-faced young dancer to someone who looked so down and out and ravaged by the years. He died, so sadly, just nine years later, at the age of only 38.

After our rehearsal period, we all drove down to Melbourne in a flotilla of cars, arriving at the Ritz Hotel in Fitzroy Street in St Kilda which was to be the home of Melbourne's Les Girls. Rehearsals continued for a few weeks until our grand opening in April 1970. The hotel had been built in 1922 and was quite the elegant venue for the first few decades of its life. It was now run by the Walker family whose fierce matriarch we nicknamed Johnny Walker. She was someone not to be crossed.

Johnny had a daughter called Lyn who would have been in her early twenties. Lyn liked to tell me that Helen Reddy had performed at the Ritz Hotel earlier in her career. She adored us but was ruled with an iron rod by her mother. Johnny did not like us queens mixing with her daughter because she and the family lived at the Ritz and, unsurprisingly, we would see quite a bit of her. However, I became very friendly with Lyn much to her mother's chagrin. She was lovely but her mother really was the bitch from hell. She reminded me of one of the ugly sisters from the story and pantomime Cinderella. At one point Sammy Lee, who was visiting the show in Melbourne, took me aside to advise me to stop being so friendly with Lyn as he did not want any aggravation from the Walker family.

For the first couple of weeks, we were put up in the various boarding houses that were located near the Ritz before being ensconced in a newly built block of flats in Wellington Street. Walking to work, I passed a company called Cocks International, which always put a smile on my face. I was lucky in that I had my own flat but some of the other queens shared with each other. Ruby had been a carpenter and she kindly drilled peep holes in everybody's door so we could see who our visitors were before we let them in. The measly wages that Sammy paid us didn't stretch much beyond the rent and basic necessities. I was earning a little bit more than the rest of the girls as the compere but not all that much more.

Sammy had us doing quite a lot of publicity for Les Girls in the press and we also appeared in drag at various events in order to promote the new show. Les Girls was the first drag show of its scale and kind to be publicly performed in Melbourne and we were quite the novelty. Of course, the headlines over the articles would often tout us as an 'all male review', even though, as I've mentioned previously, most of the girls performing in the show were at various stages of transitioning. The opening night was a huge extravaganza with many of Melbourne's best-known personalities attending including Jimmy Hannan, Stuart Wagstaff, Tommy Hanlon Jr and Vi Greenhalf. The night was a great success and we got lots of great publicity from it.

At the end of opening night, I walked into the busy foyer out of drag and there was Tikki Taylor and John Newman, who owned the very popular Melbourne institution and pioneering theatre restaurant called Tikki and John's. As I walked past them, I heard Tikki comment, 'Darling, they can't even sing!' She was telling the truth as we all mimed but I was slightly bemused as they had been given a free invite.

That same evening after the show I caught up with Stuart Wagstaff who I had got to know as we were both regulars at Caulfield Sauna and had met a couple of weeks before the opening night of Les Girls. I often went on a Sunday evening, which was my night off.

Stuart and I introduced ourselves one night as we were sitting wrapped in our towels and he asked me what I was doing in Melbourne. I explained that I was about to start working on the Les Girls show. I think he rather liked me, but he was not my type as I found him a bit too posh, and he spoke with a plum in his mouth.

However, Stuart was a thorough gentleman and told me how lovely it was to meet me. At the end of the opening night, he came up to me and said, 'I must apologise. You should have told me that you were the star of the show!'

Sammy used to come down to Melbourne occasionally, but he was pretty hands off, leaving the running of the place to Don Williams and Albie Franks. I was never keen on either as I found both a bit two faced. Don was a former touring manager on the Tivoli circuit and Alby was a real estate agent cum singer. They could be very friendly to you one moment, particularly if they wanted something, but could turn on you the next.

Don was a short, fat man in his fifties who was full of shit and would tell me what he thought I wanted to hear just to keep the peace. Alby was a tall, strong man in his sixties who could be quite intimidating. He had a terrible temper and was even known to threaten people with his gun if they dared to cross his path. One incident even resulted in us having to leave the Ritz Hotel a few years later but more on that in the next chapter.

Our choreographer, Sheila Cruze, would come down for a month at a time to rehearse the new shows before returning to Sydney after opening night. Kenny Williams also travelled to Melbourne from time to time to measure the girls for their costumes. These he would make in Sydney, in a huge room above the back of the stage. The costumes would then be sent down to Melbourne.

Before the show opened one of the guys who pulled the curtains and did comedy drag was caught by the police at a public toilet. The cops contacted Sammy and told him that if he put the man on the next plane back to Sydney no charges would be laid. And indeed, he was on the next flight out and a scandal was avoided which could have really messed up our opening night. Funnily enough, the performer re-joined Les Girls many years later in Melbourne, hopefully with his reputation intact.

I was very much the spokesperson for Les Girls in Melbourne and so I had to be very careful what I said and how I behaved. I was under strict instructions from Sammy not to reveal my sexuality and come out publicly as gay. Homosexual law reform in Victoria was still a good ten years away and I can understand why Sammy did not want to court controversy. Any wrong move or wrong word on my part could affect the show and lose Sammy money.

Newspaper stories that were written about the show often referred to me as having had many girlfriends and even having been engaged to a woman. Sammy was concerned about how it might affect the show if I came out as gay publicly though it could hardly be said that I was ever really in the closet. I spent my time in a frock camping it up, for goodness' sake! This is one reason why in interviews I would send myself up by talking about my string of female lovers and fiancées. I wonder if many readers cottoned on to how ridiculous it all sounded.

Soon after I moved to Melbourne and had started with Les Girls I wrote to my lovely friend, Bert, who I had met on the ship taking me back to the UK in 1965. Within a few months he started coming down from Ararat to see the shows and stay over at my home in St

Kilda, near the Ritz, for the night. Bert worked as the head tailor at J Ward Asylum for the Criminally Insane in Ararat, making uniforms for the inmates and guards. Bert once gave me a tour of J Ward. It was very frightening as the prisoners were housed basically in cells resembling cages. Bert told me not to look any of them in the eye in case it upset them and made them angry. I can assure you I was not even tempted. However, I did notice a couple of prisoners who had their trousers in between their legs sewn up and their sleeves sewn to their sides. It was akin to wearing some sort of straitjacket. As they walked around, they moved like penguins. It seemed very strange.

Bert was a regular visitor to my flat during most of the 70s, but he stopped visiting and I received a letter in which he told me had been diagnosed with cancer, which had now spread throughout much of his body. My then partner Phillip and I drove immediately up to see Bert. I wanted to help cheer him up and told him that I would love to do a show for him and help raise money for a charity or cause of his choice. He told me he would love to donate the money to the cancer ward at the local hospital.

The show sold out and I had to put another one on a couple of weeks later for people who had missed out on tickets. They were such great nights filled with love for Bert, who actually performed as part of the local theatrical group as the fairy queen, of course. Bert had been an active fund raiser for many years for various causes in Ararat and so I decided after the first show to write to the Melbourne Lord Mayor, Ralph Bernardi, and asked him if he would write a message of thanks for all the work that Bert had done for the community, which could be presented to him.

I was moved emotionally when I received a large scroll in the mail from Melbourne's Lord Mayor. This is what he wrote: *'Dear Mr Bates, I've heard through your good friend Stan Munro, of the excellent work and dedication you have shown for many years in your support of local charities and in particular the Ararat Hospital, in organising a drama group and theatrical productions. May I say how indebted the community is to people like yourself who so unselfishly devote their time and energies and talent in helping those in need.'*

At the end of the second show, I asked Bert to come back up on stage and I presented him with the scroll from the Lord Mayor. He and his family were delighted and had it framed. The shows were not only a success as events, but we raised $4000 for the local cancer ward.

My final memory was of Bert and his mother waving me and Phillip goodbye. I remember leaning over to Phillip and saying I felt it would be the last time that we would see him. He had lost so much weight and was getting weaker. He died a few weeks later. Everybody in Ararat seemed to love Bert, as did all my friends to whom I introduced him. He was just such fun and so easy to get on with but above all kind and generous.

There was a certain mystique and magic to Les Girls, particularly during the 1960s and 70s which endeared us to our audiences. 'Men' creating the illusion of being women was very much an enigma with straight audiences back then and Sammy was of course keen to preserve that illusion. It was one thing for people to wonder about our private lives, but it would have been quite another for me to have told the world I was gay. I was a man who dons a frock on the stage. In fact, part of my act for the final show of the night would see me come back on stage in a suit, without any hint of makeup, The crowds loved this. In our own way we were all pioneers at Les Girls, and I suppose that being on stage, either as men in drag or living as transgender women, we were making our own statement and testing and pushing boundaries.

Sammy had taken a gamble opening Les Girls in Melbourne as there was nothing like it at the time, at least not outside Sydney. The impression that Sammy and we all had, rightly or wrongly, was that Melbourne was rather more conservative and traditional than Sydney. We saw it as Victorian by name and Victorian by nature. Sammy knew that the newspapers, particularly the popular tabloid *Truth*, were watching us closely and probably following our every move. Therefore, Sammy was very keen to avoid any whiff of a scandal.

He need not have worried about people coming to Les Girls, however, as patrons frequently had to join a queue that snaked right around the block. The district was hardly the entertainment quarter that Kings Cross was, but this did not stop people flocking to St Kilda for our show. I heard that at one time the Melbourne show was making more money than the Sydney one and by the late 1970s was even helping to keep it afloat financially.

It was not only Melbourne's tabloid press that was watching our every move. Our security men at the Ritz Hotel were often off-duty police officers moonlighting for a bit of extra cash. They seemed friendly enough though I never had much to do with them; at least they kept us safe and out of trouble. I cannot remember any particular difficulties with customers or the police during my years at Les Girls in Melbourne. If it happened, I was never made aware of it but the approach that I tended to have towards work was that I was there to do a job; I avoided gossip and kept out of 'office politics'.

Although I did not have any problems with the Boys in Blue in Melbourne, on one occasion I certainly let one of them take down my particulars and helped him with his enquiries, so to speak. One year, my fellow queens and I were invited to a fancy-dress ball at St Kilda Town Hall. The party had been going for a few hours when we arrived around 10.30, in our glamorous costumes, after having performed our show at the Ritz. It was a fabulous party even though we did arrive very late. A uniformed police officer at the event recognised me as I was leaving and said, 'Hello Stan! Would you like a lift home?' I eagerly obliged as I really did not want to stand outside in drag waiting to hail a taxi. It was only about a three-minute drive away to my unit in Wellington Street, but the rest is history. I invited him in, no warrant required, and we had some of the best sex that I have ever had. In later years he became an actor playing detectives on television shows. He never became famous, but he was certainly recognisable in support roles.

While at Les Girls in Melbourne I must admit I was not always liked by a lot of the cast members. I needed to be strict with them. If they ever played up on stage the management would come down on me like a ton of bricks for letting them get away with it. I always approached my job in a professional manner, and I expected my girls to do the same. I had quite a burden of responsibility. Thankfully, the queens tended to be professional as they also wanted a successful career, but if they messed around or rubbed me up the wrong way I would scream at them – and I certainly know how to scream when required. I wanted the show to be a success and I also wanted to keep what was a steady job for me.

Years after I left Les Girls in Melbourne, I was doing a one-man show at a gay bar in St Kilda when a voice called out from the audience, 'You're a cunt, Munro!' It was Renee Scott who had joined Les Girls at the Ritz Hotel in Melbourne in its second year. By this time, we were very good friends, and I took her comment in good humour, but she did have a point.

From my experience working in Hong Kong onwards I had really come into my own, particular in terms of my confidence and humour which was becoming bawdier and more risqué with a fair amount of innuendo. I was at my best in Melbourne and in my mind's eye I can see Sammy looking up at me from the audience laughing at my jokes and looking so proud.

The Ritz Hotel was on a street corner facing about four lanes of traffic and there was a billboard on the façade of the building saying in huge letters, 'Les Girls starring Stan Munro.' Thousands of drivers would see that sign every day and night. It really was the perfect spot. I had made it and I was at the top of my game. I hope this doesn't come across as conceited, but I do not think that that it would be an exaggeration to say that I was Sammy's star performer in the 1970s. I really felt that I had made it.

We were working six nights a week and I did not get a lot of time to go out and socialise with the other queens from the show. Some of the girls would go a nightclub in South Yarra called Winston Charles but it was not really my scene. After a show I often just wanted to go home to put my feet up and unwind.

However, on Sundays, our only day off, we often went to an after-hours café called Mae West's in South Yarra which was run by a very camp queen whose drag name was Giselle. It looked like a shop front with the curtains drawn. Inside was quite narrow and filled with tables and chairs. Down one end was a little stage where queens would perform. It was a fun place to hang out. Before long, Giselle was taking hormones and living as a woman. She actually ended up working at the Ritz as part of Les Girls. She was always fighting with the manager Don Williams and on one occasion I remember him throwing a chair at her. Office politics!

From time to time, we performed lunchtime shows at shopping centres to promote Les Girls which would attract a good crowd of very curious onlookers. We even appeared in the audience of *The Mike Walsh Show* and Mike came over to the audience and did a quick interview with me about Les Girls. As part of our public relations, we also got involved with community groups. There was a Jewish organisation called WIZO, the Women's International Zionist Organisation, and two or three of us would go to a home of one of the members every few Sundays where the owners of the house would prepare a huge buffet. I often found it intimidating as we would sit in the centre of the room answering questions such as when did we realise we were homosexual, when did we start to wear women's clothes, that kind of thing. I know, it sounds bizarre. Sometimes there were as many as 100 people attending these Q&A sessions. This went on for about a year and we never got paid for it. After all, it was largely for public relations. But why the members of this organisation wanted drag queens to come to lunch every few weeks is beyond me.

One time I was unable to attend one of the lunches and someone went in my place. One of the women grilled the girls about what they did not like about dressing up. One of the queens responded quite boldly that she did not like having to tuck her cock between her legs. Apparently, there was a room full of shocked people and that was the end of our Sunday appearances in Jewish homes, much to my relief.

My contract with Les Girls in Melbourne was only for 12 months as I always intended to go back to Sydney. And so, after my 12 months was up, I returned and moved in with Neville who was now married to Dawn and living in a four bedroomed house in Lidcombe. Shortly after my return I slipped comfortably back into the role of compere of Les Girls in Kings Cross.

One night I saw a most beautiful man of about 20 in the audience, with blond hair and when he stood up, he was about six foot three. We spoke after the show and I found out that his name was John, he was Dutch, and he was working in a strip show run by a man called Bill Munro…no relation!

As old habits die hard, it was love at first sight for me, and I took him home that evening. He explained that he did not have a permanent address so I spoke with Neville who kindly said he could come and live with me. He moved in right away into our place in Lidcombe. Talk about moving fast!

At first things were great between us but soon it became clear that he was struggling with his sexuality. He just never seemed to feel comfortable with being gay. I still loved him, but he was becoming more distanced from me. Then, one morning he took his stuff and left, which devastated me. I really had fallen for him, big time.

I had been with John for about four months before we split up. I was reeling from the end of our relationship, and I was a not in a good place mentally. I wanted to be anywhere but Sydney. Fate intervened and Sandy Taylor who did the sound and lighting back in my early days at Sydney Les Girls as well as in Hong Kong and Les Girls in Melbourne appeared in Sydney out of the blue. He told me that he had been sent to Sydney to persuade me to go back to the Ritz in Melbourne. Apparently, the compere who had replaced me in the Melbourne shows had not been working out and the regulars had been asking after me.

The person in question was a fabulous performer and talented dancer but just not a great host. Essentially, the management wanted me to come back and save the show. The timing was perfect, and I was totally chuffed that the punters wanted me back in

Melbourne. It felt amazing to be wanted and to be regarded so highly. I said yes immediately and negotiated to work one more week in Sydney. After that I went back to Melbourne with my dear friend Glyn in a converted ambulance driven by his sister Jean as neither Glyn nor I could drive. I think Sammy was happy for me to be growing the big audiences in Melbourne because at that stage, Melbourne was pulling in bigger crowds than Sydney.

I slipped back into my accustomed role as compere immediately and spent about a week staying with Sandy before I moved into my own second floor one bedroom apartment in Inkerman Street, quite close to the Ritz Hotel. It really did feel wonderful to be back and to be truly appreciated.

CHAPTER 14
The Love of My Life and Alvin Purple

I have had many lovers over the years and, as you have read, I often 'fell in love' very quickly. But I have had only one true love. He came into my life a few weeks before Easter 1972. I was compering a show when I looked out from the stage and saw a table full of younger men. One in particular caught my eye. He had dark hair and was slim and beautiful. He also had a twinset of eye lashes like Elizabeth Taylor which I found mesmerising. I found him incredibly attractive.

During the interval I decided to approach his table. It turned out he was called Phillip and he and his mates were all gay. He said that he was visiting from Tasmania for the weekend. There was a shyness about him that I found very endearing which added to the initial attraction.

I asked him he if would like to go for coffee after the show and he seemed keen. Sadly, when I went out into the audience at the end of the evening he and his friends were nowhere to be seen. I was really disappointed but thought little more of it. 'Oh well, you win some and you lose some,' was the phrase that sprang to mind.

However, a week after the show a call came through for me at Les Girls just before the show started. 'I don't know if you remember me, but I was there last week. I'm so sorry I didn't wait until after the show, but my friends wanted to go straight away.' It was Phillip and I told him, 'That's ok. Drop me a line.'

After writing to each other for a few weeks I suggested he come to Melbourne at Easter, which he did, staying with me at my Inkerman Street flat for a couple of nights. On the Saturday evening he came to see the show, and as we were walking back to my place, he told me that he was going back to Tasmania to hand in his notice so he could live with me in Melbourne. And about a week later that is exactly what happened, and it made me very happy.

We were in love from the get-go. We kept growing closer and our love kept getting stronger. We seemed a natural match. Phillip and I loved spending time together. We never really did the gay scene as Phillip found it superficial and still does to this day. I have to agree and as we have both got older, we have found it rather ageist too. For most of those early years in our relationship I was working most evenings at Les Girls and only had Sundays off. On those evenings we would often cook for each other. Our favourite dishes were those containing prawns. I had never had them in the UK, and they seemed more readily available in Australia. Phillip and I adored them. We also loved making curries. The hotter the better! In later years we would invite friends around for our curry evenings. Phillip is a particularly amazing chef, and our guests would always praise his cooking highly. They still do.

It may sound unusual for a young couple, but we enjoyed going to op shops and auctions. Phillip loved anything made from sterling silver. I found it a joy to buy gifts for him and on one occasion I purchased some George Jensen silver rings from Georges department store in Melbourne which he still wears today. He always did have great taste!

After a year together, we put down a deposit and got a mortgage on a terrace house in St Kilda. Then, two years later we bought a three bedroomed house in the Melbourne suburb of Springvale where we lived for about eight years. I really enjoyed living there because it did not feel like living in or too near the big city while at the same time being a reasonable distance from the city and work.

Towards the end of 1974 I took a month off from Les Girls to take Phillip on his first trip over to the United Kingdom. We spent part of the time staying with my mother in Wales. She and Phillip got on well, though I do suspect that my mother was a bit envious that I had found someone while she was alone. She was always very sensitive, so I felt that I had to tread carefully and not rub my relationship in her face.

I spent the next 14 years in a relationship with Phillip. It is difficult to put into words why our relationship lasted so many years and why he is my closest friend today. I just find him so beautiful and his kindness to me and my friends is what stands out. He always makes an effort with them and, being a splendid chef, will often cook them the most delicious meals. I have always felt safe if I knew he was around even when we split up romantically. I have kept in contact with him every day wherever he has been as I have always needed to know that he is with me, even if not physically. He really is my life to this day, and I have never loved anyone else since we met. We are a team, and all our friends know us as 'Stan and Phil'. He has seen me through ups and downs of which there have been many.

His mother gave birth to 22 children, and I have not even met all his siblings. The ones that I have met have always been lovely to me and have treated me better than most of my own family. They really have become a surrogate family.

Phillip was never easily impressed by showbiz and never fawned over the fact that I was the host of Les Girls. He never gushes and will speak his mind to me. He will tell me if I do a show where he thinks I did not perform at my best. However, he will also tell people that 'Stan was the best'. Phillip can be my fiercest critic but greatest friend. I love his honesty. He does not suffer fools gladly either and has warned me many times to be careful of some of the people I have met. He is an astute judge of character and has never yet been wrong about someone. He has kept me grounded and I am very grateful to have Phillip in my life. My guardian angel!

One of the characters who has very much become associated with the Melbourne gay scene was the entrepreneur Jan Hillier. We first encountered each other soon after I became the compere at Les Girls. She was delivering bread by day, but she hosted popular gay dances at the Prince of Wales Hotel very late on a Saturday night. She asked me to do a couple of shows which I did after I had finished for the night at Les Girls, although I'm still waiting for payment!

Sometime in 1977 Jan rang me and asked me to meet her upstairs at the Prince of Wales Hotel in St Kilda. Phillip came along with me. We were enjoying a few scotches together when she told us that she was planning to launch a new night on Sundays at the Prince and asked me if I would be interested in compering.

Phillip immediately put his foot down and said he knew what I would be like if I was let loose. By that he meant he was concerned that I would have too much temptation to mess around behind his back with customers. To be honest, he did have a point. I loved Phillip very much and have always thought the world of him but throughout my life I have struggled to be faithful in relationships.

I also thought that working seven nights a week would have been a bit too much for me and it would have also meant that I would have seen less of Phillip. Jan suggested I sleep on it, but I still turned it down.

Jan's Sunday nights at the Prince of Wales Hotel, which became known as Pokeys Nightclub, were a huge success. Phillip and I started going there soon after it opened, and it was always packed. We had many wonderful evenings there. Although the food was at best bland and at worst pretty dreadful, the amazing shows more than made up for it. The compere, Doug Lucas, whose drag name was Ellie, was brilliant - he was so outrageous and flamboyant. He had a huge following among gay men. Performers in the shows at Pokeys included Renee Scott, Debra La Gae, Michelle Tozer, Terri Tinsel and Wanda Jackson, some of whom had strutted the boards at Les Girls.

In March 1973, one of the managers of Les Girls, Don Williams, came backstage to tell me there was man at the club who was keen to talk to me. Intrigued, I went into the main bar area and met the gentleman who turned out to be film director Tim Burstall who had recently directed an Australian comedy called *Stork*, based on a David Williamson play. He told me that he was looking for someone to play the role of a 'transvestite' in a movie that he was making called Alvin Purple. My immediate response was that I thought that it was an odd name for a film. Anyway, he told me he was looking for a blonde person to play the role with lots of personality. The queens at Les Girls tended to wear dark wigs whereas I wore a blonde one. Tim said that I fitted the bill perfectly.

He warned me that there would not be a lot of money in it for me. I think I was offered about $150 for the role. With hindsight I wish I had taken a percentage of the royalties instead as the film proved a huge hit in Australia even though many critics were not so keen. However, *Alvin Purple* became the most commercially successful Australian film released to that time, even breaking the box office record set by Michael Powell's comedy film *They're a Weird Mob*.

Tim asked me to meet him at his office the next morning for an audition to read through my lines with him. He gave me the script that night, so I was able to familiarise myself with my part. We did a read-through the next day and I must have impressed him - or he was desperate to find someone to play a blonde 'transvestite' - because he gave me the part. He told me we would film my scenes a week later.

Alvin Purple, played by Graeme Blundell, was a door-to-door waterbed salesman who proved irresistible to women who all lusted after him. Alvin tried his best to resist their charms but, happily, he rarely succeeded. The film is essentially a Benny-Hill style sex romp. It has even been credited as introducing full-frontal nudity to mainstream Australian audiences. Other cast members included Abigail, Jacki Weaver, Noel Ferrier and Penne Hackforth-Jones. I was in very good company.

A pre-shooting party was held at a fabulous house in Toorak where I met many of the cast and crew who I thought were all lovely. Many of the guests asked me about my role as Mrs Warren. One man that I got along with particularly well was Jon Finlayson who played a lawyer. He was very friendly and easy to get along with. The party was a great way to break the ice.

About a week after my audition, I arrived at a swanky two-storey house in South Melbourne where my scenes were to be filmed. This was when I first met the star of the film Graeme Blundell, who was fabulous right from the start. He was very easy to get on with. After all, we had to be at ease with each other as I would be seeing him naked. A sight for sore eyes!

I brought along my own wig and my own hairdresser, John. I put on my own foundation, but the makeup department did the rest because they wanted me to look as feminine as possible rather than looking like a drag queen. Given that my career was as a female impersonator, my makeup was always much more like that of a glamorous woman than a drag queen, anyway.

We filmed from about eight in the morning to ten at night. In one scene, Alvin stands up in the bath and I stare right at his genitals; in another we are romping in bed together – he is naked, and I am still in my dressing gown. It was certainly an interesting experience having half a dozen members of the crew watching us, but it was great fun and a good laugh.

In our opening scene my character is sitting in a large cane chair and sharing a drink with Alvin who is sitting on the bed. The props department had nothing that resembled alcohol, so they just grabbed a bottle of brandy out of the drinks cabinet belonging to the owner of the house. In another scene, Alvin is sitting in the bath. A crew member had to keep adding dish washing liquid to it while they kept beating the bubbles to make them froth. It clearly was not working, and you do not see any bubbles or even the bath itself in the final cut.

At the end of our main scene Alvin discovers, predictably, that I am not quite as feminine as he at first thought and leaps naked out of bed and runs down the stairs. My character, Mrs Warren, appears once more, where she is interviewed by a reporter at her front gate about Alvin. She explains, to the reporter with barely a hint of irony, that she thought that Alvin was terrified of sex. Working on Alvin Purple was a great experience, and I am so glad to have been a small part of Australian cinema history.

In 1974, after four years at the Ritz Hotel, Les Girls moved to a nightclub and restaurant called Olivia's on the Upper Esplanade in St Kilda, overlooking Luna Park.

At the time we were told we were moving because Olivia's had made Les Girls a better offer, but I later found out that the real reason was rather more sinister. About two years after Les Girls began at the Ritz another family had taken the hotel over from the Walker brood. I found out about six months after moving to Olivia's that our manager Albie Franks had allegedly had an argument with the owner of the Ritz Hotel and had drawn his gun on him.

Interestingly, a couple of days before we left the Ritz Hotel the owner offered me my own show as he knew that I would bring in customers. However, I was under contract to Les Girls and there was no way I was going to do another flit, let alone one in the same suburb, and not one where my former boss could be after me with a gun!

However, it was not long afterwards that I was to have my very own run in with Albie and a firearm. Above Les Girls at Olivia's was a large venue which held wedding receptions and other events. If the music was loud and lots of people were dancing, it made putting on a show downstairs a real challenge. It was not so bad when we were doing music numbers as our own music would often drown out theirs, but it became unbearable when I was doing my comedy patter. Sometimes, audience members could not even hear my jokes.

One night, it all got too much, and I snapped. After finishing my spot, I bee-lined straight to Albie at the front desk and screamed, 'What are you going to do about the fucking noise up there?' and stormed off. Albie saw red and immediately raced after me. I slammed the dressing room door in his face and locked the door as a good diva should. Locked inside with me was Pat who was living with Phillip and me and helped with my costume changes.

Fortunately, Pat was a big girl and she put all her bulk against the door as Albie tried to break in like a maniac. It dawned on me that he may have wanted to get hold of his gun, which he kept in a briefcase in a cupboard in the dressing room. I was absolutely terrified, but thankfully, after a while, Albie calmed down and I am still here. Nothing was ever said about it again.

Olivia's was trendier than the Ritz as it had been renovated when we moved in. It had been painted red – remember - Sammy Lee's favourite colour - and it included fixtures such as plush red curtains. However, as much as the new venue was more upmarket, I preferred performing at the Ritz as it felt more intimate, and I could be closer to my audience. At Olivia's, the audience was on two levels, a bit like some theatres, so I kept having to look up and down. The noise from upstairs did not help either but at least I had my own little dressing room which I lacked at the Ritz, and which came in handy from time to time when I needed to avoid Albie.

I was lucky to have worked with some wonderful names at both the Ritz and Olivia's, who were very talented and gave their all. Two performers in particular stood out - Cinnamon Brown and Renee Scott - both brilliant dancers. They excelled at their craft and were perfectionists when it came to their performances. They shared my aim of treating the audience to a fantastic night.

Cinnamon and Renee became great friends of mine. When I make good friends, I hang on to them so when they died, I felt part of my history had been lost. I was shattered. However, I am grateful that we were part of each other's lives.

Funnily enough, I almost did make it in television as a star in the 1970s and one newspaper reporter even wrote an article asking if I could become the next Graham Kennedy. Perhaps I could have been the Queen of Australian television. A journalist had written a review of my act in which he kindly described me as a 'TV natural.' Soon after, Channel Nine got in touch and invited me to an audition to fill in on one of their Graham Kennedy shows.

I was given the names of various personalities and I was asked what questions I would ask them in an interview situation. I was very nervous, and things went even further downhill when the television executives made it clear they wanted me to perform as a guy and not in drag. As you know, drag is my security blanket that I use to perform. It is my prop and gives me the confidence to go on stage. Asking me to compere a show out of drag is like asking a prude to walk down a street naked. I am known for being a female impersonator and that is what I do. That is when I am at my best. Clearly, Australian television, Channel Nine anyway, was not yet ready for a drag queen as a chat show host on prime-time TV so, alas, it was not to be. Close, but no cigar!

Les Girls in Melbourne really was the place to go and be seen and over the years we had many well-known personalities in the audience. These included the likes of comedians Frankie Howerd and Dave Allen as well as actor Frank Thring. Yvonne De Carlo, who had played Mrs Munster in *The Munsters*, came along one night in 1972, when she was starring in the play, *No, No Nanette*. I would have dearly loved to have met them but they all disappeared straight after the show. However, some did hang around for a couple of drinks. Actor and singer Barry Crocker came over one night and said how much he loved me. 'You were brilliant. Don't ever go on television,' he said. On another occasion actor Michael Pate sent me a note stating, 'I think you're something else.'

The socialite Lillian Frank was very over the top, flamboyant and theatrical - every second word was 'darling'. The writer, reporter and entertainer John-Michael Howson was always friendly and wonderfully camp and colourful, and we got on very well. He reminded me a little of John Inman. On one occasion we even had Jean Nidetch the founder of Weight Watchers who had flown over from America in our audience. She was there with radio and television personality Jimmy Hannan. She was very tall and had quite a commanding presence. On the occasions when Melbourne theatre critic, Howard Palmer, was in the audience, I had to make sure he was well looked after.

Another person who came to Les Girls at the Upper Esplanade who I would have dearly loved to have met was Barry Humphries. Despite being a drag queen myself it was always his character Sir Les Patterson rather than Dame Edna whom I admired. I loved his filthy sense of humour. I was performing one night, and I saw Barry standing at the bar while our two managers were schmoozing with him. I recognised him because of his hat that came down over one eye and his long coat, which was very much his trademark look. By the time I had finished my show he had vanished.

One of the more unusual projects that I was involved in was a photography exhibition involving the then Lord Mayor of Melbourne, Irving Rockman, who was a keen photographer. The exhibition featured photographs taken by different personalities. Irving seemed charming and friendly, and he took a picture of me in drag at Les

Girls. I attended the opening of the exhibition, in drag, and got to chat with former Australian Prime Minister John Gorton, who was lovely and seemed very interested in me and my photograph.

Two of the loveliest people were Bert Newton and his then girlfriend Patti McGrath who went on to marry in 1973. The cute couple came to Les Girls quite a few times and would sit in a corner in the shadows watching the show. We got on very well and they were always lovely and very supportive of Les Girls.

In 1974 while we were still working at the Ritz Hotel the management of Les Girls received a call inviting us to appear on *The Graham Kennedy Show*. Graham was very much the King of Australian television at the time. It felt great to be invited on such a popular show. I was so nervous but excited at the same time. I think I was shitting bullets as not only was I performing but I was also going to be interviewed live - no editing and no cutting out embarrassing scenes or bloopers.

Most of the cast toddled off to the Channel Nine television studio. I was very anxious as my only previous television experience had been on the *The Mike Walsh Show* where I was sitting in the audience and Mike had a quick chat with me to promote our show.

I need not have been too worried as I found out that my friend Bert Newton would be interviewing me on *The Graham Kennedy Show* as he was a co-presenter. When we arrived at the studio I changed into my costume and did my makeup. Bert came into the dressing room and really helped put me at ease. 'Stan is there anything special that you would like me to do during the interview?' he asked.

He really was so sweet. I told him that when I get nervous, I usually need a cigarette. Bert said that would be fine. It seems odd these days but back then people could smoke on television. Pete Smith really talked us up as he introduced us while sitting with Kennedy at his desk, emphasising the fact that the 'girls' who were about to perform were in fact, 'men'. The curtains opened to reveal five showgirls with fabulous feather head pieces and high cut costumes who could have been straight out of a Las Vegas show. About halfway through the number, 'If You Don't See What You Want Up Here' from Jackie Barnett's Showgirls album, released in 1964 (and still a mainstay of drag queens all over the world, today), I appeared and mimed to the rest of the song, along with the girls.

The performance went really well and judging by the applause, the audience thought so, too. After a brief cross back to Graham and Pete, Bert appeared and walked down the line of dancers, asking each of them their male names. Two of the performers were called Dave, and Bert actually asked them for their last names. Talk about awkward. I was last of course so that Bert and I could have a few minutes of camp banter and I could get some plugs in for Les Girls. I asked Bert during the interview if I could have a cigarette and if he could light it for me. I puffed away and we camped it up using the cigarette as a prop and an excuse for a bit of suggestive banter. When I look at the clip of this performance on YouTube it's clear that Bert is somewhat uncomfortable; he tells me he's a little uncomfortable talking to me in drag and he doesn't know what to call the girls and settles on 'performers'. At the very end, I pull my wig off to reveal my masculine haircut and plonk the wig on Bert, who, as always, is a very good sport.

Bert and I continued to bump into each other every so often and in 1978 I received a phone call from him asking me what I was doing the next night. I said that I had nothing planned and he replied that he had two tickets to the opening night of *A Chorus Line* and asked if I would like to go. I took my hairdresser friend John to the show and the cast party (Phillip was just not all that interested in going to see shows). We had a brilliant evening.

In the early 1990s I appeared on *Good Morning Australia* which was hosted by Bert. He interviewed me about my memories of Les Girls, and I discussed with him how I was not allowed to say that 'I was a Friend of Dorothy' and that I needed to pretend to have relationships with the opposite sex during my days as compere. I then performed Divine's 'You Think You're a Man'. Bert really was a most beautiful person who was always very good to me, and I was so sad when he passed away.

Another person who I feel very privileged and honoured to have met and known was the internationally renowned dancer and actor, Sir Robert Helpmann. As a boy I was taught dancing at the Mitchell & Hammerton School of Tap and Ballet at the Tin Platers Hall which belonged to the Tin Platers Factory where my father had worked when he was younger.

I was being taught a routine which involved a rather complicated dance step and a cane. I just could not master this particular step and I got the shits. I was about 11 and I could be the bitch from hell.

I threw down the stick and started to walk away when I heard one of my teachers saying, 'He thinks he's Robert Helpmann.' My immediate thought was 'Who?' Years later I got to know him when he came to visit Les Girls shortly after we had moved to Olivia's on the Upper Esplanade in 1974.

Sir Robert came to see the show and afterwards I was introduced to him. I sat with Sir Robert, and he was very complimentary about me, telling me that he loved my material and timing as well we as my rapport with the audience which he said was amazing. He could not have been friendlier and gave me a real confidence boost. At the time he was co-director of the Australian Ballet and came with a friend called Peter Bain who worked for the ballet.

One evening a photographer from *The Age* newspaper saw a photo opportunity on seeing Sir Robert in the Les Girls audience and suggested he and I go to the entrance of Olivia's and have our picture taken. Sir Robert was all for it and was such a good sport about it. Shortly afterwards, the photograph of Sir Robert and me made page three of *The Age* and the front page of the *Sydney Morning Herald*. In the background of the photograph, you can see Keith Murray who did the bookings at Les Girls. People sometimes mistake Keith for Gough Whitlam in the photograph as there is certainly a likeness. Talk about being photo-bombed!

Sir Robert sent me a letter with a doctored version of our photograph that he had been sent for his birthday by some of the young cast of a production he was working on. Our heads had been swapped over on our bodies and we both found it hilarious. He wrote, 'Isn't it wonderful!' He had a wicked sense of humour and was always very down to earth.

Sir Robert had been to Les Girls a few times and we'd developed a friendship, so I decided to invite him to a party at the home of my friend Keith Murray in East Hawthorne. Keith had exquisite taste and his house was full of antiques. Anyone who knows me will know my love of antiques. The party was a wedding reception that Keith was hosting for a couple of his friends. I did not have contact details for Sir Robert, so Keith suggested I go through Peter Bain and invite them both which I did.

Sir Robert loved parties, so he came with bells on. I can only imagine what the young couple who had only just got married thought of having such a star at their party. I made the two-tier cake which had lots of icing on it and Phillip helped with the catering as he was a fantastic cook. When Robert arrived, he made such a fuss of me and everyone else. He really made an effort to mix with everyone and we all loved him. We gave him some really good wine, albeit out of a cask that we were really desperate to hide. We had a fabulous time.

He had a wicked sense of humour and loved a good party. Some friends of mine told me that on one occasion he was in the kitchen at a party in Melbourne where trays of hors d'oeuvres were being prepared. He took a tray and got out his rather large *schlonger* which he put on the tray among the hors d'oeuvres and covered it with a large lettuce leaf. He then went among the guests with the tray offering them his delights. Their reaction on lifting the lettuce would have been priceless. Some sights can never be unseen.

Sir Robert became a dear friend of mine, and I would call him Bobby and he would refer to me as 'my dear boy'. He never behaved with any airs and graces like I might expect of a man with a title, and he treated me like a friend. He was never boastful and was always very modest about his achievements. He never got on his high horse probably because he was very secure in his abilities and talents and knew he had nothing to prove. I saw him a few times during my time at Les Girls but after leaving we lost touch as often happened when I moved on to new adventures. I am so grateful that he was a part of my life for a few years and would often have to pinch myself that the young boy learning to dance in South Wales who was told he 'thinks he's Robert Helpmann' by his dance teacher, was now lucky enough to count Sir Robert as a friend.

By the end of 1977 I felt as though I had gone as far as I could with Les Girls. I had run my race and I had done my time. I had been getting more and more offers of solo work and was increasingly taking on daytime and evening gigs on Sundays at sports and RSL clubs where my act seemed to go down well, and I was certainly paid better than I was at Les Girls.

The founder of Les Girls Sammy Lee had also died a couple of years earlier. It was clear that on some of his visits to Melbourne shortly before his death that his once formidable mind was not as sharp, and he was losing the plot. He had always been a supporter of mine and was one of my mentors who had given me my big break with Les Girls in both Sydney and Melbourne. I will always have fond memories of him and be thankful that he was a part of my life. His death felt like the end of an era.

It was time for me to move on and allow a whole new world to open up to me. In December 1977 I handed in my notice and left without any fanfare or so much as a whimper. This time I was not doing one of my famous flits and nobody asked me to stay. I had made a lot of money for Les Girls over the years. Now it was time for me to make more money for myself and to put my own career first. I was out on my own!

CHAPTER 15
Going Solo: TV Beckons

It felt liberating to be going solo at last and not having to turn down gigs because I was performing at Les Girls. I was now my own boss, although that also meant that I was no longer earning a weekly wage. I had built up quite a reputation and a network of contacts while performing at the Ritz Hotel and Olivia's, so work was not too hard to find. My various television appearances on programs such as *The Graham Kennedy Show* had also given me a wider audience.

I was also lucky to have had exposure on other television shows including the morning talk show *Vi's Pad* while I was still working at the Ritz. The show was hosted by the larger-than-life character Vi Greenhalf. She used to come to Les Girls quite often with Lillian Frank and as they were both well-known personalities, they would always get the best service.

It was the opening edition of a brand-new series, and everyone was keen to get everything right, particularly Vi. I was out of drag but was there to plug Les Girls. She was being a bit of a bossy boots and told me to hold her scripts while she opened the show. I sat out of shot fiddling with them before clumsily dropping there all over the floor. I'd created a disaster and I picked them up hastily to give them back to her but, of course, they were all in the wrong order and as a result I had messed up her cues. As someone who understands the importance of cues, I felt very bad that I had done this. Not surprisingly she was not too happy and her interview with me was rather brief. I do not think she liked me much after that. Let us just say that I never appeared on her show again.

Going Solo: TV Beckons

However, thankfully, it was not my last television appearance. A producer of an ABC show featuring personalities singing songs from musicals got in touch with me. He asked me to dress up as Carmen Miranda and perform 'Tico Tico No Fuba'. At the time I was having singing lessons with a teacher in Dandenong and so I told her that I had three weeks to learn the song, which I did.

We recorded the vocals at a studio in North Melbourne and then on another day I had to turn up at the ABC studios at 6am to do my makeup and dress up as Carmen Miranda and mime to my recorded track for the television show. Singing live was a new experience for me and I was quite nervous. Miming to my own voice took it to another level. It was all rather surreal, and I am not sure I was that good. It was, though, an honour to be working under the show's musical director, the Australian composer, Brian May, who went on to write scores for television programs such as *Return to Eden* and *Countdown* and films such as *Gallipoli* and *Mad Max*.

But easily one of the most enjoyable shows that I worked on before I left Les Girls was *No Man's Land* hosted by Mickie de Stoop. Mickie was a frequent patron at Les Girls and had said to me that she'd give me a little bit of work on her show, although, she couldn't pay me very much. I became a roving reporter on the afternoon program alongside the likes of Susan Peacock who was then married to Liberal politician Andrew Peacock. I worked on about six shows and the team and I would meet up in the morning and decide what subjects to cover that afternoon. All I got paid was $25.50 per gig but it was a fun experience.

On my first afternoon on the show, I was sent to Bourke Street and wandered around near the department store Myer. I had a microphone in my hand, and I was wearing a short brown wig, a denim jacket, a smart pair of jeans and high heels. I asked passers by what they thought of female impersonators. Thankfully most told me that it did not worry them while I was standing there staring at them right in the face. The funny part of it was that not one of them appeared to have a clue that I was a female impersonator myself!

On another occasion I was assigned the Melbourne Cup and I was there from 6.30 in the morning in full drag downing champagne at the Channel 9 marquee. Once the race was over, I had to go around during the afternoon asking people what they thought of it. It was all so camp.

On one occasion I entered a sex shop near Acland Street in St Kilda with the cameraman in tow to ask customers if they came there often. Not surprisingly they all freaked out and fled. Being caught in a sex shop on camera in the late 1970s was a bit of a no-no and to be honest it was not a very good thing to have done, but I just followed what the producer told me to do. I finished all my reports with a gag or some memorable shot or tag line and it drove me mad trying to think of something catchy and memorable sometimes. On this occasion the closing shot was of me walking up Acland Street with a blow-up doll under my arm. I had some fun times on that show.

When I went solo, I was fortunate to have three excellent agents. They included Wally Bishop who had a reputation for promoting and

Going Solo: TV Beckons

bringing big names to Australia. My other two agents who got me lots of work were Richard Rushton and John Robinson who ran 3RRR Promotions.

I first met them at Les Girls when the owner of the building invited me to perform at the venue above Olivia's as part of that night's entertainment. The band performing on stage just before I did my thirty-minute comedy spot was one of Richard and John's. It marked the beginning of a beautiful friendship, which also developed into a business relationship. John's two sons are now successful musicians in their own right. I consider Wally, Richard and John family as they have always been good to me.

My solo stand-up drag comedy shows at sports clubs and RSLs seemed to go down well with the audience as I attracted big crowds who remembered me from my Les Girls days. I tended not to have much to do with the venue management as I would arrive for my show, perform and then leave. There were rarely any problems. However, there was one occasion which led to a bit of a problem, and it involved the comedian Ugly Dave Gray. By the late 1970s, Ugly Dave had built up quite a large following thanks to his appearances on the game show *Blanket Blanks*, hosted by Graeme Kennedy.

I had first met Dave at the Ritz Hotel when he was in the audience of a Les Girls show. I said hello to him after the show and he seemed friendly enough. At that stage his television career was starting to take off. A few years later when I went solo, I was booked to do a club in North Melbourne on a Sunday evening.

A few days before the show, the venue manager called to say that I would be on a double bill with Ugly Dave Gray. I was excited to be on with such a star and mentioned to the manager that I had met him a few years before. However, I did find it odd to be up against another comedian as two comics were not often booked on the same night in the places that I performed.

My friend Pat, who lived with Phillip and me, and who drove me to gigs, helped me with costumes and had saved me from a run in with Les Girls manager Albie which I mentioned in chapter 14, drove me there early as I always liked to have time to do my makeup and put on my costume. I was just about to start applying my makeup when the manager of the club appeared in the dressing room to introduce himself and asked me to come to his office. He said that he was sorry to have to tell me that he was paying me now because I wouldn't be performing. He explained that he had had a call from Dave's agent saying that he would not perform that night if I shared the bill. I asked the manager why and he said he did not know, and no reason had been given.

The manager gave me my money and I returned to my dressing room in quite an angry mood and told Pat that we would have to pack up and go. I explained what had happened and she was shocked. The next day I phoned the agent who got me the gig and recounted my experience. He reckoned that Dave or his agent may have seen me as unhealthy competition as we were both big names in Melbourne at the time.

Around this time, I also had a funny incident involving a Roman

Catholic priest. One Sunday a couple of younger good friends of ours invited us for a drive in the countryside. They suggested we could meet a friend of theirs, but they were very vague about who it was. We arrived in a country town near Ballarat and approached a Catholic church. I am a lifelong atheist and certainly did not want to spend my Sunday in a church in the middle of nowhere. 'What are we fucking doing here? I am not stepping into a church. Forget it!' However, they explained that their friend was the local priest and that we would be going to his private dwelling next door.

We stood at the front door, and we knocked several times but there was no answer. This went on for quite some time, but my friends insisted he was home as he would be getting ready for the 11am service. I was getting a bit irritated and made a tasteless joke that he was probably doing something wicked with a choir boy. Thankfully that made them laugh and to be honest I was not too far off the mark. Eventually, we heard footsteps down the hallway and the door was opened by their friend the priest who would have been in his 40s.

He apologised for keeping us waiting and explained that he had been listening to music and had not heard us. We walked to the kitchen at the back of the house and lo and behold who should be in the kitchen, but an altar boy aged about 15 or 16 with a joint in his hand puffing away. We could smell it before we entered the kitchen. The priest had been smoking a joint too and offered us some, which we all declined. I believe my friends refused as they were driving, and I said no because I was astounded by the hypocrisy of the priest who was smoking cannabis with an altar boy minutes before he was about to give a sermon moralising about people's lives. I have always had little time for that holier than thou attitude when so much goes on behind the lace curtains. I just wanted to get out of there.

We made some awkward small talk and then the priest noticed the time and said he had a sermon to deliver in about ten minutes. He had one more drag of the joint and took off in the direction of the church. He and the altar boy were so stoned and off their faces. Goodness knows how either got through the service!

While at Les Girls I had been introduced to the entertainer Mary Hardy who became a regular at the shows. I always thought she was fabulous, and we got on very well and after I left Les Girls my agent Wally arranged for me to appear on three episodes of the popular Channel 7 show *The Penthouse Club*, which Mary hosted along with her co-host Michael Williamson who was later replaced by Ernie Sigley.

I used to listen to her afternoon Melbourne radio show, which was hysterical and very near the knuckle. She could be so naughty, and her wit and style have been described as caustic and irreverent. She certainly spoke her mind and did not suffer fools gladly. She was once suspended from her television show *The Penthouse Club* for dropping the F word.

She liked a drink as did I and she could often be found at Murphy's Pub in South Melbourne from where she would go straight to her radio show. Many a time I could sense in her voice that she had had a few too many. We became very good friends but behind her boundless energy and huge stage presence I could tell there was a vulnerable woman who, like me, also suffered from depression.

She always appeared as if she was on stage, everything was a performance, a bit like my dear friend Larry Grayson. I find that as someone with depression I can often spot other people who have it and I saw it in Mary pretty early on. She was often quite manic and hyperactive, but I could see this was partly a symptom of her condition. I was very sad to hear that she had taken her life in 1985 but I cannot say that I was surprised. I have known many creative and entertaining people who appear bubbly and excitable but deep down are struggling.

Not many people know this, but Mary told me that when Lucille Ball was making the film *Mame* (which was released in 1974) she had gone over to the United Stated to audition for the role of the maid. She had already performed the role in a big stage production of *Mame* in Melbourne and her agent thought she stood a good chance. Lucille Ball was actually at the audition and heard her sing her piece, but unfortunately Mary missed out on the part.

The Penthouse Club was one of the old-style TV variety shows that crossed live to harness racing or the 'trots' as we called it. Melbournians loved their horse races! I appeared on three episodes performing five or six minutes of comedy each time. On one episode Mary Hardy, the larger-than-life Maria Venuti, a folk singer whose name escapes me, and I recorded a track called 'This is the Thing that Makes the Men Smile'. Later in the afternoon we were filmed miming to it at the Channel 7 studios.

It was a big production number filmed in several takes in different parts of the studio for various scenes. It was then swiftly edited together and shown on *The Penthouse Club* that evening. Spending time with Mary and Maria was such a laugh and we had a great time recording it. The musical director on the program was the very talented Ivan Hutchinson who was also a popular film critic with his own shows where he would introduce and review movies and interview visiting stars.

My appearance on *The Penthouse Club* led to me appearing on a television show in Adelaide hosted by Ernie Sigley, who sadly died recently in 2021. Rather coincidentally, I actually sat next to Ernie on the plane over from Sydney and we had a good chat and were able to break the ice. It was the only time that I have ever flown first class. Not perhaps as exotic as flying to Dubai or New York but there's a first time for everything.

While I had been performing in Les Girls at Olivia's I had a couple of weeks off and went to Adelaide where I performed at a club on Hindley Street. Before I did my first show, I went to a local hairdresser to get my wig done. The hairdresser was a man called Ian and we ended up having a short fling. At the time I was on a break from Phillip as we had had a bust up and he had moved out. However, by the time I went on Ernie's show in Adelaide our short romance had long fizzled out.

But when I appeared on Ernie's program Ian was in the audience with his then boyfriend and I suggested to them that they come and see me the next night at a venue in Elizabeth. So, the next night I

Going Solo: TV Beckons

was just about to go on stage when I had a sudden need to pee. There was no time to go to the bathroom. I was desperate and just could not hold it in, so I ended up peeing in a large wine glass, which I left in the dressing room.

As I came off stage after my show Ian told me that he had brought me a glass of white wine which he had left in my dressing room. I fetched the glass of wine and re-joined him and his boyfriend to chat and socialise. As I sipped the wine, I immediately realised that I had picked up the wrong glass. I was far too embarrassed to admit my mistake so for the rest of the evening with them I kept sipping my pee from the glass until it was empty. Finally, when I got a chance, I went back to the dressing room and saw the actual glass of wine that they had bought me on the other side of the room. I downed it pretty quickly to drown the taste. An experience that I have no plans to repeat!

In late 1978 my agent Wally Bishop put a variety show together with actor and singer Ron Challinor who had appeared on *Cop Shop* and *Homicide*. The name of our show was *The Stan Munro Show* and I was to be the compere in drag, Ron would sing, and we had two female dancers and a piano player. Our season lasted about eight weeks at the Dorset Gardens Hotel in Croydon. It was great fun and gave me regular work for a couple of months and made a change from the solo shows that I had been doing.

Sadly, my next experience of working as part of a variety show was not such fun. In late 1980 I was contacted by a man called Alain who had previously worked for a short time in the chorus at Les

Girls. He was a choreographer and a very good dancer. Alain affected a French accent and called everyone 'darling' but we were pretty sure he actually came from Eastern Europe.

He told me that he had been compering and choreographing a drag show called Les Coquettes at a club known as La Tenda in Perth which he was sending on the road to tour. At the same time, he was also putting together a new variety show to replace it at La Tenda and wanted me to be the compere. He assured me that it was not another drag show but one which sounded similar to my previous show with Wally and Ron featuring female dancers and singers. I thought it sounded a wonderful opportunity and I jumped at the chance. I phoned my agent Richard who was getting me bookings at the time and agreed to pay him a commission for the next few months.

Before arriving in Perth, I booked a small flat for six months and paid a month's rent in advance to hold it. I arrived in the Western Australian capital on the first of January 1981 where I was met by Alain and his business partner Frank. I was so excited about the new show but perhaps I should have smelt a rat - if things sound too good to be true, they often are!

Later that day I received a phone call from Alain inviting me out to dinner with him and Frank. During the evening Alain dropped a bombshell telling me, 'Darling, I've got a surprise for you. You're not going to compere the show here in Perth because I am sending you on the road with the drag show.' Another bloody drag show and one that was going on tour! This really pissed me off as by that time I had worked with so many different drag shows. I was so over them. I had done my years with Les Girls in Sydney and Melbourne and had really wanted to move on and spread my wings. I had also gone to the trouble of finding a home in Perth and had paid advance rent.

My agent Richard had also organised some gigs for me on my days off in Perth. I was frantic and phoned Richard who reassured me that he would cancel the shows that he had booked and would clear my diary for the next six months. I was so angry, but I also needed the money, and I knew this would be regular work for me.

We spent a month rehearsing for the tour during the day at La Tenda and in the evenings, I compered the show. The day before we went on tour, we all had a meeting with Alain who told us, 'Listen queens. Your weekly wage will be paid to you in half so that when you get back to Perth at the end of the tour the rest of your money will be waiting for you here so that you will get a lump sum of money.' His reasoning was that apparently drag queens like to spend too much on tour, so he was doing us a favour! Bullshit!

'Just a moment, Alain. Not me! I get my wages up front every week. What you do with the rest of the cast is your problem. I have an agent's commission to pay,' I shot back. He agreed and said in his phoney French accent, 'I wouldn't do that to you. You're a star, darling.' To soften the blow of going on tour Alain had told me that we would be travelling in a comfortable air-conditioned bus. Another fib. It was all too much but it was what it was.

The day our tour bus arrived it turned out to be a single-decker old school bus with no air conditioning. It was just awful. I could not believe it but then again at that stage I am not sure anything would have surprised me. As we got further and further into the tour the bus started playing up, so we had to hire a new one, thankfully with air conditioning.

I think that our first show was in Bunbury and in the early days of our tour we used to attract big crowds and the venues would be booked out. The audiences seemed to love me and some of them remembered me from their visits to Les Girls in Sydney. Some of my fellow queens were not so keen on me as they all knew each other and seemed to see me as little more than a blow-in from Victoria. They almost certainly saw me as coming in and stepping on their feet or invading their territory which had never been my intention. To me it was simply a job. A girl has got to earn a living.

One time during the tour there was an argument in the dressing room between a couple of the performers. I was caught in the middle of it and became pretty pissed off. Frank called a meeting of the cast and said firmly, 'We don't want any more bullshit because if it was not for Stan there would be no show.' Even though part of me resented being on the tour, I appreciated his words and, indeed, I always did my best to hold the show together. I was not paid much, and I was still paying my agent Richard, but I took my role seriously and always gave it my best shot.

On one occasion we visited Geraldton and I was asked to visit the local prison on a Sunday afternoon and entertain the prisoners. They wanted someone to do comedy, which is what I did in our show. I was picked up from my motel and I arrived at the prison and

Going Solo: TV Beckons

was shown to the recreation area where I saw about 400 prisoners waiting for me.

The temperature must have been about 45 degrees and I was sweltering. I was actually given one of the cells which belonged to one of the inmates to use as a dressing room to change into my costume and put on my makeup. I then went onto the stage and was introduced to a sea of hundreds of prisoners. Unfortunately, my jokes went right over the heads of the audience which just did not seem to get my humour, and nobody watching seemed to have a clue who or, perhaps, what, I was.

I realised early on that I had to change my tactics, so I walked into the audience with a microphone and joked along with the prisoners who then started to warm to me. I think the personal touch helped rather than talking down to them from a stage and it gave us all a closer connection. I finished with a song, and I took a bow.

Then from the audience I could see this man walking towards me who was wearing a pair of shorts. He looked a lot like Sir Les Patterson with a big *schlonger* in his pants. He got on stage and said, 'Come on boys. Let's give a big hand to the Dame.' The audience cheered and clapped, and I felt great. What could have been a disaster became a success. That was probably my highlight of the whole tour. That, and the time I cajoled the bus driver to pick up a good-looking hitchhiker who was heading south to Perth. I convinced my new friend to stay the night in the motel we were staying at as he could share a room with me. He had some hooch and it turned out to be quite the night.

Anyway, I went back into the prison cell to get changed and I pressed my lips on the shaving mirror above the sink and gave it a big kiss with my red lipstick covered lips. Before leaving I sprayed the prisoner's pillow with the lovely perfume that I was wearing in order to give him something to dream about. I really hope he slept well that night.

After about five months, our tour of Western Australian, which had gone as far north as Port Headland and east to Marble Bar, fizzled out as our audiences were dwindling because our road manager who was supposed to go ahead to let people know we were coming was not very good at getting us publicity. As a result, we had some very small audiences.

I was glad to get out of the tour as I felt that I had been conned into it. I was also missing Phillip who was the other side of the country. Before I left Alain asked me if I would be willing to work for a few more months on a show that he was putting on at the Tudor Inn in Launceston, Tasmania. I must have been a glutton for punishment as I agreed. I let my agent Richard know and he said it was fine as he had no work lined up for me.

I flew back to Melbourne to spend a couple of weeks with Phillip before arriving in Launceston. The show was like the one in Western Australia. However, at least in WA we enjoyed beautiful weather, even if it was a bit hot at times. I hated my time in Launceston. It was in the depths of winter, and it felt so cold and dreary. It was as if I was at the end of the earth.

Our season in Launceston came to an end after about three or four months and it could not have come soon enough. I was glad when it was all over. My only respite while in Launceston had been a weekend that I spent in Hobart at the home of one of my agents, John Robinson and his family, where we watched the wedding of Charles and Diana.

CHAPTER 16
The Cheeky Chaps and Carlotta Returns

The Cheeky Chaps and Carlotta Returns

While staying with John and his family he managed to persuade me that Hobart would be a great place to live. Phillip had family on the west coast of Tasmania, which meant he could be a bit closer to them so, a few months later, we sold our home in Springvale and moved down. I often wonder why I moved there. Tasmania is a beautiful place, but I love warmth and sunshine and the winters there can be pretty tough. My earlier experiences in Launceston had not exactly been great, so I still struggle to find an explanation for the move, beyond it being part of a mid-life crisis as I had hit the grand old age of 40 at the beginning of that year.

Looking back, I think it was a mistake to move as there was simply very little, if any, work for me. Hospitality has long played a major part in Phillip's life, and he soon found work as a maitre d' at a revolving restaurant. However, there was nothing for me, so I spent most of my time feeling bored. To get work I had to go the mainland and I often ended up performing in Melbourne, so selling up and heading south had been rather pointless.

In early 1982 I was hired as a compere at a ladies' luncheon in the Melbourne suburb of Frankston. I was still quite a big name thanks to my work at Les Girls and various television appearances. On the same bill was a male stripper whose stage name was Sorrell. Male stripping was only just starting to take off in Victoria and Sorrell was one of the first. At the side of the stage watching on with pride was his boyfriend Guy Barton who took me aside and told me that he loved my act.

He explained that he was a promoter who had a show every

Wednesday night at a club in Fitzroy which featured male strippers, and he wondered whether I would like to be the compere for a night. I agreed and one night led to more nights and then on to visiting various venues across suburban Melbourne. I was getting regular work and I was really enjoying it.

This format led to Guy forming the Cheeky Chaps which became one of the first touring male strip shows in Australia. It consisted of me and three strippers. I spent the next three years or so from 1982 touring Victoria, New South Wales, Queensland and South Australia as a compere with three handsome hunks who had audiences of women in the palms of their hands. Of course, our lusting female audiences had little idea that they were barking up the wrong tree as two out of the three original strippers were gay. Over the years, as the show progressed, more straight strippers joined the show who could have the pick of any women they wanted…and they often did.

Guy Barton was the best boss that I have ever worked for because he kept me in solid work for more than three years and he paid me very well and always on time. He was very organised and always ensured our shows were well advertised in the towns and cities that we visited.

I was on stage for most of the evening as my role was not only to introduce the strippers, who would each do a set of about 12 to 15 minutes, but to also perform gags, sing 'You Think You're a Man' live and do my trademark tin can strip. The women would go insane for us. They loved us and we would often have bookings six months ahead of time, which was great as it allowed us to plan ahead.

The Cheeky Chaps and Carlotta Returns

I recall our strippers very well in those early days of the Cheeky Chaps. Guy's boyfriend Sorrell was tall, had blond hair and was a tad feminine. He dressed as a clown to begin his routine and would strip out of his outfit. He had a white face, a large red nose and big red lips. When he did his makeup he would wear Johnson's Baby Powder, which I can still smell just thinking of it.

Another stripper called Ray Wilde is still a friend of mine today and is a very dear soul who recently celebrated his 21st wedding anniversary. He dressed as an American Indian, was about five foot eight and had a muscly physique. He was a brilliant performer and the women loved him. He was probably my favourite stripper that I worked with over the years as he was so down-to-earth, and we got on so well. A dear soul and a good friend.

Then there was Roberto who was a Romeo type with naturally curly hair. He came on dressed as a tramp and stripped down to this magnificent body. He was very agile and balletic in his leaps and movements.

Of course, over the years we had our tiffs and up and downs. I was probably not easy to work with as I had had a lot of experience compering shows and wanted everything to be brilliant.

On one occasion we were performing in a town in South Australia. About an hour before our show, we heard that a group of local Christians were protesting outside with placards. I told our manager and Guy that I would get ready and go out in full drag and talk to them. I spoke with the demonstrators to try and reason with them and to ask them what their issue was with our show. They explained, perhaps unsurprisingly, that they thought it was immoral. I decided to invite them to the show so that they could see it for themselves and then make up their own minds.

We were doing two shows in that town and on the second night I came off stage after doing my opening spiel when Guy came into the dressing room to tell me that the woman who had led the protest was in the audience. He suggested that we give her a bit of her own medicine as the night before she and her cohort had tried to disrupt the show. He told me where she was in the audience and suggested that I point her out from the stage to the rest of the audience and he would shine the spotlight on her. That is exactly what happened, and she jumped out of her chair and took off like a rat up a drainpipe.

A few months after joining the Cheeky Chaps Phillip and I felt that it was time to look at moving back to Melbourne as I was hardly in Tasmania and most of my work was around Melbourne and other parts of Victoria. It really made very little sense staying in Hobart. However, we could find no buyers for our home, so we ended up renting a couple of places in the Melbourne suburb of Fitzroy for the next year.

After about six months of touring Victoria, we did a show in Albury in New South Wales when an agent and promoter called, believe it or not, Dougie, who had flown into see the show, suggested that he could market it across the state and other parts of Australia. This led to work in Sydney and rural NSW in RSL clubs. In Sydney we would often have three male dancers in addition to our strippers and would do lunchtime, late afternoon and evening shows.

The Cheeky Chaps and Carlotta Returns

Some of my costumes were being made by my former Les Girls co-star Electra. She was a brilliant dressmaker and had her own studio in Newtown with two girls working for her. Electra went on to make costumes for so many people including for some of our strippers in the Cheeky Chaps like Sorrell.

At one stage, about halfway through our three-year run, we all had a month off. I took a short trip back to Wales to catch up with friends and family. Of course, I managed to get some work there, including a gay bar in Swansea. As I was walking down the main street of the day of my performance, I spotted a poster with the headline, *Vintage Drag in Mint Condition*. This is what I used when I first started doing solo shows in and around Sydney! I looked a bit closer and the drag queen who also happened to be performing in Wales that night (although at a different bar) and who had stolen my headline, was Kandy Johnson, who used to run the Purple Onion. Such cheek! My nephew and his wife and I decided we would see his show (he was performing at 9.30 and I wasn't on until 11pm) so I hid behind a post in the club until he came on and began miming to a Shirley Bassey number. When he saw me, he was so gobsmacked he actually stopped miming and said, 'What are you doing here?' Apparently, he later caught my act, which went really well, and had said to one of the barmen, 'Isn't Stan wonderful!' Although we had our differences over the years, we respected each other's work.

I then returned to Australia with Mum, who stayed with Phillip and me for a short time. She came to see the Cheeky Chaps, but goodness knows what she thought of the show as she did not say much. Coming from a small village in rural Wales and seeing her son dressed in drag introducing three gorgeous men who stripped down to their G-strings must have been a bit of a culture shock.

We were performing somewhere like Tamworth when the British journalist Janet Street-Porter came to see the show. Soon after, she interviewed me at the Windsor Hotel in Melbourne for a publication. I remember her as being lovely and quite quirky, but I will never forget those teeth!

The audiences loved us, and it was fabulous to be back in the city where I had started my Australian career. I was working increasingly in New South Wales and so it made sense to move back to Sydney, which Phillip also thought was a good idea. Eventually, I received a call from my agent Richard telling me that Phillip had been in touch and wanted him to pass on the message that he had finally sold our place in Hobart. As I was often on the road, I was not always easy to get hold of so Richard would sometimes have to relay messages between Phillip and me.

The sale of the house in Hobart was brilliant news and I spoke to Phillip to let him know that I would start house hunting in Sydney. I found a lovely two storey terraced house in Erskineville close to the Imperial Hotel which of course has been immortalised in the film *The Adventures of Priscilla, Queen of the Desert*.

On the day we were due to move in I went into our new home and found that the previous tenants who had been renting the place were still in bed. I could not believe it and I had the task of getting them out of bed and moving them out as Phillip and our truck of furniture were on their way from Melbourne and due later that day. I gave the tenants a bit of time to make their exit.

When Phillip arrived with our friend Doreen, I took them both to the pub and bought them drinks in order to soften the blow when I explained what had happened. Phillip was understandably not too happy and when we did move into our tiny new home later that day we were up to our neck in furniture. I was so happy to be living back in Sydney and Phillip went on to become the manager of the Koala Motor Inn on Oxford Street. The lovely Karen Chant lived around the corner, and sometimes popped in for a cuppa and a chat.

One of the highlights of my time with the Cheeky Chaps was a ten-week tour that we did from Newcastle to Cairns. We hired a bus that had, at various times, belonged to singers Marcia Hines, Julie Anthony and Simon Gallagher. It was a huge black vehicle that we called 'The Bitch'. I loved it as it had all the mod cons that we needed such as beds, a microwave, and even a television. It was so different from my disastrous and unhappy tour of Western Australia a couple of years before. We were packing out the RSL clubs with female audiences and it was a very successful tour. I loved it.

But all good things must come to an end and after about three years or so with the Cheeky Chaps we disbanded as other similar shows featuring male strippers were taking off and our novelty had worn off. However, our show was a pioneering one as we were one of the first. The last time I saw Guy Barton was at the same ceremony in Melbourne in the 1990s where Simone had called me the dreaded 'C'-word.

Sadly, he died some years later. Guy really was an amazing boss who kept me in regular and happy work for a few years. I will always be grateful.

Shortly after the Cheeky Chaps ended, I did two short tours of New Zealand in 1985 which included Auckland, Wellington and Christchurch. The first was with a group of male strippers for about a month and the second was with a group of female strippers for about three weeks. It was fun though it did not compare to my time with the Cheeky Chaps, which I adored.

It was at some point during this period that I made my notorious appearance on *The Mike Walsh Show*. This was the afternoon program to be on thanks to its high ratings and television awards, and it had won many Logie Awards. Everyone loved Mike Walsh. I was invited onto the show to do an eight-minute set of comedy in drag. Before I went on, I spoke to the musical director Geoff Harvey to ask if he had the music for 'The Stripper'. I did some gags and as Geoff and his orchestra performed 'The Stripper' I started to remove my costume.

At the end of my set, I went to the dressing room where my friend Glyn, who had accompanied me, told me that I had been cut off and they had gone to a commercial break. I had been oblivious to this while performing. The next thing I knew a floor manager ran into my dressing room shouting, 'What the fuck do you think you are doing? You've blown your chances of appearing on this show again!!!'

I had made a joke during my performance that I was wearing a feather boa because there had been a cockfight in the dressing room, which in fact was something that I had borrowed from Larry Grayson who had said it on British TV years before. The floor manager could not believe that I had come out with such a line, and to make matters worse, I had started removing my clothes to 'The Stripper' on national television during the daytime. I knew that my act was a bit risqué, but I found his reaction so over the top. What I had not realised was that it was the school holidays, and they were worried about kiddies watching. I was never invited back.

After my tour of New Zealand with the strippers I got a gig compering a strip show in the room above Les Girls in Kings Cross. Jack, the manager of Les Girls, came upstairs to see our show and we chatted after it finished. I went down to have a peek at Les Girls, and it seemed to be a similar format to what I remembered all those years before. By this time, Jack was running the place with his Scottish business partner Alastair. The 'Boss of the Cross' Abe Saffron, owned the building.

A few weeks later Jack asked if I would like to come back to compere Les Girls for as long as I liked. I was delighted, as once again I had walked into regular work almost straight away. But I was also nervous because I had not performed at Les Girls in Kings Cross since the beginning of the 1970s and was concerned how the Sydney audiences would take to me coming back as the compere in the mid-1980s.

I had last worked in Sydney at Les Girls during the glory days of Sammy Lee and the place had certainly changed. The management seemed to be trying to make as much money as it could by cutting corners and the venue had certainly seen better days. It needed a good paint job, and the food was shocking, being little more than slop. The shows were still good, but the customers no longer dressed up like they used to, and the audience seemed to be mainly made up of tourists, particularly from Asia, who just sat there taking photographs. They had limited understanding of English so they didn't get the humour and they would rarely laugh or smile.

Those running the joint did not seem to care as the steady streams of tourists were bringing in money and that is all they were interested in. I just accepted it as I was getting a steady income. However, it was not much fun performing to people who barely reacted beyond the clicks and flashes of cameras. We had become little more than a freak show by this stage. It was very sad.

One night as I was in full flight among the audience, I began to feel a panic attack coming on. I had actually started having these attacks a few months before, but this was the first I had while performing. Somehow, I continued with the show, but my legs were like jelly. Luckily, I managed to conceal my state from the audience, but it scared me a lot. From that moment, I became very wary and paranoid when performing, as I never knew when another attack would arise. I will write more about my panic attacks and how they affected me later.

Perhaps my paranoia was justified because, after a few months, Alastair, one of the managers of Les Girls, came backstage during the first show of the evening and said to me, 'Guess who's in the audience. Carlotta!' Apparently, Carlotta was visiting from Brisbane where she had been working. Call it a drag queen's intuition, but alarm bells rang immediately, and I had a strong feeling that my days at Les Girls were numbered.

It was quite the night because during the second show Alastair came backstage again and told me that Carlotta was in tears and asking to come back. As he told me this, I knew that was the nail in the coffin for me. I had starred in Les Girls in Melbourne, but Carlotta was a much bigger name in Sydney. I knew that I could not compete.

It went from bad to worse. The following Monday I was told that Carlotta was returning but, they said, only as part of the management, not as a performer. Whenever I saw Carlotta, she kept insisting that she was only coming back to manage. I felt the 'lady doth protest too much'. As a compere myself I knew that someone of Carlotta's stature would not settle for anything less than the spotlight.

A couple of weeks went by when I received a call from Jack asking me to come to his office. I knew what was coming. He told me that Carlotta was going to return as the front of house manager for six weeks and would then take over my job, which meant that they would have to let me go. Those six weeks would give Carlotta enough time to rehearse for the new show. I was totally pissed off though not surprised and I agreed to work off my notice as I needed the money, and it would give me a chance to find work elsewhere.

Jack said that he would give me a reference, which he would get typed up soon for me, saying that I had done a fabulous job. As I was walking out of his office he said, 'Oh hang on. Here it is.' He had already had it typed out and ready to give to me. It had not even been typed by Jack but by someone who worked in his office and who had never really liked me. It was hardly a glowing reference and simply said that I had worked for Les Girls and that they were satisfied with my work.

That night Carlotta was there when I came in early as usual to get ready. She followed me backstage and said, 'Oh darling, I don't want you to think that it is my fault that you are getting the sack. The management have been down on their knees begging me to come back.' Carlotta may not have meant it, but I felt as if I was a dog that was being kicked when it was down. What could I say!

I felt so insulted by the way that I had been treated, and the fact that someone with as many years of experience as I had had with Les Girls was let go with little more than a mediocre reference. It was all so belittling. Only a few months ago I had been reassured that I could stay in my role as compere for as long as I wished. It seemed like an utter contradiction. I felt terrible and felt I had been treated with contempt.

I had been stabbed in the back, but it is all water under the bridge now. For a long time, I was unsure whether to believe Jack or Carlotta's version of events, but with the passing of time I feel more inclined to believe Carlotta's. I genuinely have nothing but love for Carlotta and will always wish her all the best.

Jack's over-riding focus was about making money and putting bums on seats. Bringing Carlotta back was essentially a business decision as she was a bigger name than me in Sydney but none of that excuses the way he treated me. I had been with Les Girls for much of my time in Australia since 1963 and it felt like a very sad note on which to end my days at Les Girls. Such is life. It was truly the end of an era and once again, I was now on my own.

CHAPTER 17

Never Meet Your Heroes: Danny La Rue

Never Meet Your Heroes: Danny La Rue

It is said that you should never meet your heroes because they are sure to disappoint you. This was, to an extent, sadly true with Danny La Rue who I got to know in 1980. I first heard about Danny in the early 1960s before I moved to Australia. I was working in Manchester when I saw a newspaper article featuring two photographs of him which had been spliced together. Half his body was in drag, and the other half was not. I was intrigued as, at the time, he was one of the first people to make it big in Britain as a female impersonator, or as a 'comic in a frock' as he referred to himself. He went on to top the bill in theatres in London's West End and across the world.

I first saw Danny perform when he played one of the Ugly Sisters in the pantomime *Cinderella* at London's Golders Green Hippodrome on my first trip back from Sydney in 1965. My friend, Des, and I were absolutely spellbound by him. Danny had teamed up with another popular drag performer Alan Haynes, who was the other Ugly Sister.

For anyone who knows *Cinderella* the Ugly Sisters are supposed to look grotesque and villainous, but not our Danny! Alan Haynes dressed rather dowdily but Danny was the height of glamour. This was not quite the image that I had of an Ugly Sister, but Danny was magnificent. He very much held the show together and, in my eyes, he was clearly the star. He gave the show that extra sparkle and magic.

I finally met Danny in 1980 thanks to my friend Cilla Black. I first got to know Cilla around 1968 when she was performing at Chequers nightclub in Sydney, owned by Chinese entrepreneurs Denis and

Keith Wong. It really was the place to hang out in the 1960s. I was taken, in drag, to see Cilla, on a date. I had to leave her show early as I was performing at Les Girls that night, but I sent a note backstage telling Cilla how much I enjoyed her performance and inviting her to come and see me perform.

Lo and behold, Cilla turned up to Les Girls a few nights later and after the show I came out to chat with her, and we got on really well. I also enjoyed meeting her boyfriend (and future husband) and manager Bobby, and her gay road manager. Cilla and I clicked so well that we arranged to spend a day together in Sydney. My costume-designer friend Kenny Williams and I showed Cilla, Bobby and her road manager the sights of Sydney, including a wonderful afternoon at Taronga Zoo. I have a black and white photograph of Cilla and me at the zoo, which I treasure as well as one of her and me at Les Girls. She wrote on it, 'To my lovely Stan. Come home soon! Love Cilla xx kiss.'

While Cilla was in Sydney, I asked her if she loved anything camp. She said that of course she did so I suggested that I take her to the Purple Onion, to which she agreed enthusiastically. When we arrived, I went backstage and asked if I could perform a number which they agreed to.

When it was time for my spot, I walked out on stage and announced that I had brought along a very special guest. When I mentioned Cilla's name the crowd went wild. I brought her up on stage and asked her if she liked the gay boys and she said enthusiastically, 'Oh yes, they're lovely,' and everyone cheered. She sat back down, and I mimed to a lesser-known Cilla song, a rather suggestive scouting-themed ditty about a Wolf Cub and a Brownie called 'Follow Me'. That night, Cilla and I had the audience in the palm of our hands. Spending time with Cilla was fabulous. Though we eventually lost contact I remained an admirer of hers for many years.

Now, back to Danny…He was touring Australia in 1979 and I flew up to Sydney to see his show at Her Majesty's Theatre, near Central Station. The show was more or less identical to the one I had seen him in at the Prince of Wales Theatre in London. At the end of the show Danny stepped forward, took his bow and thanked the audience, before saying, 'I've got a very good mate in the audience, and she is sitting down here. Please give a big hand for Miss Cilla Black.' The spotlight shone on Cilla, and she stood up and waved to the audience.

After the show I raced downstairs, and I spotted Cilla walking across the foyer. Thankfully, she remembered me well and asked if I had ever met Danny. I said that I had not, and she kindly invited me backstage to his dressing room which was packed with his friends and admirers. He still had half his makeup on, and he was talking mainly about himself. This was something he was rather good at.

Cilla introduced me and I was really flattered when he said that he had heard of me. To know that the world's greatest female impersonator had heard of me was high praise indeed. I stuck around for a few drinks and Danny took me aside and said that I must look him up when he was in Melbourne and come to his show.

He emphasised that it was a personal invitation, which I thought was very kind considering that we had just met.

When he eventually came to Melbourne, I contacted Danny's manager and partner Jack Hanson. He was a former commando, very handsome and a beautiful person. He offered me a couple of tickets to the show and because Phillip wasn't interested, I brought along my hairdresser friend John. We had a great time and enjoyed the show.

I suggested to Phillip that we ought to invite Danny over for dinner as he had been very kind in inviting me to see him at the theatre. I got in touch with him, and he gladly accepted our invitation to come over to our home in Springvale. Being an anxious person, I was worried what we were going to serve Danny for dinner; but I need not have been concerned as Phillip was, and still is, a wonderful chef. Phillip drove to Danny's flat in the affluent Melbourne suburb of Toorak to pick up Danny, his manager and partner Jack, and his Australian pianist Wayne King.

Phillip and I gave them the best evening we could, including delicious food and champagne, as we had been told that all he ever drank was champagne. I later discovered that he would drink pretty much anything. We all had a wonderful evening and Danny said that he would love to see me perform but it would have to be on a Sunday as that was his only day off. I told him my next Sunday performance would be in, of all places, Moonee Ponds. I said it with a smile and wink, but he did not appear to get the reference, so I explained that it was the birthplace of Dame Edna.

On the evening of the show, I had my wig coiffured fabulously by John. He and I arrived early at the club to ensure that Danny and his guests could have one of the best tables. I really wanted the evening to be perfect for Danny. The table was laid out neatly when a family arrived early and plonked themselves down and started eating.

On seeing this from backstage I ran like a maniac to the manager and told him they had to be moved. I was going spare as this was the last thing I needed. Thankfully, the management shuffled off the family to another table. I was worried that Danny would walk in any minute on this and so I asked John to help the staff to clear the table, put on a fresh cloth and lay it with cutlery.

It did not help my anxiety that in typical drag queen style Danny was running late. When Danny did arrive, he whizzed around the full length of the club like a Duchess with his entourage so that he could be seen by all and sundry. Danny and his companions just managed to fit around the table.

Things only got worse as Wayne and John's eyes met across the table and it was clear that they obviously fancied each other. Apparently, they even started playing footsies under the table and it did not take Danny long to cotton on to this. Danny and Wayne went on to have a relationship though I did not know the situation between them at that stage as Danny was still with his lover Jack Hanson who unfortunately died of a brain haemorrhage in 1984. However, Danny was clearly not happy with what was going on under the table.

I had of course made a big fuss of Danny in the show, which I thought had gone well. Afterwards we all went back to Danny's flat. He was in a foul mood and had had quite a bit to drink earlier at the club. Throughout the night he would call out, 'Jack, champagne, champagne!' I often felt sorry for Jack as he was at his constant beck and call. Jack fetched expensive bottles of Veuve Clicquot, and Danny continued to get more and more pissed. With each sip he became cattier. He started making digs at me and I felt that he was trying to get at me in order to get at John.

To my utter shock, at one point in the night Danny announced loudly in front of everyone, 'I could do your show right now standing on my head!' This was a side to Danny that I had never seen. I felt very hurt and really upset by his comments, but I said nothing as I was in awe of him and felt honoured to be at his home. It is strange what you let people get away with when you admire them. However, it was time for us to leave so Phillip, John and I decided to make our excuses and head home. As we were leaving Danny called out after us, 'Stan and Phillip, you are welcome anytime but don't bring that hairdresser!'

No romance developed between John and Wayne though John ended up having a fling with Danny's hairdresser. Not long after the incident at Danny's house I went to see the cabaret singer Frances Faye do a show in Melbourne. It was a wonderful show and Sammy Davis Jr, entertainer Don Lane and comedian Ronnie Corbett were all in the audience. Don and Sammy did an impromptu number with Frances which we all loved. Danny was also present as was John and Danny's hairdresser. That evening Danny accused John of only being with his hairdresser so he could steal as much information on wigs as possible. It was a throwaway line, but one designed to sting. It was clear that once you crossed Danny, he never forgot or forgave.

I learnt quickly that there were two sides to Danny. There was Danny with the drink in his hand who could be obnoxious and a braggart and then there was Danny who was sober, generous and charming. He was definitely not a jolly drunk and clearly had a drink problem. He was also bitter with it. I think some of that bitterness came from the fact that he was one of the first female impersonators in the post-war era to crack it internationally and perhaps he resented to some extent those who had come along and done well after him. He certainly wasted no opportunity in regularly reminding me that he had worked in some of the biggest theatres in London's West End.

In 1984 I was on a trip to London and saw Danny star in *Hello Dolly* at the Prince of Wales Theatre in the West End. Before the show I bumped into Danny's manager and partner Jack in the foyer, and he kindly invited me up to the green room afterwards. I was there with my friend Des and my Australian travelling companion Glyn. It was a shockingly awful production and Danny seemed ill-suited to the lead role of Dolly Levi. I found, for instance, that his rendition of the title song sounded flat and bland and left a lot to be desired.

Des, Glyn and I went to the green room after the show and Glyn made a beeline for a man with grey hair perched in the corner on a stool and told him, 'Danny, I loved the show.' The man responded loudly, 'I'm not Danny La Rue!' The man was Danny's showbiz partner Alan Haynes who I had seen all those years ago as one of the Ugly Sisters in Cinderella. Glyn's case of mistaken identity was all a bit embarrassing at the time, but we had a good laugh about it later.

In the green room we could see Danny greeting everyone and lording it over his guests reminding them what a star he was. He was telling some Americans that he planned to take his production of *Hello Dolly* to Broadway and would have the audience at his feet. As we left Des said to me, 'He'll have the audience at his throat if they see this!' Unsurprisingly, it only lasted for a short run at the Prince of Wales Theatre.

I remember writer and entertainer John-Michael Howson telling me that he was at a dinner party with Danny when he stood up and told everyone loudly that he should be knighted for the things that he had done for English theatre. John-Michael said it was all very embarrassing, but it was typical Danny. I found him so different to my friend Sir Robert Helpmann who was great fun but also so modest and down to earth despite being internationally renowned.

Danny always had to be the star and get his own way and show people that he was the boss. I was touring Queensland with the Cheeky Chaps and we were booking into a motel in Rockhampton when I saw Danny in the foyer. He explained that he had his Four for the Road show on at the local theatre and I told him about ours. He said it was the last night and he wanted to know if my boys and I would like to join him for dinner at the Chinese restaurant across the road.

By this time Danny had gained a reputation in show business for going to parties, getting drunk and then bragging about his crowning achievements. I invited the Cheeky Chaps for dinner, and it turned out that they already knew of Danny's reputation when alcohol was involved. One of them responded, 'No way! I don't want to see that fucking old queen!' Nobody wanted to join Danny for dinner.

I was so embarrassed that nobody wanted to come along with me, and no amount of persuasion would change their minds, so I ended up going alone. It must have been about midnight and the Chinese restaurant was still open. I could see Danny sitting there with the cast and crew from his show. As I walked in, he was lording it over a male dancer telling him, 'Well, darling you know I've topped the bill on the West End stage…' Goodness knows how many times I had heard him deliver that line.

I cringed as I knew what I was walking into. Danny engaged me in some small talk, but he was four sheets to the wind and seemed more focussed on the young dancer. As the night wore on one of his dining companions advised Danny that the restaurant had to close as the staff needed to go home. Danny hit the roof and started screaming blue murder about the restaurant's owner, yelling things like, 'How dare he! Does he have any idea who he's talking to? Does he know who I am?' He was apoplectic with rage, and it was terribly embarrassing. My Cheeky Chaps had been right to stand their ground.

We all left, and a very drunk Danny held on to my arm as we walked back to the motel. I am not knocking him for being drunk as I have been there myself, but it was what happened next that I found tragic. As I was saying goodnight and leaving the lift on my floor, he told me that he would have loved to have invited me up to his room for a drink, but he needed to sleep. As I looked down, I could see that he had wet himself. I felt so sad that this star of whom I had been in awe had been reduced to such a state.

There were, of course, times when Danny would make me chuckle. I went to see the opening night of a new drag show in Sydney in the mid-1980s. It was compered by a well-known and popular performer who shall remain nameless. There were lots of bouquets of flowers on the stage after the first show of the evening. I was sitting up in the balcony when the singer Tony Monopoly came up to tell me that Danny was in the audience. Tony said that Danny had told him that I was a much more sincere performer than the compere.

I went down to Danny's table where he was sitting with some friends. He gave me a kiss on the cheek and said, 'Oh darling, I have to fucking sit here and watch her. How do I get out of here???' He had clearly had a bit to drink. I thought he was quite mean about the host as I knew that she had always been a superb performer but what made me laugh was that the next day Danny was on morning television on a segment where they had covered the opening night. The reporter went among the audience. Danny said something along the lines of, 'What a marvellous show. The compere is such a wonderful performer. It's fabulous that she's back!'

The last time I saw Danny was in Wales in the early 2000s at a manor house which had a large reception hall where he was performing in an old music hall-type show that featured two male dancers who looked rather past their prime. The show started reasonably early at 5pm. Most of the audience members were quite elderly.

I went with my nephew Mark and his business partner John. Before the show I saw Danny's dressmaker, confidante and long-term assistant Annie in the foyer, and I asked her to let Danny know that I was there. She kindly invited us to come upstairs after the show.

We went into Danny's dressing room where he was holding a glass of champagne and was alone apart from his beloved pooch Jonti, which was a Chinese Hairless Crested dog, a rather unusual-looking creature with hair on his head and around his tail and paws but was otherwise hairless. Danny was absolutely devoted to Jonti and was known to say when offered gigs, 'No Jonti. No Danny!'

Seeing Danny alone in this dressing room in the middle of nowhere seemed like such a contrast to the days when he appeared in the dressing rooms of large West End theatres after a show surrounded by an entourage of admirers, friends and hangers-on, all wanting a piece of him and hanging off his every word.

Danny had also aged quite a bit since I had last seen him and put on a lot of weight. He also seemed quite frail and there was no boasting by him of his showbiz credentials. I am unsure why, but he started ranting to my nephew and his business partner about how promiscuous men were on the gay scene. He kept repeating himself until he told us, 'Sorry darlings I cannot offer you any drinks tonight as this is all the management have sent up.' He said this while holding his glass of champagne. He seemed a shadow of his former self and such a solitary figure. I am not sure if there were genuinely no more glasses of champagne or whether he simply did not want any guests. That was the last I saw of him.

I felt very sad for the way he ended up because during much of his career he had it all: adulation from the public and a lot of wealth. We had a love/hate friendship and though I thought that he lived in an ivory tower I still thought that he was a wonderful star. However, he did have a vicious streak particularly when alcohol was involved.

Perhaps his moods were partly influenced by being ripped off by two Canadian conmen in the 1970s, or by the deaths of his much-loved Jack and Wayne. I feel that Danny wanted to be loved and adored but, sadly, some of his behaviour could drive people away. I find it very difficult to write what I have about him, but I feel it is important to be as honest and as candid as possible and not gloss over my own experiences.

None of the above is to deny what an amazing performer he was but, perhaps, at times I would have been better off admiring him from afar. One promise I have made to myself over the years is not to end up like the Danny I witnessed when it comes to alcohol. I, too, could be catty and judgemental when it came to liquor and have lashed out at people and have said things I regret. Maybe, Danny did teach me a valuable lesson after all. I gave up drinking several years ago and haven't touched a drop since.

CHAPTER 18

The Nervous Breakdown: A Career in Tatters?

Who could forget the terrifyingly sinister Australian Grim Reaper or British black tombstone adverts in the 1980s warning us of the dangers of AIDS? It was a terrible time for the gay community, and I have lost so many dear friends to the disease over the years. The AIDS crisis really was a painful period of my life and that of so many others.

I first read about what was sometimes referred to as a 'gay cancer' or 'gay plague' in the newspapers in the early 1980s while performing with the Cheeky Chaps. We would have conversations about it and our promoter Guy Barton studied the gay and mainstream press to keep us informed of the latest stories and developments. At first, I thought it wasn't really true or was exaggerated sensationalism as the press was not kind to gay people in its reporting.

Some of the reports were horrific, and I have a feeling that audience numbers at some of the RSL clubs where I performed in the 1980s dropped off because they did not want to see a show with gay men. They were terrified of the Grim Reaper who featured so prominently in the AIDS TV campaign.

As homosexuals we had been thrust into the public eye and demonised and our sex lives provided the source of much gossip and innuendo. We were no longer simply drag performers providing entertainment to our adoring punters, but disease-spreading poofters with rampant and shameless sex lives who would sleep with the first man who glanced our way.

There was so much fearmongering, so many rumours and untruths during the AIDS crisis. A man who worked in the kitchen at Les Girls in Sydney also had a job at a hospital. He insisted that you could catch the disease simply by touching someone who had it. Having always been a worrier this terrified me.

When I first heard about the link with AIDS and unsafe sex, I immediately started taking precautions and always used condoms. For many years, while I still had a sex life, I would get tested for HIV every three months or so as I was so worried about it. Every test came back negative, and I was always thankful and surprised because in the pre-AIDS era I had been quite promiscuous and had never used protection.

I consider myself very lucky yet people I know who were not as promiscuous as me or not promiscuous at all did fall sick and were sometimes among those who died. I often wonder if the patron saint of drag has been looking down on me. That's my dark humour for you!

It really was a devastating period for me and for our community. All those who lived through the AIDS crisis have so many stories to tell. One instance sticks out in particular. I was on a visit to Sydney in the late 1980s from Dubbo, where I was living at the time, when I went for a drink at the Oxford Hotel on Oxford Street. A young man approached me and asked if I was Stan Munro. He looked so ill and thin, and I was shocked by his appearance. He had sunken eyes and his face was so gaunt.

He told me he was the boyfriend of a Greek guy that Phillip and I had known called Alex, who I had first met when he came along to watch Les Girls at the Upper Esplanade in Melbourne in the 1970s. Alex and his previous boyfriend had become quite friendly with us, and they had taken us to see their friend the dope-smoking priest I wrote about earlier. Phillip even went on a holiday to the Greek islands with them in the late 1970s.

His current boyfriend explained to me that Alex had told him fondly all about me and how he had loved my act. I asked after Alex, and he said that he was desperately ill in hospital with full-blown AIDS. This came as such a shock to me. Both were so young, and I worried that it would not be long before the boyfriend would also find himself in hospital.

I asked if I could go to the hospital to see Alex and he said he would ask him as he was on his way to visit. We agreed to meet the following night. It was so heart-breaking what he was about to tell me. He told me that Alex did not want to see me as he would prefer me to remember him as the healthy young man that I knew, and not the person that I would see dying in a hospital bed. I felt so sad, but I understood.

I gave him my phone number so that he could pass on any updates to me. A few weeks later I received a phone call telling me that Alex had died. Phillip and I went to the funeral, which was attended by four other people. His partner was not there. Alex had been such a vibrant guy and must have been no more than in his mid-thirties when he died. I found out that his boyfriend passed away not long after.

I have felt so sad for all the people that we have lost through AIDS over the years as well as their lovers, families and friends. It has decimated our community and I am so grateful that, thanks to medical advances in HIV treatments, people with the virus can now live long and healthy lives.

Over the years I have done many charity shows to raise money for HIV/AIDS organisations such as the Bobby Goldsmith Foundation. I suppose it is partly my way of giving something back to the gay community and a means of paying tribute to the beautiful friends who I have lost. I had a great night, once, performing at the Albury Hotel on Oxford Street with two of Sydney's best known drag queens, Miss 3D and Cindy Pastel.

I was very nervous as I had never performed at the Albury before because I had almost always done shows for straight audiences at non-gay venues. It was very noisy, and I had to perform behind the bar as there was no stage. It was a challenge doing stand-up comedy and singing live in front of hundreds of noisy queens, but they seemed to really enjoy the show.

Shortly after leaving Les Girls in the 1980s, I toured again with a couple of strip shows up north, one male, one female. Both were run by a woman called Jackie, whose son was a stripper in one of the shows. I worked for her for about three or four months. The male strip shows were quite fun as I had had a lot of experience with them during the days of the Cheeky Chaps.

However, the female shows were a different story. When Jackie told me I would be touring with a group of female strippers I had my doubts, but I said yes because I needed the money. I have always found it easier to perform to female or mixed audiences than all-male ones, although those early gigs in Newcastle with Monique St John always went well. Yes, women in the audience can be wild but the men watching strip shows can be very rough and pretty much just want to see the women get their tits out. They have little interest in seeing a drag queen and they take no prisoners.

At one venue in Queensland, I arrived with the girls and the manager asked me who I was. When I explained that I was the female impersonator who would be compering the show, he responded, 'No fucking way. The place is booked out with men tonight!' He insisted that the contract had made it clear that they were sending up a woman to host it. It turned out that Jackie had not told him that she was sending him a drag queen. Thankfully, the show went well but when I took it up with Jackie, she denied it, of course, but I knew that she was telling porkies.

Not every show we did went as well. During that tour I endured the roughest crowds that I have ever experienced. At an army base in Darwin, members of the audience started pelting me with beer cans. I just drew on all my years as a performer and kept going. It takes a lot more than a bunch of arseholes to force me off the stage! However, things went from bad to worse. At another venue audience members were banging their cans of beer on the table and yelling out 'poofter' and 'faggot'.

I never felt comfortable on the tour or working for Jackie. Before the tour she had told me that I would be sharing a bedroom with one of the female strippers. I felt uncomfortable about this as I was not used to sharing a room with a woman. I was also concerned that I might have a panic attack like the one that I had had while at Les Girls in Sydney; not something that I wanted anyone to witness.

I got out of having to share a room by telling Jackie that I talked in my sleep. It was not true, but I got my own room. I later found out that she had told another woman that I could not share with her because I had schizophrenia. I was so happy to leave that tour and I have not worked for Jackie since.

Not long after I finished touring with the strip shows, Phillip and I moved to Seven Hills in Western Sydney in the late 1980s. We had friends there and I wanted to get out of the city now that I was no longer working at Les Girls, and I was also having increasing numbers of panic attacks. I needed to be out of the rat race for a bit, but I did end up making an unwise business decision while living out west.

When I moved to Seven Hills Simone Troy asked me if I wanted to buy half of Simone and Monique's Playgirls. She explained that she had left the show and that Monique wanted out. She said a performer called Stephanie had bought her share and that I could buy Monique's for three grand. I spoke to Phillip about the offer, and he encouraged me to go for it as their show had a good name and reputation.

We sorted out all the legal stuff and I ended up buying half the show, but it was a big mistake. The costumes were stored in this huge warehouse in Alexandria. Before each show we had to go to the warehouse to pick up the costumes from a lock up storage area, put them in the car and drive to the venue. Then, after the show, we would have to do the same thing in reverse. I found it torture. It was so tedious, repetitive and tiring.

The costumes had seen better days and I would go as far as to say some were even tatty. There were about eight of us in the show, but without Simone and Monique it had lost some of its sparkle and magic. We were not getting a lot of bookings and audiences seemed to be dwindling. This was during the AIDS crisis of the 1980s and I think a lot of shows featuring trans and drag performers were suffering. People in the RSL clubs were staying away from us. This failing business venture was only adding to my increasingly depressed and anxious state, so after about a year I ended up selling my share for very little money to a drag queen with whom I had worked when touring Western Australia with Alain.

All the travelling back and forth between venues was getting to me and my panic attacks were increasing. Sometimes I would have three or four a day. I felt awful and my feelings of depression and anxiety were getting worse. These would happen without warning, and I became nervous about working. One moment I would be very busy and flat out with shows; the next minute I would have periods without work when I would spend time at home on the couch overthinking everything and worrying about what was happening to me and my life.

I was heavily into marijuana as well as wine and scotch which many of us in showbiz circles were. I first got into dope while performing with the Cheeky Chaps as many of the strippers were into it. At Les

The Nervous Breakdown: A Career in Tatters?

Girls, during the latter years, for instance, it was commonplace. I was really abusing my body and I think my panic attacks were its way of saying that enough was enough.

I will never forget my first panic attack. It took place a few months before I re-joined Les Girls in the mid-1980s. Phillip and I were driving home to Erskinville after visiting friends when I suddenly felt my heart pounding out of my chest and I struggled to breathe. I thought I was having a heart attack and was going to die. I begged Phillip to stop the car, but he could not as we were on the freeway near Blacktown.

He drove me straight to the nearest hospital where a doctor diagnosed me as having suffered a panic attack. I had never experienced one before and knew nothing about them. I had thought that I was going to die. It was terrifying for me, and I had little idea what it meant for my future.

I kept going to different doctors and psychiatrists to find out the root of the problem. I had an MRI scan to see if there was anything wrong with my heart.

Nothing wrong was ever found with my heart but I was later diagnosed with depression and anxiety, which contributed to my panic attacks. The fact that I constantly worried about my depression, anxiety and the panic attacks just made me feel even lower and exacerbated my problems.

My depression and anxiety worsened, and my panic attacks increased. I was getting so desperate that I was prepared to try anything. I even went to see a radical health practitioner whose advert I had seen in a newspaper. He told me to lie down before putting a crystal on a tray that he placed under the bed. He then stood over me holding another crystal tied to a string, which he was circling over my head and told me to try and free myself of my emotions. This lasted ten minutes. I did not feel any better!

On another occasion, in Broadway, I was shown into a room where a group of people were sitting in chairs. We were all told to close our eyes, meditate and try and shed all our negative thoughts. The people hosting the event were wearing robes and it felt very cultish. It turned out to be a religious group, though I had no idea of that until I went along.

None of the conventional or alternative treatments were helping me and I was becoming really desperate. After I sold my share of Simone and Monique's Playgirls, I spent much of my time depressed at home. I felt unable to work because I was terrified that I would have a panic attack and be unable to perform. So, I was no longer earning any money and I was unable to contribute much financially at home.

Phillip found my change in mood very difficult to live with and we were becoming more distanced. I was living in a bubble and would often just close myself off from the world. Communication between us broke down. I do not blame him at all for feeling frustrated; depression is very hard to understand unless you have experienced it yourself. It cannot be easy living with someone who has depression as it can be very draining. Phillip now works in the caring profession, so he has been around depression a lot more. However, back then, he did not really get it; nor did other people I knew.

It got to the point when in 1990, after 14 years as a couple, Phillip and I decided to split up. We continued to live together, in Seven Hills, though we were no longer sharing a bed. Of course, our split only added to my woes and by this time I was at my lowest ebb. I was feeling worse and worse, and life no longer seemed worth living.

My doctor gave me some medication, which had little effect except to make me very drowsy. In the meantime, I felt that I was being engulfed by a dark cloud. My depression and anxiety, which I used to refer to as my black dog, was taking over my life. Everything about my life seemed hideous and I felt that the black dog had won. I felt well and truly beaten.

Things had snowballed and I felt helpless. This was before the days of support organisations such as Beyond Blue which do great work. Depression was not something men tended to admit to.

I was, however, seeing a sympathetic psychiatrist in Blacktown who kept asking me if I could cope. I broke down and confessed that I was getting more and more intrusive thoughts and wanted to kill myself. I told him that I needed to be somewhere where I could be taken care of. He realised that I was in the throes of a nervous breakdown and organised for me to be admitted to the psychiatric unit at the nearby Westmead Hospital.

One of the first things that the staff at Westmead did was wean me off the anti-depressants that my doctor had given me. It was a torturous process as I had the shakes, hot and cold sweats and headaches. One day, I went to have a bath and I just wanted to put my head under the water and drown. I could have easily done so as nobody was around at the time. I think some sort of willpower must have stopped me. It seemed that I had to get worse in order to get better.

Once the anti-depressants were out of my system, I was put on different medication. However, at first, the dose was so high that I was constantly zonked out. Thankfully, it was lowered, and I felt a little more active again. Some of the patients were having electroconvulsive therapy, as my very own mum had so many years ago, but I refused after a female patient told me she believed that it was affecting her memory.

I shared a ward with three other people, and we would have daily group therapy sessions with other patients. I found the sessions helped a bit as it was a relief to know that I was not alone and that there were people who understood what I had been going through. A lot of the young women there were suffering from eating disorders.

I was so focused on fixing my own depression and panic attacks that I did not think to mention my own history of eating disorders. I never thought that discussing them might help some of the women there. It also never occurred to me that my obsession with food might have in some way contributed to my own depression, anxiety and panic attacks.

I had some of my shows on VHS tapes and I showed them to the other patients. They loved them and it seemed to help cheer them up. The other patients asked me sometimes how someone who had

had a successful career and seemingly had every reason to be happy could end up in such a place. I used to simply respond, 'Life is like that.' Anxiety and depression can affect anyone from the richest to the poorest. It takes over your whole existence. Sometime during all this turmoil, my beautiful friend Des came over to visit me. He had travelled to see me a couple of times previously, but I really appreciated his visit as seeing him really helped me at a time when I was very low. It turned out that I think this was also his way of saying goodbye to me as I think he had known by this stage that he had cancer and died not long after he returned to the UK.

Before being admitted to Westmead, Phillip and I had agreed to sell our place in Seven Hills as our friends who lived nearby were moving to Dubbo and we had decided to join them. Soon after I was discharged from hospital Phillip moved up to Dubbo and lived in a caravan on their farm, as we were still paying our mortgage for the house that we had bought in Seven Hills.

It may seem odd for me to want to still live with Phillip after we had split up as it would have been the perfect opportunity to make a clean break and start afresh. The truth is I was still in love with him and attached myself to him like a limpet. My treatment at Westmead helped me to understand some of my problems but I was far from cured and my mind was still all over the place. I had spent many years living with Phillip and though he struggled to understand my problems in those early days, he at least offered a sense of consistency and familiarity. This gave me some comfort, though I must have been very difficult to live with, at this time, as I was still feeling low and helpless.

To give you an idea of my state of mind I was worried that if I went up to Dubbo on the train, I would have a panic attack and throw myself off it. If this sounds extreme, it should. I stayed a few weeks with my friend Glyn before, finally, plucking up the courage to board a train and join Phillip.

Another reason I was happy to go to Dubbo was because I heard that there was a clinic where I could be a day patient. I went to this clinic for four days a week for about a year. They did not give me medication, but I would sit with other patients like I did at Westmead, and we would talk about our problems.

Once again, it did feel good knowing that I was not alone but only up to a point. After a while, though, I found that hanging out with people that also suffered from depression could bring me down further. This is why I try and surround myself with positive people who are optimists and love a good laugh as I find that I am very sensitive to the moods of others. I have been known to cut people out of my life who show any sign of negativity or toxicity. It may sound selfish, but I cannot afford to go down that path again. It is my survival mechanism and a form of self-protection. My period of depression, anxiety and my nervous breakdown was one of the worst times of my life. It was horrendous. To be honest, I would rather kill myself than ever have to go through that part of my life again.

It took many years to get my medication right and I still take a very mild anti-depressant to this day. It did not help that I was still drinking heavily while on medication. I had spent many years working in bars and clubs where alcohol was plentiful and often free. I would also drink to help drown my sorrows, but it only made me feel worse. I was never diagnosed as an alcoholic, but I think that I probably was. I would drink at every opportunity, day and night. I gave up alcohol in late 2018 and it has been one of the best things that I have ever done. My moods have improved and so has my energy. I also feel the need to sleep less.

Anti-depressants can have side-effects and one of them was that they took away my sex drive. To make matters worse, not long after I started taking medication I developed prostate problems, though neither were related. It was just bad luck. When my doctor and a specialist checked my prostate, I asked if they could use two fingers. When they asked why I explained that I would like a second opinion. My GP got the gag, but the specialist remained stony-faced. You cannot win them all!

Sadly, following surgery I lost the ability to ejaculate which, of course, did not help my frame of mind. I continue to get my occasional dark days when I do not want to get out of bed but I have found the best treatment has been exercise. When I moved to the farm outside Dubbo, I would ride my bike about 20 kilometers into town and go running daily. These days, here in Kyogle, I perform up to 100 star jumps at home every day and go to a local gym regularly. Not too bad for an 85-year-old drag queen! Exercise really improves my mood and general well-being. Sometimes, I wonder if I would have been better off going to an exercise boot camp than a medical centre.

I found keeping myself occupied also helped. In Dubbo I took a part-time health food industry course at TAFE for about two years, and I also worked in the kitchen at a local bistro in the pub where I had done a few shows. However, Dubbo was a culture shock to me as I found it to be red neck territory. It felt so unlike Sydney and Melbourne as it was so homophobic.

The woman who ran the bistro told me that she had been at a market one weekend where a man had asked her why she had 'the poofter with the earring' working for her. I asked her who it was, and I phoned him at work. His secretary explained that he had just left work for the day, but she managed to catch him as he was walking to his car. When he came to the phone I told him in no uncertain terms, 'How fucking dare you, you homophobic piece of shit,' and he hung up. I felt good letting off some steam.

One day I went to see my doctor and his receptionist, who was in my aerobics class, handed me a file containing my medical history to give to my GP. Written across it was the word 'Homosexual'. Understandably, I never felt particularly at ease in Dubbo.

Even though there were homophobic attitudes in Dubbo, I nevertheless performed a few shows in the area. Sometimes, audiences were so unresponsive that I think they would have still ignored me if I had fired a gun in their direction. Dubbo really was a hard place to live.

Thankfully, Phillip and I were still good friends, but I felt that it was time for me to move on with my life and meet Mr Right. I often thought of my Dutch boyfriend, John, who had run out on me just before I left Sydney to start work in Melbourne. He had actually found me in Melbourne during my Les Girls days and we caught up at my flat. He was keen to try again with me, but I was in love with Phillip by this stage and there was no way I was going to do anything to hurt him. Had I been single, things would have been very different. So, on the very slim chance that it might work, I placed an advert in a magazine column for finding lost friends and loved ones.

Would you believe a friend of John's son saw my advert and tipped off John, who phoned around the various pubs in Dubbo to try and locate me as he guessed that I would probably be performing in at least one of them. We eventually spoke on the phone, and he told me that he had gone on to marry a woman in Adelaide. I tried to talk with him about the old days, but he made it clear to me that those days were long gone and were firmly in his past. He refused to give me his phone number or address in case his wife found out. It was evident that he wanted no more contact with me, and I felt hurt and rejected. I wonder why he even decided to reach out to me again in the first place.

At around the same time I began placing adverts in the personal column of a gardening magazine called Grass Roots. What an appropriate title! I received a letter from a man called David who lived in the Victorian town of Castlemaine. We decided that I would take the ten-hour bus journey and visit him for a week. David had booked us into a hotel for the first night and then, for the remainder of my stay, we stayed at a local camp site.

In the advert I had not mentioned how old I was, and nor had he ever asked, but when we met, I told him in order to nip it in the bud. It turned out that I was 22 years older than him. He was not happy about it, but we still had sex every day. David was living with his mother who I met, but it was clear she did not like me. She was cold around me and did not make me feel welcome. David later confirmed my suspicions, telling me that she felt that he could do a lot better.

One night, we stayed with a lesbian friend of mine in Melbourne who decided to show him photographs of me. There was a photo of Phillip which immediately caught David's eye, which I later found out he had resolved to keep and take with him. At the time I did not have a clue that he had immediately fallen in love with Phillip based on that one photograph.

A couple of weeks later, David asked if he could come up and stay with me. He had ulterior motives which did not involve me, as I would soon discover, to my disadvantage. By this time, Phillip was sleeping in a converted shed on our friend's property where we kept the caravan, though he was still using the caravan's kitchen and other facilities. At first, things seemed fine between me and David and we enjoyed sex together, but after a couple of days it was clear that his affections lay elsewhere.

David never left and Phillip and he became an item. It all felt a bit too close to home for me and I was devastated. At the time, it really hurt as I was struggling with my depression and not only had I lost an opportunity with David, but he was now involved with the one man I had truly loved, and they were living together on the same property as me! I must have been hell to live with as I became even moodier and made snide comments to both of them at every opportunity. I just wanted to get out of there.

Thankfully, after living in Dubbo for about a year, a pianist with whom I had done a couple of shows told me that he had recently returned from performing in Newcastle where there was a lot of work. I decided to put an advert in a local Newcastle newspaper which read, 'Stand-up comedian, female impersonator requires work in this area. Please ring....'

A week later, I received a phone call from a man called Gary who asked me if I was 'the Stan Munro' that he remembered from Les Girls in Sydney. He explained that he and his partner Martin were in charge of the catering at the Workers Club in Wangi Wangi, a suburb of Lake Macquarie south of Newcastle.

They ran the Dobell Room, a restaurant featuring a small cabaret stage, named after the painter Sir William Dobell, who had lived up the road, as well as a second larger entertainment room for bigger shows.

Initially, Gary offered me a couple of weeks work in the smaller cabaret room to test the waters. I travelled five hours or so on the coach down from Dubbo and stayed with them at their house. The shows went down really well, and the audience loved them. Importantly, they helped me recover my confidence in performing and it was not long before they offered me a permanent gig in the Dobell Room at weekends. During the week, I helped out at the restaurant that Gary and Martin ran at the club. I found it valuable as it helped keep me occupied and my mind focused. One day I was serving tables when in walked Mickie de Stoop. I felt so embarrassed and was worried that she might think that I had had some spectacular fall from grace. However, I need not have worried as we had a catch up and it was good to see each other.

I spent about three months at a time working in Wangi and then headed back to Dubbo for about a month to spend time with Phillip and David whose relationship I was growing to accept and understand. After a while, I realised that Phillip was happy. To me, that was what really mattered. My bitterness turned into happiness and respect for them both. Time really can heal. This arrangement of me living between Wangi and Dubbo continued for about nine months and it worked really well. I was feeling really good again.

One night, Gary told me that there was a singer called Steve Holly performing in the next room who had previously worked with me. At first his name did not ring a bell but then it clicked that I had worked with him a few years earlier in a show in which he had been a stripper. He had given up the stripping and was now a professional singer. Not only was he handsome but he also had a beautiful voice. He was living in Newcastle with his male partner where they owned a big nursery.

We met up after his show and after chatting I thought that that it would be a good idea if we team up and perform shows together at the venue. Steve and Gary loved the idea. Gary suggested we put on some Christmas shows, which would start in November and run through to January. I organised for two young female dancers and two young brothers, Garon and Mathan Michalitis, to be part of our variety show. At one point in the show, I would come out in drag and tap dance with them. It was such a hoot. Garon and Mathan went on to join the internationally acclaimed show Tap Dogs in 1995. I was so proud of them.

In early 1994 Phillip announced that he and David were moving to Chewton in central Victoria, which was near Castlemaine where David was from. They told me that there was a room for me if I would like to move down with them. I could hardly say no as I adored them both, and Phillip was my best friend and soul mate. The timing was good because Gary had told me that they would be taking a break from doing shows until later in the year so I decided that it would give me a good opportunity to take on new challenges. I worked for about another month at the club in Wangi and then Phillip and David came down and took me to their new home in Chewton.

However, I continued to perform with Steve at a club in Newcastle every month. This meant taking the train from Castlemaine to Melbourne and then catching an overnight train to Sydney which took many hours and then taking another train to Newcastle before doing it in reverse on the return journey. I enjoyed doing the shows even if the journey did seem to take forever. I did it because it kept me in work. I enjoyed working with Steve and it kept me in showbiz circles, which I loved. However, after about five months, I found the very long commute incredibly draining and Steve and I felt that our shows had come to a natural end, so we called it a day. I did love working with him, though. It was now time to focus on my new life in Chewton and the challenges ahead.

CHAPTER 19
Back On Track

I arrived in Chewton and moved in with Phillip and David but, just like my return to Eddy in the UK, things just did not feel right. I was still jittery with my nerves, and I felt as though I didn't belong. It really was a matter of three being a crowd. They were still going through their honeymoon phase, and I felt that I was intruding on their space. After a couple of months, I stuck an advert in the window of the local milk bar saying, 'Accommodation wanted!'

A man got in touch who explained that he had a house in nearby Castlemaine and asked if I would like to have a look. It was rather small and not particularly attractive from the outside. It was also at the top of the hill on George Street – the climb from hell as it was so steep. However, the rent was cheap, and I needed a clean break.

During this time, in 1996, one of my brothers rang me to let me know that my mother had died in Wales. I felt very upset but was not in a position to go back, either financially or emotionally, for her funeral. At the time I had no regular income, I had rent to pay, and I was still getting anxious about travelling a few hundred kilometres. It just was not feasible and to be honest I was thankful that I had spent quality time with my mother on her three visits to Australia. We had always had a difficult relationship, but I knew that she loved me and that I loved her.

I was still doing the shows in Newcastle on a Friday and Saturday at this stage, but I needed something to occupy my time as I found that making myself busy helped keep my anxiety and depression at bay. I ended up volunteering at the local Salvation Army op shop in Castlemaine four days a week for about seven years.

My role was to price everything that we sold. I enjoyed volunteering there as I liked meeting the many people who visited our shop. I also liked many of the women with whom I worked and formed friendships with them, but unfortunately some were very homophobic, finding any excuse to make a snide comment. On one occasion, the gents toilet was not working so I had to use the one for the women and they did not like it one bit. Their problem wasn't that I was a man but that I was a gay man, and they were worried that they would catch something from the toilet seat. This was at a time when there was still quite a bit of stigma surrounding HIV and AIDS.

Thankfully, most of the other volunteers only did one shift a week so I would only have to cope with the hostile ones in small doses.

David and Phillip had, by this stage, bought a house in Chewton which they had done up. David is a master of all trades and a brilliant builder and carpenter. After I had been living in Castlemaine for about six months, they told me that the house next door to them was up for rent as the elderly woman who had lived there was now in residential care.

David suggested to her son that he rent it to me. I had been so lonely living alone in Castlemaine that I jumped at the chance as it meant that I could be close to Phillip and David again but also have some independence. The house was 150 years old and the woman who had lived there had brought her family up in it. It had an outdoor toilet as well as an outdoor bathroom. The son used to come over regularly to mow the lawn, which was a bonus as it saved me worrying about it. After a few years, the son said he was selling the property and gave me first refusal. I took out a huge mortgage and bought half, and a female friend of mine bought the other half as an investment.

When I moved next door to Phillip and David, one of the local women I became great friends with was Bettie Exon. We first met when I did a show at a pub in town. We understood each other and we just hit it off. She loves gay men and can camp it up with the best of them. We developed a very close bond, and she still refers to me as her brother.

About a year or so later David and Phillip announced that they were leaving town and moving to Byron Bay after David had a falling out with a family member. I had to make a decision as I knew that if I stayed in Chewton, it would be the first time that I had lived long-term without Phillip for many years. After a lot of thought I felt that it was important to give them the space that they needed and start afresh.

It did not take long for me to miss them terribly as they had been my rock and the reason that I had moved to Chewton. I felt so alone and isolated. Thankfully, with the help of locals such as Bettie I was able to get my life back on track. Bettie got me involved on the committee of Chewton's monthly newsletter, the *Chewton Chat*, as she thought that I would bring a lighter touch.

I was also part of the committee of the Chewton Domain Society, and we organised some wonderful events including the 150th anniversary of Cobb & Co coaches passing through the area. We held the event at the Chewton Community Centre and people came along in period costume. We put on a show featuring tap dancers, an opera singer and folk singers. During the second half I came on in drag and was introduced as the 'Queen of the Goldfields'.

I made some great friends in the town. One such friend was Jimmy Lynch who was a real character. He always sat on the same seat in the pub, and we would have slanging matches in front of everyone which were little more than banter. Everyone loved our verbal jousting, and they knew when we were there they would be in for some fantastic entertainment.

Whenever Jimmy left the pub he would say to me, 'You know I'm only joking.' I did and I always gave as good as I got. Jimmy was big into horse racing and when he died his funeral took place at the local football club. His horse's rug was draped over his coffin and many of us took turns in getting up and sharing our memories of him. I told a story of how I was walking into town when he pulled up beside me in his Ute and called out, 'Get in this car, you fucking poofter.'

After he dropped me into town, he poked his head out of the window and said, 'Don't tell those bastards down the pub I gave you a lift because they'll think I'm fucking porking you!' When I told this story everybody burst into laughter and gave a round of applause. Jimmy was a rough diamond but kind-hearted and sincere.

After about a year of living in Chewton I asked the director of the Castlemaine Festival to see if I could do a show, and he suggested that I perform as part of a trio. I approached a keyboardist and singer called Steve Virtue with whom I had previously worked and through showbiz contacts I found a singer called Christopher Goodall. We performed at the festival, and we went down so well that we decided to work together on a more permanent basis.

We created *The Stan Munro Show* and would you believe spent the next five years performing together on Fridays and Saturdays in clubs and RSL venues throughout Victoria and New South Wales. We all got on so well. Steve had a beautiful voice. Christopher was something else. He was so handsome, and the women adored him. He used to flirt with them something rotten even though he was gay.

We sang together as well as performing our own sets, which included me doing my comedy drag routine. Steve and Christopher were fantastic performers. I had been singing live for many years but working with them helped me become a better singer and gave me the confidence to sing live more regularly. In effect, they had become my de facto singing teachers. They were both so brilliant they even made me shine.

During my time with them I had to take a few weeks off to recover from hip surgery. While living in Dubbo and Wangi I had done a lot of cycling and running. Sadly, in my obsession to keep fit I started feeling pain in my right hip, which had been taking the strain from all those heavy workouts. The pain kept getting worse. Eventually, I saw a doctor who got it x-rayed. He said that I would need a hip replacement. Sadly, I did not take his advice and kept running regularly in Chewton.

The pain got so bad that I had to have hip surgery at a hospital in the Victorian town of Echuca. I was in hospital for six days and my recovery took about six weeks. I only needed crutches for a short time because I did the exercises every day that my doctor and physio taught me. I was also pretty healthy and fit. All that exercise had been a double-edged sword as my hips had taken the strain, but my overall fitness helped with my recovery following surgery.

The Stan Munro Show continued successfully for five years but all good things must come to an end. I was in my early 60s and I eventually found all the travelling to and from venues in Victoria and New South Wales exhausting and Steve and Christopher were also involved in separate projects, so we called it a day in 2001. However, occasionally I would perform with one or the other.

On one occasion, Christopher and I did some shows at the Star Hotel in Melbourne. Molly Meldrum was in the audience of our final show, and he came up to me and said, 'Stan Munro! The legend!' I had not seen him for many years, but he used to come and see Les Girls when we were at the Ritz Hotel. He invited me for drinks at the Peel Hotel, but I have no memory of the rest of that evening. I only remember waking up in my hotel bed alone the next morning and then Fritz who managed the Star Hotel drove me to Spencer Street Station to catch my train home. It must have been one hell of a night!

To this day I continue to perform solo or occasionally on the same bill with other performers, but what I love most is doing charity shows because I feel that I am giving something back to the community. I am not a doctor, I am not a social worker, and I am not wealthy, but I can still put on a good show and entertain people.

Back On Track

I have done a lot of charity work for causes such as cancer, AIDS and organisations such as Beyond Blue, which help those with depression and anxiety. One cause that is close to my heart is that of young LGBTQI people taking their lives. I was lucky that my own coming out experience went relatively smoothly and that my parents seemed accepting. But that is not always the case for people coming out in rural communities. It is so crucial that young people get the support they need. If I can make any difference in their lives, then it has all been worth it.

I was ever hopeful of finding someone special and I continued to place ads in magazines and newspapers looking for love. A fellow from Bendigo saw one of my adverts in the *Bendigo Advertiser* and arranged to meet me on a Friday night at the railway station in Bendigo. I arrived at seven in the evening and waited for around an hour for him to show. I gave up waiting and asked a staff member sweeping the platform what time the next train was for Castlemaine. He told me that I had just missed it.

I tried calling my date several times, but I kept being put through to his answerphone. Feeling frustrated and disappointed at being stood up and missing the last train I went to the taxi rank and asked one of the drivers how much the fare would be to Castlemaine. He told me that it would be seventy dollars. I had no idea what to do as I only had twenty dollars in my pocket and very little cash at home either.

I decided the simplest and cheapest solution was to attempt to walk home. This may have seemed a practical option, but it was certainly not the most sensible as it was raining, and I was getting soaked. I managed to walk for about half an hour to a place called Kangaroo Flat, where in desperation, I rang a friend in Chewton to ask him to pick me up.

He told me that he could not fetch me until ten o'clock as his wife had the car, but he suggested that I wait for him at the pub over the road. It was quite a rough pub full of ocker types and I felt quite uncomfortable but eventually my friend collected me. I never did hear from the man I was supposed to meet and never had an explanation for his no-show. Sadly, he was not the only man who has stood me up over the years. Usually, I never find out why.

Another person who responded to my advert in a newspaper when I lived in Chewton was a young carpenter from Bendigo who was very slim and taut. He clearly looked after his body. When he first arrived, he asked if he could get some of his stuff out of his car. He came in with paper bag full of women's clothes and a wig that looked like something out of *Worzel Gummidge*.

He then put on the wig and clothes that he was carrying in the bag. These consisted of a corset, pantyhose, a bra, a blouse and a little mini skirt. Unfortunately, he looked dreadful, but it would have broken his heart if I'd told him that. We never had sex, but he would just sit there in drag having a wank while I got on with my household chores and we chatted. It did not bother me as I had some decent company, and he would ask me a lot of questions about my career in drag performing at Les Girls and elsewhere.

He asked me if he could visit me again, so I told him to always ring me first as sometimes I had people over. One time he arrived, and he went to the one of the bedrooms to get changed. He had been gone a while, so I decided to check that he was fine. There was no sign of him and then I took a look outside. There he was, in the garden, taking in the sun in full drag. I told him to get inside in case my neighbours saw. I would have hated the prices of their properties to go down.

He told me that he would often go into the bush and dress up in women's clothing and play with himself. I guess we all have to get our thrills somewhere and it takes all sorts to make a world. Many people think what I have spent many years doing for a living is strange, so I am hardly one to talk or judge. He was married with kids, and his wife had no idea about his double life.

The men who get in touch are not always closeted. I went back to one man's home several years ago and when he took me to his bedroom there was his wife sitting up in bed. I was out of there in ten seconds.

While living in Chewton I performed at Tarrangower Women's Prison in Malden thanks to Christopher who taught singing there once a week, and I also did three shows at Castlemaine's Loddon Prison thanks to a staff member on whom I had a massive crush. The shows went over very well, and the inmates were a great audience. Performing a show in a prison certainly makes you appreciate what you have. I may not be rich, and I may not have everything I could wish for, but I have my freedom. That is truly something!

In 2001 I was nominated by a woman called Mary Keily who had interviewed me for the ABC in Victoria to be part of the Peoplescape exhibition in Canberra. It was the final event in a year of celebrations in the national capital marking the centenary of Federation. The exhibition was to feature the images of about 4000 people who had helped to change the face of Australia.

About a month later I was told I had been accepted. It was a wonderful feeling that people out there believed that I had somehow had a role in shaping the country that I was proud to call home.

A government vehicle delivered a flat packed parcel to the post office. It contained a corrugated plastic life-size cut-out of a person. I asked my friend Maggie Jacobs, who was an interior decorator, to create a collage of images of me from newspapers and magazines to stick onto the figure. She also found a life-size image of my head to stick on the cut-outs.

Once it was complete, we took it to the post office. Another government vehicle took it to Canberra where it was displayed on the lawn outside Parliament House with a few thousand other life-size representations of Australians from various walks of life, each one having played a role in shaping our nation.

Sadly, I never made it to the exhibition though several of my friends did and they showed me photos of my cut-out. I felt so proud and genuinely humbled to have been nominated and included in the Peoplescape exhibition. It was exactly the sort of confidence and recognition that I needed. Not bad for a boy from the Welsh valleys!

In the early 2000s while living in Chewton I had a nasty accident. I was friends with a guy called Gary who was renting a house near to me and we used to hang out at the pub together. He was building a two-storey home for himself and his girlfriend and I used to help him out about four days a week. I was basically a gofer and doing things like painting.

One morning Gary asked me to turn on the switch, which was on a pole, as he wanted to do some sawing. When I hit the on button the circular saw on the ground near my feet suddenly sprang into action. It slid across both my feet. I was in agony. I have never known physical pain like it. I should have had work shoes on, but I was only wearing runners. I took off my right shoe and I was shocked to see that most of my big toe was still in the shoe.

They drove me to hospital with the missing part of the toe wrapped in a handkerchief. Gary's girlfriend also had to be treated for shock; the nurses and the doctors seemed to be fussing over her more than me. I thought to myself, 'Whose fucking toe is missing here? Hers or mine!'

Unfortunately, the doctors told me that they could not save my right toe. At the time I just felt like I had to get on with it as my main concern was to be free of pain and to recover. The next day I went into surgery where they stitched up my left big toe, which had also been injured, and they sewed up the gash where my right toe had been. It was only a few weeks later that I felt a sense of loss as I found myself physically stumbling due to the absence of my right toe.

I spent five days in hospital. During my stay, surgeons took a strip of skin off the top of my left thigh in order to try and patch up the gash in my left toe. Sadly, the skin graft did not take, and I still have a large scar there. Nothing more could be done for the big toe on my right foot either. After I was discharged from hospital I was shuffling around on crutches and then used a walking stick for about a month. The loss of my right toe has affected my balance and I have fallen over in the street and at home hundreds of times. Eat your heart out, Norman Wisdom!

When the accident happened, I really did wonder what else could go wrong. Luckily, I was surrounded by amazing people and my friend Bettie Exon ensured that my house was locked up and that my dogs - I had three back then - were taken care of. Bettie also put large collection tins around town while I was in hospital to help raise money to get me back on my feet financially. She really is a dear friend who, despite having had her own health problems with her back, was there for me. That is true friendship!

Not all my memories of people in the Chewton and Castlemaine area are good ones, though, as I did experience a couple of incidents of homophobia beyond the Salvation Army op shop. There was a man at the pub who was always giving me filthy looks and I was told that he was out to get me. One night I was in the pub when I heard a loud argument taking place between two women on the footpath outside. I recognised one of the voices as being that of a woman that I knew so I went outside to see what was going on.

I had just stepped outside the pub when this nasty man from the pub came right up to my face and said, 'What do you think you're fucking doing here, you poofter fucking queer cunt?' He then jabbed me in the chest violently and I fell backwards onto the ground, hurting the base of my spine. There were a few witnesses but not one person helped me up or asked if I was okay. Nobody seemed to want to know, and I think that hurt as much as the physical pain. I was in such discomfort that I went to see a chiropractor, but I think he just made it worse. I saw the man in the pub many times afterwards, but he never spoke to me again and we just ignored each other.

This incident happened just before I was due to visit Phillip and David at Byron Bay. A friend drove me to the nearest airport which took around an hour and a half. I could barely get out of the car when we arrived. Goodness knows how I checked in. When I arrived at Coolangatta Airport I could barely walk. Thankfully, Phillip and David's doctor prescribed me some good painkillers and I also went for some massages. It took almost two weeks for my back to feel right again.

On another occasion I was in Castlemaine when a couple of men yelled at me from behind, 'Poofter poofter.' I just carried on walking, but it left a nasty taste in the mouth. I had seen a lot of changes in social attitudes towards gay people in my lifetime but examples such as the ones that I have mentioned just demonstrated to me that we still had a long way to go.

Those incidents of hostility in Chewton and Castlemaine were, of course, exceptions to the strong friendships that I made in both towns. This was never clearer than when I made the decision to leave Chewton and move to be with Phillip in 2007 after living for 12 years in the area.

Phillip was now living on a five-acre farm in Roseberry Creek which was about a 35 minute-drive from the town of Kyogle in the Northern Rivers region of northern New South Wales. I had spent a couple of Christmases in a row up north with Phillip and David but by this time they had split up. I spoke with Phillip quite a few times on the phone and he sounded so low.

I suggested that I could sell my house in Chewton and move in with him. Phillip was quite resistant to the idea. He was insistent that it would not work and that he could not see it happening. I did not blame him as I had not exactly been easy to live with when we had previously been housemates a decade before. However, I was stubborn and would not take no for an answer. Thankfully, he relented. Despite ten years living apart I still cared for Phillip deeply, and looking back, I think I not only still loved him but was also still in love. I do not think that has changed.

However, I was not going to leave Chewton without a bang. At least, the residents were not going to allow me to. I walked into the pub one evening where I saw a group of locals standing in a circle. They all went quiet when I entered, and it transpired that I had interrupted them and their plans for a farewell party for me.

I felt genuinely touched by the gesture but asked them not to go ahead with it as I said I would break down and there would be lots of tears. I have never liked goodbyes. However, they were having none of it. They told me that I could invite anyone I liked.

My farewell do - which was even advertised in the local paper - was held at the Senior Citizens' Centre and a few hundred people from the Chewton and Castlemaine areas turned up.

I did a 45-minute set featuring gags and songs. Finally, the inevitable happened and I had to give a speech. There was, indeed, plenty of tears but it was a truly beautiful occasion, a wonderful evening. Not long after I left town, I was sent a DVD showing all those who had been at the party saying goodbye to me. It showcased our community at its best and made me see how much I was loved and appreciated. I was ready to move to pastures new but, as an adult, Chewton was the place where I had lived the longest and where I had made many friendships which I cherish to this day.

Two or three days before I left Chewton, a gay friend of mine approached me and told me that he wanted me to know that I had made life so much easier for gay men in the area since I had been living there. All I had done was simply be myself because I have never felt the need to hide away. Being so open has, of course, not always worked in my favour but I do think visibility and exposure are ways to break down barriers, prejudice and taboos. If I have helped other people's lives by simply being who I am then that is truly something that I am glad that I was able to do.

CHAPTER 20
To Kyogle with Love

To Kyogle with Love

I spent about a year living on the farm in Roseberry Creek with Phillip while he and David tried to sell the place. When they had lived together, they had kept cattle and a horse which Phillip fell off, breaking his arm in three places. By the time I moved up there the farm animals had all gone as had David; it was just me and Phillip. Roseberry Creek was very pretty, and it was lovely to be living with Phillip again, but I was so isolated there. Not being able to drive did not help. There really was nothing to do except admire the views, which are, admittedly, very beautiful.

When they finally sold the farm, Phillip and I moved to the nearby town of Kyogle which has just under 3000 people. Phillip was working, and still is, in aged care in the town so it made sense to move there. We bought a two-storey house about five minutes' walk from the centre of town and even though we live together, we also lead quite separate lives. Phillip lives upstairs while I live downstairs. We have a beautiful garden where the local wallabies and bush turkeys hang out; the biggest danger is the occasional brown snake. I have also been fortunate to make some good friends in the town.

One of my early setbacks in Kyogle was not being able to continue teaching tap dancing. I had run classes twice a week for about three years through the TAFE in a hall in Chewton. All my students were women, and I loved it as we had great fun.

I made very little money from it, but it was enjoyable, and it allowed me to keep physically fit. It also gave me something valuable to do to occupy my time, which has always been very important to me. It also felt good to be needed and to be able to playing a role in the community. This is particularly crucial in small towns and, in my case, as someone living alone. I like and enjoy the company of other people.

When I moved to Kyogle I tried to teach tap dancing, but the cost of insurance proved too much so I had to abandon the idea. There is a misconception that I have made a lot of money over my many decades of performing. The truth is I have not. My work as compere at Les Girls never paid very well, though it was consistent. Most of the money that I earned went on day to day living expenses such as food or my mortgage or paying off crooked cops. I also had to pay for my costumes, wigs and makeup. There was very little money left over. My breakdown obviously impacted on my earning ability and the fact that I was now living in small towns away from major cities also reduced opportunities for good paying work. The best paid job I ever had was touring with the Cheeky Chaps but that was an exception.

A couple of years before I moved to Kyogle a woman got in touch and wanted to know if I would like to tour Victoria every few weeks with a Roy Orbison impersonator who she managed. I was very happy at the chance to earn some extra money and keep a foot in showbusiness. It sounded like a good opportunity. During the show I did two thirty-minute spots which included me telling gags and singing live crowd-pleasing songs such as 'You Think You're a Man', 'I Don't Care If the Sun Don't Shine', 'Big Spender' and 'I Will Survive'.

The impersonator was a great musician and an excellent singer who sounded just like Roy Orbison, but we were like chalk and cheese. He had quite an ego and could be vain. We never performed in RSLs because he refused to remove his hat in tribute to the fallen servicemen as he was bald on top. Before each show, he would put on a Roy Orbison style wig in the dressing room.

Why he could not have worn a hairpiece into the venue as a compromise is beyond me. We mainly performed in sports and country clubs, but I believe that not working in RSLs cost us quite a bit of potential work and, therefore, money.

When I moved to Kyogle in 2007, the Orbison impersonator's manager persuaded me to continue doing the shows. She told me that the money that we made from doing the shows would pay for my flights to Victoria. This proved not to be the case. On a few occasions I flew to Victoria to be told that we were doing only one show instead of the expected three. After spending money on flights and food I would often have very little money left over and, on some occasions, none.

A mutual friend of our manager confided in me that some venues only wanted me to perform but that our manager would tell them that the Roy Orbison impersonator and I came as a package. I really felt that I was being used in order to promote the impersonator, and I knew where the manager's loyalties lay. In my view they were simply riding on my coattails. I never confronted her about it because it was regular work, and I wanted to keep performing. There are few things worse than an out of work performer and nobody wants to be a starving actress!

However, after about six or seven years I called it a day. It simply was not profitable, and I was not enjoying it.

My last show with him was shortly before one of my trips back to the UK, around 2016. On my return to Australia, I simply never went back to doing our shows. My overseas trip gave me a good excuse to start afresh. In show business giving up work is often a gamble but if your heart is no longer in it and you are not making money, you have to reassess what makes you happy. I knew it was time to leave.

I continued to do occasional solo and charity shows, which I do to this day. However, in my early 70s I also took on an entirely different career. One day I was talking to my friend Josie Jay with whom I had worked in Sydney, Hong Kong and Melbourne and asked her about a performer who I knew from my days at Les Girls in Sydney in the 1980s. Josie told me that this person was living in the Blue Mountains and working for a sex line.

Josie gave me her phone number, and I rang my friend for a catch-up. During our conversation she mentioned the sex lines and said that she was moving on to work for a psychic phone line because, despite being a transwoman, her voice was just too deep for the sex lines. According to her, you did not need to be psychic to work for the psychic lines as you only needed to tell people what you thought they wanted to hear. Who knew! However, she suggested that I would be great for the sex lines as I had a more feminine-sounding voice. This meant that I would be more convincing as a woman. I was intrigued and she reassured me that the pay was reasonable, so I thought, what the hell, and decided to give it a try.

I gave the agency a call and negotiated that I would work from around 10am to 4pm four or five days a week. This meant I could keep the evenings and weekends free for any local shows that I might do.

Over the years the calls would come through thick and fast with as many as a dozen a day. It really was a full-time job, and I could never be far away from the phone, which in those days was just my home phone, not a mobile. Someone from the agency would phone and tell me that the person on the other end of the line wanted to speak to a granny or someone who was trans or a dominatrix, for instance. Sometimes, people would even want to speak to a hot chick. I would then be connected to a phone client after 'getting into my role'. I was nothing if not versatile!

The job required a lot of imagination and I disliked pretending to be a dominatrix the most as I would have to talk rough to the client and would run out of things to say when in fact my role was to keep them on the phone for as long as I could so that the business could make as much money out of them as possible. It was certainly an interesting job though it could get yucky at times. I had to be creative and improvise a lot. Occasionally, people would ask me to imagine I was urinating on them, and I used to tell them that I was taking the phone to the bathroom to have a pee. In reality, I had a jug of water next to me which I would trickle into a bowl.

I would often have very butch-sounding truck drivers phone to chat with me after they had pulled up by the side of a road while pleasuring themselves. I had my regulars too. There was one young guy who phoned a few times who always wanted to speak to a 'transsexual'. The first time he rang me I could hear what sounded like a lawn mower in the background. I asked him if he was mowing the lawn and it turned out he was sitting on a tractor at his father's farm plowing a field!

Many elderly men would phone me up and I would pretend to be a granny. Occasionally, lesbians would phone and ask me to talk in detail about my vagina and what I liked doing sexually with other women. As you can imagine that scenario really challenged my imagination. One lesbian commented, 'That's the best phone call I've ever had.' Whatever I said or supposedly did clearly hit the right spot, so to speak.

One woman even phoned me and explained that she and her boyfriend were packing up all her belongings as she was planning to leave her husband, and that she wanted to leave him with a hefty phone bill. I think she simply left the phone off the hook for around two hours. It must have been a huge phone bill for the husband, but it was the easiest money that I have ever made.

I stopped doing the sex lines several years ago because I was finding the fantasies were getting darker and the role-play increasingly sordid. One regular caller, for instance, was a man in his late twenties who wanted me to pretend to be his own mother. The nature of what he wanted me to do with him became more and more graphic. Working on the sex lines had been fun to start with but I found that some of the fantasies and role-play were starting to affect my mental health and I did not want to go down that road again. It was time to quit but I must say that during all my years on the sex lines not one person twigged that I was a man.

Despite all the beauty of Kyogle and the friends that I have made, it can be a challenge being a single gay man of my vintage as it can be very lonely. There are gay men here, but they tend to either be in couples, in the closet or not interested in me romantically. It can be very easy to fall into a trap of feeling stuck in a rut or socially isolated, made even more difficult by not being able to drive. At times I have felt lonely, but I do what I can to keep myself occupied.

Thankfully, I spent several years in a local choir which was great fun. We met every Friday morning, and I loved the people there. The choir members always made me feel welcome and I sang as a tenor. One of the highlights of being in the choir was performing concerts every six months or so in venues such as the Kyogle Memorial Institute. Sadly, I had to give up the choir to focus on my autobiographical stage show *Vintage Drag in Mint Condition* but more on that later. However, I think that without the choir I would have had quite a void in my life.

A typical day will begin with 80 star jumps at home and then about twice a week I will go to the gym for around an hour. Following this, I will do some shopping for groceries at my local supermarket and have a gossip with folk in the street and at the supermarket. I sit regularly on a bench outside the IGA supermarket to chat with locals. I joke often that the council should put a plaque with my name on it after I die as it is where I have been holding counsel for many years. After shopping and having a good chinwag, I head home and spend the rest of the afternoon watching television and chatting online. Facebook has been an invaluable lifeline to the outside world and a way to stay in touch or reconnect with my friends and family here in Australia and overseas.

Since early 2020 one subject more than any other has made headlines and has been on many of our minds – COVID-19! I was one of the first in line to be vaccinated here but to be honest the pandemic did not affect my life that much because I spent most of my day at home on the computer anyway. I still made my daily trips to the local supermarket and become an even more familiar sight wearing my rainbow masks which were made by a local seamstress. People have complimented me on them, so I have given some away to gay friends.

There were times when the choir could not meet but it was only for short periods. During much of the first two years of the pandemic I was unable to go to the UK or visit Sydney or Melbourne.

However, the recent catastrophic flooding in the Northern Rivers in early 2022 had rather more of an impact on my life. I was woken up at 3.30am one night in February by the sound of relentlessly heavy rain and had this strange feeling that water was coming into our house. Almost immediately, I saw my bathroom was flooding and it looked like it was being engulfed by a fast-moving river. I spent a few hours using a plastic jug to bail out the water and pour it into the toilet. The water was also flooding from the bathroom into the living and costume rooms, so I had to put down piles of towels and blankets to prevent any further water flooding from the bathroom.

Phillip came to the rescue and built a channel on one side of our home which redirected the flood water down the hill. I had to do a lot of mopping. Thankfully, there wasn't too much damage to our home though the muddy water had stained the bathroom wall which needed to be repainted. My costumes were hanging on racks which saved them. The heavy downpour was nothing compared with that of areas such as Lismore but the whole experience left me so frazzled and exhausted that I went back to sleep for a few hours, which is unusual as I rarely sleep in the day. Further heavy rain and flooding meant I had to cancel a long overdue trip to Sydney to attend my first Sydney Gay and Lesbian Mardi Gras parade as we were unable to drive through Lismore to fly out of Ballina. However, I have very recently been able to make trips to the Emerald City and have loved it! I have caught up with friends I haven't seen in decades and one of my friends even gave me two front row tickets to *Phantom of the Opera* that was being performed on the Harbour. I felt very spoiled!

Long before the floods and during the pandemic, in 2020, a producer from the ABC's *Back Roads* TV series, which visits local towns in Australia, got in touch to say they were coming to film in Kyogle and asked if I'd be interested in taking part. You can guess my answer!

In August that year host Heather Ewart, a cameraman and a sound recordist came to our town and spent several days filming an episode of the series. I was one of the local characters featured and was filmed in my home with my doggy Prince and at other locations.

As part of the filming, I visited the recently constructed circular brick labyrinth for the first time. It was built by community volunteers and contains 600 inscribed bricks featuring phrases or dedications, many paid for by townsfolk. I was particularly touched that one was donated and dedicated to me by the community. The inscription reads, 'Kyogle applauds Stan Munro. Long live the Dame!!' I felt so touched as it was such a wonderful gesture of acceptance and love from the town.

At the end of the documentary, I am shown performing in drag at an event at Kyogle Golf Club to raise money for the Country Women's Association. I was actually singing live to a backing track of 'I Don't Care if the Sun Don't Shine' but the edited version of my episode of *Back Roads* shows me dancing on stage to another tune, for copyright reasons, with the audience clapping along enthusiastically. I finish the program saying about Kyogle, 'It's given me a sense of worth and a place to live. A place to call home.' I meant every word.

When *Back Roads* was shown on the ABC in February 2021 I received very positive feedback regarding my appearance. Many people contacted me on social media from around Australia who remembered me from my days in Les Girls in Sydney and Melbourne and wanted to know more about what I was now doing. I felt very proud being part of *Back Roads* and one of my highlights was meeting host Heather Ewart who was fabulous. She made me feel very relaxed as if I was talking to a very dear friend.

I am very grateful to *Back Roads* as I believe it has led to further work and other performance opportunities. One of those performing highlights was hatched after a chance meeting with academic and author Kevin Markwell at the Kyogle Readers and Writers Festival. Kevin has been an integral part of the festival as Co-convenor and later went on to become one of the editors of this book along with Keith Howes.

We decided to put a stage show together about my life and call it *Vintage Drag in Mint Condition*. The show features Kevin interviewing me about my life and it includes photographs and television footage from throughout my career. I also perform a couple of numbers, and we have a segment called 'The Farmer Wants a Husband' which is great fun and involves members of the audience. It is so camp!

Lynette Zito from the Village Hall Players in Kyogle directed our first show which we put on at the Village Hall. It sold out and the audience loved it. It was so popular we had to allow for extra seating. I was thrilled. Following the success of our first show, Kevin and I then decided to take it on the road, and we took it to Castlemaine, Newcastle, Lismore, Katherine, Sydney and back to Kyogle.

Kevin and I are very different. I am camp and flamboyant while Kevin is more serious, but we made it work. Our humour is at times quite different, and he certainly read me the riot act over a few of my more risqué jokes. During rehearsals Kevin also had to rein me in as I found it tempting to go off on a tangent when sharing anecdotes, but I needed that discipline. Otherwise, the show would probably have gone on all night. We were like the yin and yang of show business. However, Kevin is very thorough and put so much work and effort into our show.

Our most popular shows were in Kyogle and Castlemaine where we played to full houses. It was particularly lovely to catch up with old friends in Castlemaine where I had previously lived. Seeing so many friends and locals attend our shows in Kyogle also meant so much to me. A truly amazing feeling of love and acceptance. However, the shows were not always plain sailing. At a couple of shows we had a poor audience turnout because of a lack of promotion locally which I found frustrating. At times technology would not work so we were unable to play a video or show a slide. At one show in particular the microphones kept letting us down despite working in rehearsals. I found this particularly annoying as I am a perfectionist when performing but I also believe the show must go on. At one show a video repeatedly would not play so we improvised and took questions from the audience. It worked well and created even more of a rapport with those attending.

At one performance we noticed the audience had significantly dropped in numbers by the second half and we could not work out why. It was only after the show that we discovered that during the show around 30 kids were seen hanging around outside the venue, some with iron bars and knives. We discovered many audience members had left early to avoid a potential confrontation, and we had to be escorted to our car for our safety. Someone in our party asked if it might have been related to homophobia before one of the local organisers casually responded that this was in fact a regular occurrence. No more was said. On the bright side it makes a great anecdote!

Thanks to the success, and despite the occasional challenges, of touring with *Vintage Drag in Mint Condition* I am most grateful to Kevin for taking a chance on me, putting up with me and helping make our show a great success. I hope we can take the show on the road again in the future.

It was thanks to our show in Newcastle that I was finally able to take part in the annual Sydney Gay and Lesbian Mardi parade in 2024 two years after I failed to make it because of serious flooding in the Northern Rivers. During our show someone approached me from Newcastle Pride to ask if I would like to take part with them on their float. I did not need to be asked twice. I had a terrific time though it was without doubt a labour of love as we were one of the last floats in the parade so there was a lot of waiting around but I was made to feel so welcome. It was an unforgettable experience and one I will never forget.

On the evening after the parade Kevin and I put on our show *Vintage Drag in Mint Condition* at a venue called Dulcie's which is only a stone's throw away from where I performed at Les Girls. We performed to a full house, and it was a joy to see so many familiar faces again. It was great to be back performing among the bright lights and neon signs of Kings Cross again where I belong. I felt like a star!

Back Roads was not the only television program in which I have made a recent appearance. In mid-2022 I received a phone call from a researcher on the ABC to ask if I would like to be interviewed in Sydney as part of a three-part documentary series called *Queerstralia* which would be shown in 2023 as part of the World Pride celebrations.

I was put up in a lovely hotel in Kings Cross and was interviewed alongside Ayesha from Les Girls at the Old Fitzroy Hotel in nearby Woolloomooloo by host and comedian Zoe Coombs Marr who was simply lovely. It was also great to catch up with Ayesha who was looking so well. I shared my memories with Zoe of my time at Les Girls but in particular my experiences of police corruption. When *Queerstralia* was shown in 2023 during World Pride I once again received a lot of positive feedback regarding my appearance.

During World Pride I was also very excited to be featured in the inaugural Qtopia Sydney exhibition at the bandstand in Green Park very close to Oxford Street. Qtopia has since moved to the old Darlinghurst Police Station of all places and is one of the largest museums in the world showcasing LGBTQIA+/queer history. When it moved to the former police station in 2024 those at the opening included the Prime Minister Anthony Albanese and the NSW Premier Chris Minns.

However, in 2023 it was a much smaller setup at the bandstand but nonetheless impressive. The exhibition included a signed photograph of me and footage of me being interviewed by Bert Newton on *The Graham Kennedy Show* in the early 1970s. However, the highlight for me was having my gold S.T. Dupont lighter featured which was given to me by the family that ran the Ritz Hotel in Melbourne where I compered Les Girls for many years over half a century ago. Sadly, I was unable to attend the exhibition in Sydney, but I felt so honoured and privileged to have been included.

Later in 2023 I was thrilled to discover that I had been nominated for an ACON (AIDS Council of NSW) Honour Award in the ARTS and Entertainment category. The awards recognise inspiring individuals, outstanding organisations, bold creative minds and dedicated activists, advocates and heroes with a passion for making a difference in the LGBTQIA+/queer communities.

I went down to Sydney for the ceremony. I put on a brave face and tried to tell myself that I had no expectations but of course I really wanted the award after so many decades in the business. I was up against some very impressive and worthy candidates. Winning an Honour Award would have meant so much to me. I waited anxiously for the winner in my category to be announced and silently hoped it would be me. It was not to be. I lost out to the brilliantly talented Courtney Act.

I felt utterly dejected and defeated though I was happy for Courtney and I could hardly think of a more worthy winner. It was especially tough putting on a brave face for the rest of the event. However, in a twist of fate it was Courtney herself who gave me words of encouragement and lifted my spirits. She told me not to give up and that she had been nominated previously and had not won. Courtney told me that my time would come.

The following year in 2024 I received a call from someone at ACON to tell me once again that I had been nominated for an ACON Honour Award in the same category. I felt overjoyed but also apprehensive after not winning the previous year. I was offered two tickets and decided to take my friend and co-author William Brougham to the ceremony as he had been one of the people who had nominated me.

A few days before the event I got cold feet. I phoned friends to tell them that I wanted to pull out and cancel my trip to the ceremony as I could not face further rejection. As you will have read, I have feared rejection most of my life. Thankfully my friends reassured me and insisted that Cinderella must go to the ball.

I flew to Sydney and stayed with my friend Jason at his beautiful home in Potts Point. He also kindly lent me his black sequined suit which I loved. William and I attended the ceremony at a beautiful venue opposite Hyde Park in Sydney. I felt so welcome and everyone there was so kind and friendly to me. They went out of their way to make me feel so comfortable and made such a fuss of me. Nothing was too much trouble from making sure my coat was hung up to ensuring I had a drink.

Once the ceremony had begun, I sat nervously awaiting my category. "Oh, not again!" I said to myself expecting another rejection. It was then announced that there would be two winners in the Arts and Entertainment category. The first winner that was announced in my category was the very talented DJ Gemma. It was then time to announce the second winner in our category. I had pretty much resigned myself to not winning. Then I heard my name.

To Kyogle with Love

I had to do a double take. I could not believe it. I was a winner, baby, and I felt like one.

It was such an exhilarating and invigorating moment. I made a very emotional speech in which I paid tribute to my dear and beloved mother who had given me so much support in the early part of my career. I still miss her very much to this day. After the ceremony so many people came up to congratulate me and I had my photo taken with the other winners. At times it was overwhelming, but I savoured every moment and felt elated. It was such a breathtaking feeling of love and acceptance.

Word that I had won the ACON award spread like wildfire as at the beginning of 2025 I was contacted by a producer to appear on a new television program on SBS called *Tell me What You Really Think* hosted by Marc Fennell. Each episode features a diverse range of guests sitting around a dinner table discussing a relevant topic with Marc. In my edition we discussed ageing.

I was flown down to Sydney and put up in a hotel in Mascot near the airport. The next morning, I was driven to the studios to begin recording. Marc was fabulous, was so welcoming and was such a wonderful host. I got on well with my fellow dinner guests including a sexologist from Bendigo with whom I am still in touch. Who knew there was such a demand for sexologists in regional Victoria!

We had a great time recording the program for about three hours though I was somewhat bemused by the concept of a dinner party as we recorded it early in the morning and hardly any of the food on the table, if any, was touched. I thought the program went well and on my way out from the studio I was thrilled to meet author Kathy Lette which added icing on the cake. She was about to record an edition of the show about menopause. We had a quick chat, and she was so bubbly and fun. She was every bit as over the top as I had hoped. I gave Kathy my business card though the phone still has not rung. However, meeting her made the trip worth it.

The program was broadcast several months later in late 2025 and the feedback I got was positive. However, to be honest I was disappointed as so much of what I had said ended up on the cutting room floor including me discussing Kyogle and my life there. It also seemed that a couple of other guests were allowed to dominate the discussion while I felt I was the support act. However, my experiences of ageism in the gay community and the challenges of finding love or intimacy as an older man were thankfully aired.

That same year I was excited to be part of a photography competition and exhibition. I first met photographer Jodie Harris at the Kyogle Film Academy where she was teaching. I was there so that the students could practice their interviewing skills with me. From there I got to know Jodie better and found we both clicked. She is a lovely person. Jodie approached me and asked if she could photograph me. Naturally, I said yes.

Jodie came to my home where I put on some colourful drag but I did not wear a wig. She took several photographs but settled on one which she thought was magic. I told her I knew that she would photoshop the photograph and make me look beautiful. That is when the clanger dropped as she said there would be no photoshopping whatsoever as she wanted every wrinkle to show. And they did!

However, it worked out well for Jodie as she entered the image in the National Photographic Portrait Prize where she was selected as a finalist. It may not have been a glamour shot but I think it worked out well for Jodie as it was the right decision to show me warts and all. I am not sure that the photograph would have done so well otherwise.

The work was exhibited at the National Portrait Gallery in Canberra between August and October 2025. The exhibition has gone on to tour nationally, and my portrait has been shown in galleries across Australia. I felt so proud of Jodie but also felt so proud that a poor working-class boy from the Welsh valleys ended up at an exhibition at such a prestigious gallery in Australia's capital city.

The photograph did not win the competition, but I am so happy to have been a part of it and even happier that Jodie's portrait of me appears on the front cover of this book. Thank you, Jodie!

The people who live locally are wonderful people and Kyogle and the surrounding areas are beautiful, but I miss being among showbiz folk and working under the bright lights of Kings Cross and St Kilda. Many of my showbiz pals and fellow performers have long since died. Those who are still alive I rarely see but, occasionally, we will chat online or on the phone. I have been out of the limelight for so long that I fear that I have been forgotten and it is often me that makes the first move to contact friends; but that has always been the way as I have always feared losing people in my life, so I hold on to them.

Very rarely I catch up with showbiz pals as I did in 2017 with Carlotta and Monique St John when they came to Kyogle to perform in a charity show at the golf club. It was just like old times, and it was like we had never been apart, but these occasions are very much exceptions to the rule.

How I long to walk the streets of Melbourne and Sydney visiting my old haunts as I take a trip down Memory Lane. My last visit to Melbourne was several years ago for a charity show. It has been a joy to visit Sydney again recently after so many years. I felt so at home. I would love to be asked to do shows in either city again but lack of finance or finding places to stay are my main challenges. I would come down at the drop of a hat if asked.

I hate growing older as I worry about losing my independence and being forgotten. I would rather die than languish in a care home where I cannot do anything for myself and where few people know my past. I would just be another face in the crowd. Please never let it happen. I suppose, in many ways, I am the Peter Pan of drag hence my constant visits to the gym to try and keep healthy.

When finances allowed it, and before COVID-19 came on the scene, I still travelled overseas, and I made a few trips to the United Kingdom and Thailand. On one trip to the UK in 2016 I stayed with my nephew Mark in Wales for three months where I did a couple of shows in Wales and in London which I really enjoyed. I also spent a great holiday with Mark and his husband in Gran Canaria. While in the UK I helped raise money for local charities which made performing even more worthwhile. Through my dear friend Alan

Bugg in London, I took part in a variety show and I helped raise funds for the charity Cancer is a Drag. In the Welsh town of Aberdare, where my nephew Mark lives, I helped raise money for a young rugby player who had become paralysed in an accident. I have always enjoyed helping others which is why I enjoy doing charity shows. As I have said before it is my way of giving something back to the community.

My last visit to the UK was in 2023. Drama follows me around and this trip started with no exception. Believe it or not I have never applied for Australian citizenship and always travel overseas on my British passport. As I was leaving Australia an immigration officer advised me that my Resident Return Visa had run out and that I needed to apply for a new one before I returned to Australia. I was stressed out even before leaving these shores. Not the way I had planned to start my holiday!

I stayed for much of the trip with the wonderful Jane, who is the younger sister of Sheila who was married to one of my brothers. To be honest, they have been more like family to me than most of my blood relatives. They really care for and love me. I struggled to apply for a new Resident Return Visa but thankfully Jane and her husband Kev came to the rescue and helped organise one for me. We all need a Jane and Kev in our lives though perhaps it is time I finally became a true blue fair dinkum Aussie in my mid-80s. Applying for a visa was not my only drama. In my wisdom I had decided to travel to Wales at the height of Winter and came down with a dreadful bronchial infection which kept me bedridden for a few days.

Thankfully, a good local doctor sorted me out with medication.

Despite the setbacks I had a lovely time staying with Jane and her husband but there was no contact with my younger sister even though I was not staying far from her.

One of the highlights of my trip was performing at a popular bar a stone's throw from Trafalgar Square in London called Halfway to Heaven thanks to my dear friend Charlie Rowling who is a seasoned performer himself. I did a set and took questions from the audience. I also caught up with my fellow performer Scott St Martin for the first time at the venue who I have known for years thanks to Facebook. He is lovely and so knowledgeable about showbiz having trodden the boards on the West End stage for many years. It was such a fun evening.

On my return to Wales I did interviews with a local newspaper and a community radio station about my memories of life in Wales and my career in Australia. Both interviews went very well. I even took out and wore a feather boa for my photo in the local paper. Sadly, all too quickly my UK trip came to an end, and I had to return home to Australia.

I am hoping at some stage to return to the UK soon and spend more time in London, catching up with old friends and making new ones. I also hope to perform at a few venues and make a few more contacts on the London drag scene. One thing that has been on my mind lately is whether to re-establish contact with my sister as I would very much like to build bridges with her and repair our once close relationship. I often wonder if she or other members of my family with whom contact has ceased ever think about me or reflect on how I am doing or even if I am still alive.

My relationship with my family has always been a difficult one and I am estranged from most of my relatives. My parents are long since dead as are all of my brothers, but I still have my sister living in Wales. Unfortunately, she still wants nothing to do with me. Sadly, I have never had an explanation. Thankfully, I do have a nephew and niece who I am in contact with and whom I adore and remain fond.

I just wish more of my family could have appreciated me more. They never understood the challenges I have faced in life. Not even my mother. At times I wonder if they could have cared less. It is sad but I feel it is true.

I have never felt that my brothers, for instance, accepted my sexuality or my life as a drag performer. Having said that one of them once came to see me in one of my shows in Wales. At the end of the show, I performed my swan song called 'Fantasy' which my wonderful friend Tim Barton, a composer, wrote especially for me. It is a beautiful and emotional song.

The song ends with the lyrics:

> What you've seen tonight
> Is just a fantasy
> It's a masquerade
> A wild parade
> It's not really me

My brother came up to me after my performance and admitted that he had been moved to tears. Perhaps there was a slight nod of acceptance on his part, but I think he and my other brothers were in denial about my sexuality.

For a while my sister was the one member of my immediate family with whom I was close, and I thought was supportive. In recent years however contact has ceased.

In 2016 I performed a paid gig on my trip back to Wales in a pub in the West End of Abercarn only a few yards from where my sister lived. Not one member of my immediate family attended. The next day I decided to phone my sister to try and sort things out. Her response was simply, 'I suppose I have to talk to you as you are my brother.' The rest of our conversation was brief, stilted and awkward so I made my excuses and hung up. I have not spoken to her since as our short conversation was not a happy or comfortable one. She has made no contact with me either. During that four-month trip to the UK I only saw the niece and nephew with whom I am in contact. That's family for you. It is sad but there you go.

I guess the main thing that stops me from initiating further contact is that I am nervous of being rejected again, but none of us are getting any younger and I do not want to lose any chance that I may have of rekindling our friendship.

My last visit to Thailand was in 2018. I usually stay with a German friend who I used to know from my days in Melbourne. He lives in a small town called Pai in the north of the country. It is very popular with backpackers and other tourists and has a vibrant bar scene. On previous trips my friend would drive to me to various bars, and I would be in costume. I would then perform at these bars and do a show. I did not earn any money, but I loved it. The crowds lapped it up and, of course, I received free drinks.

One night I was camping it up on a small stage in a bar when a group of British tourists came in. One of the men in the group was laughing his head off at my jokes but he had his back to me, which I found rather rude. After a while I said to him, 'Hey, look at me when I'm talking to you!' One of his friends responded, 'He is blind, but he loves your jokes.' Oops! Talking about putting my foot in it. Thankfully, we all had a good laugh about it.

Sadly, my last holiday to Thailand in 2018 ended in disaster when I fell over and split my head open after a drunken night on the town. The doctor who saw me in A&E told me that I should be ashamed of myself, getting drunk at my age.

On my return to Australia, I started getting dizzy spells which led to vertigo. As a result, I had to get regular physiotherapy. It took a few months to feel better. It was a wake-up call with regards to my drinking. Before my holiday I consumed as much as a bottle of wine on an almost daily basis - from three in the afternoon until bedtime - and I was falling over at home after getting drunk.

I remember, on at least one occasion, we had a few friends over for dinner and I snapped at them after getting inebriated. The drinking and the falls continued for a short while after my return from my disastrous trip to Thailand. I decided that enough was enough and simply gave up the demon drink in 2019 and went cold turkey. I also gave up smoking at the same time as I was finding myself increasingly out of breath. I have so much more energy and feel happier and more fulfilled since giving them up. The truth is I do not miss either.

What I do miss is having someone special in my life. Living with Phillip is wonderful, but I would dearly love a partner. I find the worst part of being gay and single at my age in a small town is that it is nigh on impossible to find a like-minded person to meet. It can be tough sometimes when you turn over in bed and all you find is an empty pillow next to you. Age can be a curse, but you have to learn to live with it.

For the last couple of decades, I have kept the personal columns of newspapers and dating websites very busy in my search for a lover. So far it has been hopeless as everyone who gets in touch is either deeply in the closet, not my type at all, a scammer, a fetishist or sick. In my search for love I seem to be meeting all the wrong faces in all the wrong places.

The majority of men that have contacted me in recent years have been married men who have wanted a bit on the side. I really would like more than to just be someone's 'bit on the side'. Then there are those men who at first seem too good to be true. They are usually young men living overseas who befriend and charm me after seeing my profile online.

They try to flatter me with compliments and before long they express their love for me. Soon, they either ask me to send them money or ask me to send them an airfare to Australia. I have, thankfully, wised up to these tactics and have had to block a few people though occasionally I play along for a bit of fun before hitting the block button. It is often pleasing to receive compliments, however empty and insincere, but I have little time for people who want to take advantage of others, no matter how desperate their own situation.

As I grow older, I find that it gets tougher finding someone, particularly living in a small rural town as I do. Whether it is a lover or simply someone to cuddle up to on a cold night I live in hope and have never given up. Perhaps one day I will wake up next to a pillow that is no longer empty.

Recently, a talented guitarist called Matthew got in touch with me. I had worked with him a couple of times when he was filling in for the Roy Orbison impersonator. On the first night we worked together he asked the impersonator's manager where he could get changed. She told him that he would be sharing a dressing room and that he would have to change with me. He looked very uncomfortable and there was a strange atmosphere in the dressing room for the rest of the night. I got negative vibes off him and wondered if there was an element of homophobia at play.

My intuition proved to be correct. When he wrote to me recently, admitting that he did not know what to expect when he first worked with me, he said that perhaps he was a bit homophobic back then. He said that working with me changed his way of thinking and his attitude and that he hoped that we could be friends.

Everyone here in Kyogle knows that I am gay, and I continue to perform for charity here and elsewhere in the Northern Rivers region. I often get involved in organising the charity shows and hand out flyers in full drag on the main street. I was even recently asked to be on the 'Kyogle Together' float in the procession at our annual Fairymount Festival. Nobody is nasty or unpleasant to me here and I feel welcomed and accepted as part of the community.

Promoting charity events and putting on a show can be exhausting as I need to get bums on seats. After each event I swear that it will be the last time I do a drag show but within a short time I am looking forward to putting on my glad rags again.

Recently, I read about an 87-year-old drag performer in Adelaide who is still going strong. I am still fit and healthy and I have no plans to retire from performing while I am still physically able to do so.

Looking back at this long life of mine I wish that I had not suffered from depression or found comfort in alcohol, which saw me through the pain. I have not always been pleasant to people around me and I must have been difficult to work with at times in Les Girls, in part because I was told by management that, as the compere, I was responsible for the behaviour of the girls. Perhaps there were occasions when I pulled my weight more than was necessary. However, for the most part I have always done my best to be good to others and do the right thing.

Life has not always been easy and sometimes I think that I have been dealt a bad deck of cards. I have mentioned depression and alcohol but there was also drug abuse, sexual abuse, physical abuse, threats and corruption by police and of course estrangement from my family. I certainly hope that the latter can be rectified, and bridges can be built.

However, looking back I also realise how fortunate that I have been to work in many magnificent and stunning parts of the world with so many amazingly talented people from all walks of life. I have been honoured to compere shows such as Les Girls and the Cheeky Chaps.

I didn't achieve the international success of Danny La Rue or Dame Edna Everage, but I am proud of my career and my life. We really were among the first to put drag on the map in Australia with Les Girls when we started from the early 1960s onwards. I doubt we will ever see the likes of Carlotta, Monique or Simone again or the sophistication of Les Girls. Every guy and his father are doing drag these days and I feel the mystery and magic of drag or female impersonation has largely gone because it is so out there and mainstream with popular television shows such as *RuPaul's Drag Race* and cities such as Sydney and Melbourne playing host to many drag performers and even having drag competitions. It is no longer seen as daring or as risky as it once was. It is no longer a forbidden fruit...not to mention having audiences dress up as they did in our day. We live in a different era.

Nevertheless, I have spent decades in regular work across the world doing what I loved doing, performing and entertaining and, today, I can say that I am happy. I still get a huge thrill when people say to me, 'I saw you in Les Girls all those years ago and you are still as good as ever,' or 'My late mother used to love you and always spoke fondly of you.' I am so happy that I have made an impression and that people still remember me. Few of us want to be forgotten, particular in show business.

I live in a beautiful part of Australia where I see the wallabies and bush turkeys playing as I look out of my front window. I get on well with many of the locals who all know me, and I feel a much-valued part of the community. Occasionally, I wonder how my life would have turned out if I had stayed in Wales, but the truth is that I will never know. I will always love the country of my birth, but I have no regrets about migrating to Australia. This country has provided me with many wonderful opportunities, and it is the place that I am glad to call home.

I have been lucky with the friends that I have made who still stand by me to this day such as my dear friend Wendy who has been the only woman with whom I have fallen in love. And, of course, there is my beautiful Phillip who, despite no longer being together as lovers, is still the love of my life, my best friend, soul mate and house mate. He is my rock and without him I wonder where I would be today. He makes my life complete.

The boy from 5 Penrhiw Terrace in Llanfach, Wales, the Queen of the Valleys, did indeed 'go far' as that performer predicted I would to my dear Mum after he had watched me in that pantomime at the age of 12. In fact, he hasn't done too badly for himself despite a few obstacles here and there. All the stories I have shared with you have been told to you, warts and all, according to the best of my memory.

If I have caused just one person to wipe away a tear of laughter, then that is my reward in life. That is how I would like to be remembered…making others happy.

Photo taken by William Brougham.

STILL CRAVING MORE SPARKLE, SCANDAL, AND SHOWBIZ?

Follow Stan on Facebook and Instagram for fabulous throwbacks, delicious memorabilia, rare photos, and untold tales from a truly unforgettable life.

Facebook: Stan Munro - Performer
Instagram: stan.munro.performer

The story doesn't end here darling, this is just the warm-up act!

www.ingramcontent.com/pod-product-compliance
Lightning Source LLC
Chambersburg PA
CBHW071953290426
44109CB00018B/2006